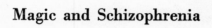

Magic and Schizophrenia

Magic and Schizophrenia

By GÉZA RÓHEIM

posthumously edited by
WARNER MUENSTERBERGER, PH.D.
with the assistance of
S. H. POSINSKY, PH.D.

Foreword by
SANDOR LORAND, M.D.

INTERNATIONAL UNIVERSITIES PRESS, INC.
New York   New York

Contents

Preface

When Géza Róheim died, he left a number of manuscripts which were more or less ready for publication. Among these were two essays which he had planned to publish together, one dealing with the psychological meaning of magic, the other with certain aspects of schizophrenic processes. In accordance with the author's wishes, we have retained the original titles for both parts.

The present arrangement, revised and edited for publication, is the result of the work of Dr. Warner Muensterberger with the assistance of Dr. S. H. Posinsky. They have done full justice to the importance of Dr. Róheim's study.

A first draft of the manuscript of the present publication I saw and discussed with Géza Róheim in the early forties, when the author had finally decided to settle in New York. Just prior to that time he had been at the Worcester State Hospital, Worcester, Mass., where he had had the opportunity to do research on a case of schizophrenia; at the same time, he analyzed several of the staff members and residents of the Hospital.

This was not Róheim's first contact with America and Americans. For a few months he had visited this country when he returned from his field expedition to Central Australia and the South Seas. And while he was in the United States, he did some comparative field work among the Yuma Indians in Arizona.

It was during these field studies that Dr. Róheim developed, on the basis of personal observations among primitive peoples, his *ontogenetic theory of culture* which became the fundamental concept of all of his further writings. According to his point of view, it is the prolonged infancy and delayed development of man which are responsible for early traumatization, body destruction fantasies, and consequently talio anxiety. If the infant's early relationships—and this means especially the relationship between infant and mother —are too deeply impaired, the ego does not become strong enough to deal with reality, and this fact may lead to psychosis. In magic, as Róheim points out, a similar basis can be observed. Yet, those who perform magic acts or rites as a countermove against regression follow an ego-syntonic technique. It is an attempt at rebuilding the world of reality with libidinal means.

I want especially to thank Dr. Muensterberger as the co-executor of Dr. Róheim's will. He has been most generous in spending so much of his time in making this work available to science.

This last psychoanalytic study of Géza Róheim will prove to be of great value. It represents a most significant contribution to our understanding of the nature of man.

New York, N.Y.   SANDOR LORAND, M.D.
May, 1955

viii

Magic and Schizophrenia

PART I

The Origin and Function of Magic

LOVE MAGIC

Though the basic or original forms of magic and schizophrenic fantasy spring from the same roots, they are not completely synonymous. Magic in general is the counterphobic attitude, the transition from passivity to activity. As such, it is probably the basic element in thought and the initial phase of any activity. Schizophrenic magic, on the other hand, is purely "imagination magic"—realistic action does not follow. In fact, schizophrenic fantasy is generally a substitute for action. Realistic action does not follow need or desire because the schizophrenic ego is markedly weak or totally absent, and we observe merely a series of diverse and fruitless attempts at restitution. To begin with I shall discuss the basic elements of magic.

The paramount love magic, or *ilpindja,* of the Aranda (Central Australia) is connected with the wanderings of the Wildcat ancestors. This is so for obvious mythological reasons, since all the Wildcat ancestors of the myth had huge phalli.

Aranda men erect a ceremonial pole decorated with tail feathers on the top. They spend several nights sitting around the pole and "singing" it. Then, gradually, the pole becomes a man who looks exactly like the man for whom the incantation is being performed. But he does not look like the man would in everyday life when he goes out hunting. Rather, he looks like the man would at his best, when he has decorated himself to attract the attention of the women.

The women then see a dream. In this dream the man who came from the pole is surrounded by a halo of lightning. The lightning pulls the women toward the man for whom the song has been sung. The magic man, or double, takes the women by force, like a whirlwind. The shell called *tjakula* is hung on the pole. This shell is mythically related to lightning; and when a man dances, one shell hangs from his neck and another covers his penis. As the women draw nearer to the pole, the lightning gets more and more frequent, until finally, when there is lightning everywhere, they have arrived.

The men who are "singing" the pole also "sing" the moon. The moon is similarly transformed into a man by the song. The moon becomes a driver of the women: they think it is an enemy on the warpath and they run, driven by the moon and pulled by the lightning.

In addition to the big ceremonial pole, a number of minor objects are "sung." The outline of a woman is drawn in the sand. They "sing" a string made of hair, which they then put on the image of the woman. The incantation is very simple:

> Long string, make her like me
> Long string, put it on
> Long string, make her like me.

Another song of this kind refers to the fire stick (*wawilija*). They swing this object from a string, the same way they swing the bull-roarer to attract women. This is an abbreviated version of the incantation:

> Fire stick, hold it
> Boys' boomerang, hold it
> Water penis [i.e., lightning], hold it
> Rainbow,[1] hold it
> Put on the rainbow
> There is the woman.

1 The word really means the band on the man's forehead.

The men also put the bull-roarers on the sand to "sing" them, but first they make the image of the desired woman in the sand. Then they put the pubic tassel on the image, the headband on this, and the bull-roarer on top. The man for whom the incantation is being performed subsequently uses all of these objects; but first they are "sung," as are the wing feathers and the nose bone. His body is painted with red ochre, and he puts charcoal on his forehead.

The headband and the bull-roarer are taken from the image and pressed to the man's stomach, thereby transferring into his body the power which has been put into the objects by the incantation.

Finally he sits down, and they "sing" his body. He rises and walks into the camp, now completely sure of himself. The women who see him also see the lightning which is encircling him and crashing down to the right and to the left. Then a woman lies down on her stomach and is deeply in love.

This type of magic would seem to conform with Jekels' and Bergler's (1949) theory of love as narcissistic, as an attempt to recapture the "autarchic" position of infantile omnipotence. Is the "singing" of an object used in love magic and then of one's own body not really narcissistic or autarchic? And the omnipotence of the incantation and the formation of doubles—are they not comparably narcissistic or autarchic?

If we look at the problem somewhat more closely, we see what is wrong with this argument. The bull-roarer, a pointed oval slab of wood swung on a string, is the typical tool of love magic. The songs frequently identify the bull-roarer with lightning (the penis of the water) , or even simply with the penis. Ursula McConnel (1935) assumes, and rightly so, that the rhythmic swinging of the bull-roarer represents the awakening of sexual feelings. The pole sung in this incantation is also a phallic symbol, as is the lightning.

Thus the autarchic fiction is only seemingly autarchic. Love magic simply amounts to this: desire creates desire, and the bearer of love magic is the erect penis.

MAGIC AND ORALITY

Saliva

Abraham (1916) has described a case of "schizophrenia simplex." The patient talked about his "oral orgasms," that is, an excess of salivation in the mouth with an accompanying sexual excitement. He used to wake from a manifestly sexual dream with the saliva flowing from his mouth. As a child his main pleasure in life was to drink milk. He had a special way of doing it, a kind of sucking, and he would suck his own tongue as if it were a nipple (pp. 75-78).

A patient of mine used to accumulate a quantity of saliva and then suck vigorously on his own tongue until it became painful. He did this whenever he was frustrated by his wife or any other woman. There was a prolonged attachment to his mother, who would play with her son as if he were her lover.

A middle-aged woman whom I analyzed was free of depression as long as she was with people. But the depression immediately set in when she was left alone, and she counteracted it by eating enormous quantities of food.

The Thonga of South Africa perform a kind of ceremonial spitting. The bride and groom are seated opposite each other on a mat. The bride's father takes a small quantity of half-digested grass which has been taken from the paunch of a slaughtered goat. He "makes a little ball of it, touches his tongue with it and emits a sound resembling 'tsu'. . . . as if he were slightly spitting. It is the customary sacramental act in most of the sacrifices" (Junod, 1912, p. 111).

Before they go into a lake to catch fish, the Thonga do not perform the full sacramental "tsu"; rather, they merely spit into the lake and say, among other things, "Let fish abound!" (Junod, 1913, p. 70). Another subvariant is the syllable "thu," uttered with an emission of a little saliva, in order to get rid of the anticipated misfortune attendant on a falling star. The sacramental "tsu" invokes the spirits of the ancestors, and is an act of respect and an offering. "Thu," however, is an insult, a spitting *at* something (Junod, 1913, p. 287).

The Masai have two ways of spitting: to show contempt or to express astonishment. In addition, the medicine men spit to heal people. When a Masai sees a child whom he has never seen before, he spits on it and says, "Grow, become accustomed to the eyes of the people." Then he says, "This child is bad"; but to himself he says, "This child is good." If he praises a child, it will fall ill. When the first Europeans gave medicine to a Masai, the latter asked them to spit on him; then the medicine would really help (Hollis, 1905, pp. 315-316).

In European folklore, spitting is used as countermagic against the evil eye.

In Szatmár (Hungary), people who have been weaned twice have the evil eye (Róheim, 1952). If such a person looks at a child, he or she must spit on the child to counteract the effect of the evil eye (Jakab, 1895, p. 414). If a child has had the nipple for seven Good Fridays in succession, no evil eye can hurt him; but at the same time *he* has the evil eye. If a nursing mother looks at another nursing mother who is suckling her baby, the second mother is deprived of her milk.

To possess the evil eye means to have oral aggression or a desire to eat the child. The thing to do, therefore, is to spit it out again (Róheim, 1952). In Göcsej (Hungary), if a child has a perpetual flow of saliva, they wipe his mouth with a beggar's hat, and this will stop it. If a woman steps into her husband's spittle, her foot will be full of sores. Rubbing "hungry spit" on any part of the body will cure a pain. "Hungry spit" is also rubbed on the neck to cure a sore throat. After saying a prayer, they use "the saliva of the prayer," that is, the saliva that has accumulated during the prayer, for the same purpose. Some Hungarian fishermen spit on the net before starting to use it.

Why should a beggar's hat cure the flow of saliva? Hungarians say, *Folyik a nyála* ("Saliva is flowing"), in reference to a person who desires something very strongly. "Hungry spit" means a desire for food; and the saliva in the infant's mouth is obviously a substitute, a symbol of the mother's milk. A beggar is a person who begs, wants; hence, *similia similibus,* his hat cures perpetual salivation. "Hungry spit" is a magical cure because mother's milk was the first cure.

Wuttke (1900) writes on German folklore:

> The breath is generally the symbol of the soul. By breathing on something, one brings it within the sphere of one's own power. Spitting has a similar significance . . . One spits on the first coin earned, on the first fodder, on the first milk given to the calf . . . Spitting—sometimes right into the sorcerer's face—is the remedy against the evil eye [p. 184].

Spitting in the face also cures jaundice, fright, and so on; and spitting into the flames prevents a quarrel (Wuttke, 1900).

The Sucking Cure

The almost universal cure-all of primitive medicine is sucking.

I saw Lelil-tukutu suck Pukutiwara's nose for a long time and finally produce a bunch of thorns. It was bigger than the whole nose. Of course, he must have kept it in his mouth. The point is that Pukutiwara was also a medicine man, and yet he underwent this treatment.

In West Australia, the medicine man, or *boylya,* sucks the patient's navel and then spits out a stone.

A lame man came to an Orokaiva sorcerer. The sorcerer, having chewed the medicine on which he relies for his power, together with some betel, sucked at the patient's leg and finally spat out a mass of chewed betel, and in it was a wallaby bone. Another Orokaiva technique is called "blowing," and the sorcerer is the "blower." He blows into the patient's ears or nostrils, sometimes into his hair, and very commonly into his fingers and toes (Williams, 1930, pp. 298-299). Here, in addition to sucking, we note two other oral techniques: chewing and blowing.

Grubb (1911, p. 150) tells us that the Lengua medicine men develop by long practice such a formidable power of suction that it amounts to cupping.[2]

We have reason to believe that the latent meaning of the sucking cure is an attack on the mother's breast. We notice another trait regularly associated with the medicine man, namely, cannibalism or necrophagia (Róheim, 1923). The sick man represents the mother, and the medicine man acts out the part of the orally aggressive suckling.[3]

Incantations

Finally, we have the magic of the spoken word. More than anything else, magic consists of incantations or of mere wishes which have been uttered. The child utters sounds, and the mother reacts to the cry or the call or the babbling (Spielrein, 1922, p. 365; Jespersen, 1922, Chap. 8).

Normanby Island is remarkable for the wealth and variety of its incantations. One of these is chanted when the people cut up the yam and plant the pieces. The following version is from the village district called Boasitoroba:

> Kaikaipepeko! Your father and your mother
> They went, they left you wailing
> You cry, sobbing, sobbing

[2] For further data see Róheim (1914).

[3] Peter Glauber gave a paper at the New York Psychoanalytic Society showing that medical students identified the practice of medicine with an attack on the breast and that this became their difficulty in obtaining the degree.

You climb up, you cry sobbing
Go up, my yam skin
Wash it, my yam skin.

Kaikaipepeko means "hunting for butterflies." This was the name of a child who was left behind in the jungle. He cried because his parents were gone, and he was so angry that he chopped down all the trees in the jungle with his little axe. As he cut the trees, the first yam started to grow. In another incantation which is derived from the same myth, the child's crying is said to be the origin of singing. I doubt whether the infant imagines that it is "omnipotent" (Freud, Ferenczi), and I doubt that we are justified in describing the child's state of mind as "childish megalomania" (Bergler). What actually happens is that the child manifests desires and emotions, and that these are then gratified.

It is obvious, therefore, that in order to achieve something in our environment, we have to want it, and we must manifest this desire. Thus, we define magic as located somewhere halfway between the pure pleasure principle and the reality principle. If it were pure pleasure principle, hallucinatory wish fulfillment would be an aim in itself. If it were pure reality principle, we would set about and work to achieve a certain goal without assuming that our wish or dramatized wish is the thing that gets what we want.[4]

Williams (1928) writes:

> . . . the fundamental element in magic consists in just desiring the result . . . desiring it in the particular way which we call *wishing* or *hoping*. One might go so far as to say that whoever hopes against hope, whoever dreams by day or builds castles in the air, has already made magic in his heart [p. 179].

[4] The air conditioning had made my bedroom too cold and that woke me. But the wish to sleep was also very strong, and I went through the motions of turning the air conditioning off in imagination (hypnopompic fantasy) and continued to sleep. However, the room *was* too cold. I awoke this time, got up and turned it off. If I had first described the motion and then got up and done it, that would have been magic.

But magic is not necessarily unrealistic. I would go further than Malinowski (1935) who, though he objects to the psychoanalytic definition of magic as "omnipotence of thought" and substitutes a concept of "constructive hope overcoming doubt and pessimism," is nevertheless able to say: "Organized magic always appears within those domains of human activity where experience has demonstrated to man his pragmatic impotence" (p. 239). This is not true. People practice love magic or war magic or canoe-making magic; but in these and many other fields of endeavor, first they perform the incantation and then they proceed to realistic behavior.

One of my native friends on Normanby Island once gave me an incantation for killing crocodiles. (It was, he felt, a very effective incantation.) Then he described how he killed the crocodile with an axe. He had both the faith that he could do it (a knowledge of the incantation) and the necessary tools. Without magic, the natives said, we could do nothing at all; we could not till the soil, make love or war, navigate the sea, or do anything else. That is, they could not do these things successfully without believing in their ability to do them.

Magic, however, as found by the field anthropologist, goes beyond this. There is also magic for rain, sunshine, and so forth, where the people cannot follow up the incantation by *action*. This proves that magic must be rooted in the child-mother situation, because, in the beginning, environment simply means the mother. Therefore, wishing or manifesting the wish is the proper way to deal with the environment.[5]

The mother is not only known by the fact that she gratifies the wishes of the child. In truth, she would never be discovered if it were not for the fact that there is a gap between desire and fulfillment and that there is such a thing as frustration.

[5] On the realism in the child's so-called "omnipotence," see Malinowski (1935, pp. 62-64) and Piaget (1929, p. 150).

The Object World and Autarchy

In the case of the spell of Kaikaipepeko, magic originates from the child's crying when he is abandoned and angry. In a sense, magic is not merely the expression of what actually takes place in the dual-unity situation but is also a withdrawal of a cathexis from the object to the means by which the object is wooed or achieved; that is, from the mother to the word, as in Jekels' and Bergler's autarchic fiction, but also back again to the mother.

A Hungarian folk tale, The Poor Man and the King of Crows, might be called the story of the origin of magic.

According to this tale, there was once a poor man who had two lean cows. The cows were to the poor man just as a mother's breast is to a child. They gave him milk and butter, for which he got a few pennies to buy salt, and he also tilled his patch of land with them.

Now the King of Crows had an army, and the army was starving. Upon request, the poor man gave the King of Crows the two cows. In return he received a salt mill and later a club. The mill would give him all he wished. He had but to say, "Grind, my dear mill," and all the food appeared of itself. If he said, "Strike, my dear club," it would kill all his enemies (Curtin, 1890, pp. 409-423).

Jack and the Beanstalk is the same kind of story. Jack sells the cow Milky White for five magic beans. His mother is angered by this and he has to go to bed without his supper. But the beans he sows grow into a beanstalk that reaches up to the sky (Jacobs, 1892, pp. 59-67).

The direction is from the nipple to the male genital organ; a frustration in reality results in a falling back to one's own resources for pleasure (Bergler and Eidelberg, 1933, p. 552); but there is also a movement from the phallos back again to the woman.

It would be a great mistake to assume that autarchy or an identification with the mother is the real reason for coitus.

For example, Jekels and Bergler (1949) write: "In coitus the male, in identification with the phallic mother, overcomes the trauma of weaning through becoming the active rather than the passive participant" (pp. 343-344). However, what about people who experience no weaning trauma? We must again emphasize the importance of reality and of object directedness in what seems to be autarchic. In the act of sucking we have the root of three different types of magical attitudes: identification, love, and aggression.

Identification with the food eaten, or participation in the imagined qualities of that which has been eaten, is well known.

In South Africa there is the powder called *umsizi*. It is made of the dried flesh of leopards, lions, and snakes. Anyone who swallows this powder will have the courage and strength of these animals (Callaway, 1870, p. 438). In Gippsland (Australia), the fat of a dead man is eaten in order to acquire his strength (Eyre, 1845, p. 359; Róheim, 1914, pp. 120 ff.). Some tribes like to eat famous chiefs; thereby they inherit the qualities that made the chief famous (McDonald, 1872, p. 179; Steinmetz, 1896). Covenant and communion rites contain this same identification and latent aggression (Róheim, 1945a, 1954).

European folklore is full of data on love magic of the oral type, such as feeding some object to a person, that is, mixing it surreptitiously in his or her food. For example, menstrual or other blood may be fed to a young man; semen, to a girl; or both sexes may be fed pubic hair, head hair, sweat, and so on (Róheim, 1925a).

Aegean Islanders prescribe the following philter: Mix mother's milk and menstrual blood with the milk of her daughter who is also nursing a baby (Paton, 1907, p. 330). In Northern Dalmatia, they bake a cake with the milk of three mothers who are nursing boys. A young man looks through a hole in the cake and expects to see his future love. In Mecklenburg, men drink mother's milk to restore their potency (Bartsch, 1880, p. 354). In Denmark, three drops of blood in coffee serve as a love potion. Vend girls sleep with an apple on their genitals; their perspiration is soaked up by the apple, which they then offer to the man whose love they desire (Schulenburg, 1882, p. 177).

Medicine is also received orally. However, in Australia we find that the emphasis is upon genital libido, just as in love magic. If a man is very sick, he drinks blood taken from the *labia minora*, and it is also rubbed all over his body. If the sick person is a woman, her sister's son may offer her blood from his subincised penis (Spencer and Gillen, 1899, p. 464; 1904, p. 601).

Black Magic

The Marind-anim of Dutch New Guinea relate the following myth: The mythological ancestors, or Dema, first acquired their magical power by killing and eating a sorcerer called Ugu (crocodile). Ugu's mother had died immediately after she had been delivered of her child; and Ugu, as a young boy, soon began to play all kinds of tricks and to beat his comrades. He knew things and could do things that others could not do, and he was the first medicine man. His skin could be extended, opened, and closed again. He could carry as many as twenty people in his skin. They killed him and divided his flesh into little pieces. All those who ate the flesh acquired the magical power of Ugu, the first medicine man, and they passed it on to others, who imbibed what exuded from their predecessors' corpses.

Destruction here is essentially oral. Everyone among the Marind-anim who intended to become a sorcerer would have to eat the corpse of a sorcerer and drink the exuded liquids. This gives him the uncanny qualities of a ghost. Furthermore, he must also eat certain other substances. By eating bird's fat, he becomes like the birds; by eating serpent's fat, like snakes.

He must also eat certain plants, one of which must be chewed whenever he performs magic (Wirz, 1922, pp. 91-94; 1925, pp. 63-64).

The practice of magic among the Marind-anim is based on the *oba,* an instrument consisting of a magic coconut and a magic arrow. The coconut is the real source of death magic. It is cut in the shape of a boar's head. The end of the magical arrow is a serpent's head, with the arrow representing a serpent, which, of course, penetrates the victim in the manner and shape of a serpent. The arrow is rubbed with semen, with plant juices, and with the exudate of a corpse.

The coconut must be shaped like a boar's head because death magic of this type is derived from the myth of the boar clan. The boar figures in these myths mainly as the animal that *bites,* that eats up what grows in the gardens; but it is also a threat to human beings. The boar spirit is also connected with thunder and lightning, with the latter being usually represented as De-heraai, an old man with a long white beard who lives in the sky.

A boar ancestor who devastated the gardens day after day was killed by Bomeid-anim; but the beast, reborn from its own liver and heart, pursued the killer. The fleeing man heard his mother shouting, "Milk, milk" (or breast)—that is, come to me, the way a mother calls her child. He ran straight into her vulva, and she grew around him and became a mangrove tree. Anyone who kills a pig for a feast also has the right to have intercourse with the girl who nurtured and tended the pig (Wirz, 1922, pp. 170-181).

In all this we can clearly see a combination of the phallic (serpent), the oedipal (father imago), and the oral (biting animal, milk). It should also be noted that hair, food, or other leftovers used in "sympathetic magic" are put into the coconut (which represents the boar's mouth) in order to ensure the success of the death magic (Wirz, 1925, pp. 68-69).

In many instances black magic is closely associated with orality or cannibalism. According to the Thonga, for example, the power of evil is imbibed with mother's milk. Sorcerers, who are cannibals, murder people by sucking out their blood. Interestingly enough, any person who commits incest is also considered a sorcerer (Junod, 1913, pp. 461-467).[6]

The Western Sudanese sorcerer is believed to have a sucking apparatus which resembles an elephant's trunk, except that it protrudes from his anus. He projects this member from his body and applies it to the mouth or nostril of his victim and sucks out all the blood (Frobenius, 1910, p. 82). We have here a condensed representation of oral and anal, of subject and object. It is at this stage that hallucinatory wish fulfillment develops.

One of the best-known forms of black magic consists of making a doll or other effigy that bears the name of, or is supposed to resemble, the original person, and of then inflicting on it whatever the victim is to suffer.

The "clay body," or *corp chreadh,* of the Scottish Highlanders is perhaps the best-known instance of this type of magic. A clay image is made and is stuck full of pins, nails, and bits of glass. Then it is placed in a running stream, with its head to the current.

Frazer (1911a), whose work is replete with many references to such behavior, clarifies the assault on the clay image:

> As every pin is thrust into the figure an incantation is uttered, and the person represented feels a pain in the corresponding part of his body. If the intention is to make him die a lingering death, the operator is careful to stick no pins into the region of the heart, whereas he thrusts them into that region deliberately if he desires to rid himself of his enemy at once [p. 68].

[6] The association of black magic and necrophagy is very frequent. Cf. Róheim (1948), and Werner (1906, pp. 84-85).

In this connection, MacGregor (1901) writes:

Catherine Ross, or Lady Fowlis, was indicted by the King's advocate for the practice of witchcraft. She was anxious to make young Lady Fowlis possessor of the property of Fowlis, and to have her married to the Laird of Balnagown. Before this could be effected she had to cut off her sons-in-law, Robert and Hector Munro, and the young wife of Balnagown . . . She proceeded to her deadly work by consulting with witches, making effigies of her intended victims in clay, and shooting at them with arrows, shod with elf-arrowheads . . . Such as were to be doomed or destroyed were formed of clay into hideous figures, or rude statues larger than lifesize. Pins, nails, and feathers were pierced into them, and fairy arrows darted against them, with fearful oaths and imprecations [p. 22].

The Malays make comparable images of wax. If they pierce the eye, the result is blindness. The same principle applies to the other organs of the body; and if they desire the death of an enemy, they bury the image (Skeat, 1900, p. 571).

A student of contemporary American magic writes: "Modern witches burn candles and mutter charms to bewitch clay or wax images or photographs; and stab with an ice pick, scissors, nails or pins the heart of an unfaithful lover's likeness so that he will return" (Lys, 1948, p. 430).

SEPARATION ANXIETY

The best-known form of magic has been called "sympathetic magic" by Frazer. This is the belief that sorcerers can injure or kill anyone by getting hold of his nail clippings, hair, blood, saliva, excrement—in fact, of anything that has been a part of a person's body or has been in contact with his body (Frazer, 1911c, pp. 258-290).

Many of these anxieties and taboos are concentrated around birth. According to the Wolmeri of North West Australia, the child gets sick if the placenta is found by men or if the navel cord gets lost. Both mother and child may be harmed if they have any contact with men before the child is four or five days old (Kaberry, 1939, pp. 240-245). The Kiwai Papuans of British New Guinea put the afterbirth in a receptacle and bury it. If the sorcerers get hold of it, they can work harm on the child and its parents (Landtman, 1927, p. 231). The Kwoma bury the placenta under the floor of the house to keep it from falling into the hands of sorcerers (Whiting, 1941, pp. 150-151). In Buka (Solomon Islands) the mother will not sell or part with a lime pot containing the child's cord lest some evilly disposed person acquire it and work black magic against the child (Blackwood, 1935, pp. 160-161).

The Dilling cut the afterbirth of the first child and bury it under the threshhold of the hut of the child's maternal grandparents. The stump of the umbilical cord which falls from the child's body is put in a gourd with the remains of the oil which was used to anoint the mother's breasts. At puberty the child is told where his afterbirth is buried (Seligman and Seligman, 1932, pp. 389-390). According to an idea which is widespread in South America, the child will die if its umbilical cord is cut with a metal knife (Karsten, 1926, p. 461).

The anxiety connected with the umbilical cord is obviously separation anxiety. It is not so clear, however, why we should use the same interpretation when a part of the body, for example, nail parings or hair, is severed from the whole. Hermann (1936) has shown that some nervous habits like nail biting are abreactions of primal anxiety, that is, separation anxiety. From the viewpoint of dual unity, the part separated from the whole would be the child separated from the mother; here the child is both a whole and part of a whole.

Strictly speaking, this fear is not magic[7] but a symbolic representation of separation anxiety. Magic is the counterphobic attitude, the transition from passivity to activity. When sorcerers actually collect the leftover scraps of food, hair, nail

---

[7] This is a modification of views I have expressed previously. Cf. Róheim (1921); also Bergler (1945a), for a summary of my views.

parings, and so on, then we have magic, an abreaction of anxiety. At least one of the sorcerers I knew, Bulema, became a sorcerer because he was afraid of sorcerers (Róheim, 1950, pp. 151-243); and this has probably been repeated many times in many lands.

Taplin (1874) describes sorcery as practiced among the Narrinyeri—or rather a type of sorcery which they call *ngadhungi:*

> Every adult blackfellow is constantly on the look-out for bones of ducks, swans, or other birds, or of the fish called ponde, the flesh of which has been eaten by anybody. Of these he constructs his charms. All the natives, therefore, are careful to burn the bones of the animals which they eat, so as to prevent their enemies from getting hold of them. When a man has obtained a bone—for instance the legbone of a duck—he supposes that he possesses the power of life and death over the man, woman, or child who ate its flesh. The bone is prepared by being scraped into something like a skewer; a small round lump is then made by mixing a little fish oil and red ochre into a paste and enclosing in it the eye of a Murray cod and a small piece of the flesh of a dead human body. This lump is stuck on the top of the bone and a covering tied over it, and it is put in the bosom of a corpse in order that it may derive deadly potency by contact with corruption. After it has remained there for some time it is considered fit for use, and is put away until its assistance is required. Should circumstances arise calculated to excite the resentment of the disease-maker towards the person who ate the flesh of the animal from which the bone was taken, he immediately sticks the bone in the ground near the fire, so that the lump aforesaid may melt away gradually, firmly believing that as it dissolves it will produce disease in the person for whom it was designed, however distant he may be. The entire melting and dropping off of the lump is supposed to cause death [p. 19].

In the Kakadu tribe one form of black magic is called *tjilaiyu*. It is concerned with injuring a person by means of his excrement. Because of this, everyone is most careful to cover and hide from view all excrement, one result of which is that Kakadu camps are considerably cleaner than those of many other tribes. The medicine man, however, will find out where it is buried and, when no one is watching, he will go to the place and rake a little into a piece of bark with a stick, because it must not be touched. A ceremony is then performed over the excrement, by which the man is killed. Or the sorcerer may secure some fragment of the food the man has been eating. He ties it up in paper bark and takes it away furtively to his own camp, where he pounds it up and sings over it, thereby projecting evil magic into it. After this, he ties it up again and takes it to an ant hill, at the base of which he makes a small hole, pushes the food inside, and closes the hole so that it cannot be seen. Within three days the man becomes very hot, constantly cries out for water, and soon dies.

Another form of evil magic is associated with the mud that attaches itself to the foot of a native when he is walking through a swamp. When he comes to dry ground, he naturally scrapes the mud off with a piece of bark. If another man who wishes to injure him comes across his tracks, he gathers up some of the mud or the paper bark to which it is attached. He wraps it in more paper bark and ties it with string. Then he pounds it up, rolls it into a ball, and places it in a hole at the base of an ant hill. In due time sores spread all over the victim's foot, the toes drop off, and the hands and feet decay (Spencer, 1914, pp. 257-261).

The Euahlayi combine the "pointing bone" method with the part for the whole. The best way to make the *gooweera* (pointing stick) effective is to tie on the end of it some hair from the victim's head (Langloh Parker, 1905, pp. 31-32).

The erection of a men's house among the Kiwai Papuans requires an elaborate set of magical preliminaries. Various medicines have been accumulated for a long time, and others have yet to be procured. The *darimo abera,* or Father of the

Men's House,[8] sends out the men to fetch the different ingredients for the medicines. One set of medicines must be brought in from villages with which the people have had previous fights and where the inhabitants are still regarded as enemies, though peace may be reigning at the time. These medicines comprise a great variety of things which are needed only in very small quantities: a few leaves from the thatch of a house, some ashes from a fireplace, a fragment of the fireplace itself, and certain things connected with the enemy's person, namely, a little of his spittle, excrement and urine, a piece of soil where he has made water, his footprint in the ground, some hair left behind when he has been shaved, and the remains of food which show his teeth marks. Some emissaries go to one village, some to another. They have to show marked ingenuity in order to avoid detection, or they must invent some pretext for their visit. In stealing the ingredients the men must pick them up, not with the bare hand, but with the claw of a hawk which they hold in the hand. As the Kiwai describe it, "All same hawk pick up fish from water, no more let him go." The Father of the Men's House receives the medicines and ties them up with a string which was also obtained in the hostile villages; by this process the enemy is tied up so that he cannot fight back.

A second set of medicines is obtained from human trophies taken in previous fights and preserved for future use. These include the skull fragments of slain enemies, tongues, eyes, eyebrows, nails, and other parts of the body.

A third set of medicines is brought from the bush. The Father of the Men's House sends out some men to kill and bring home a wild pig. He also requests some grass from the lair of a pig and pieces of soil with marks of its feet and snout. A snake is necessary, and the teeth of a dog that was known to be fierce. Also brought from the bush are thorny

8 He and his wife will be killed, or are expected to die, when the house is completed.

scrubs, creepers, and leaves; these serve to block the road against sickness, so that it will not enter the house.

Then there are also the medicines from the shore: a piece of fish that has been bitten by a shark and shows the teeth marks; remains of another fish caught and eaten by a hawk; the claws of a certain crab which always snatches at people from its hole; and part of the skin of a "suckerfish" which clings tenaciously to its enemy (Landtman, 1927, pp. 9-12).

In another ceremony the house itself and also the Father of the Men's House and his wife are identified magically with a wild pig which is brought in, killed, and eaten. Now comes the erection of the central post. The hole is ready, and a mat stolen from the enemy is spread on the bottom of it. On top of this they put a bundle of all the "strong things" collected from the bush and the sea. Underneath the post they also put the eyebrows, finger nails, and parts of the tongues of slain enemies as a "good medicine belong fight." These human trophies have specific purposes: the eyebrows permit the men to find their hidden or scattered enemies when on a war expedition; the nails help them to seize and hold the enemy; and the tongues refer to, if they do not also anticipate, the shrieks of enemies who are being killed.

After the roof has been completed, the builders lay the fireplace. The old couple who supervise the construction of the house then light a fire in the principal hearth, that is, in front of the central post; this is done by drilling or rubbing a stick against a piece of wood. The fire must be freshly kindled, and it may not be brought from another house, or else there would be eternal quarreling in that house. The old couple, in lighting the fire, burn some of the things which were stolen from hostile villages in the past and which were kept for this purpose. The idea is that the smoke shall fill the entire house, and that "He want make plenty people"; that is, there should be so much talk that the people cannot hear each other (Landtman, 1927, p. 15).

This latter explanation is certainly an accretion which fits in with the ceremonial complex of the feast, since the feast brings together many people. Originally, burning the spittle, excrement, or urine of the enemy must obviously have meant burning the enemy himself.

Little children's hair is not cut until they begin to walk. The cutting is done with a shell or bamboo knife; and the hair which is cut off is carefully collected and thrown into the water, which is stirred up so that the hair cannot be found by anyone. Sometimes the hair from the first cutting is kept by the parents and shown to the child when he has grown up. Care is taken that no hair should fall into the hands of sorcerers, who can make *puripuri* (bad magic) with it. In some cases, care is also taken that nobody should find a child's nail parings (Landtman, 1927, pp. 234-235).

Among the Mafulu the use of food remnants for sorcery is confined only to those victims who have passed the stage of very young childhood. An adult never carelessly throws aside his own food remnants, even those which are inedible, for fear of sorcery. He throws them into a river, after which they cannot be used against him.

Urine or excrement are also a medium for sorcery among the Mafulu, but this applies only to an infant or a very young child. The mother picks up her little child's excrement and wraps it in a leaf; then she carefully hides it in a hole in the ground, or she throws it into the river, or she places it in a raised nestlike receptacle where it is also considered safe. To protect urine from sorcery, she pours some clean water on it (Williamson, 1912, pp. 280-281).

Phyllis M. Kaberry (1941) writes about the Abelam tribe:

Infancy is the most vulnerable age of all, and, during this period, the parents of the child are careful to remove and burn pieces of food left by the child. If it urinates upon the ground, water is poured over the spot, and faeces are gathered up with leaves and buried in the bush. Natives take a pride in keeping their piazzas free from rubbish, but in the case of a child still feeding at the breast, there is always a fear that a person evilly disposed towards the parents may take scraps of food, or earth where urine and faeces have fallen, and send it to a sorcerer in Waigagum village. If such a person wishes action to be taken immediately, he also sends a ring; otherwise the sorcerer keeps the "dirt," as it is also called in pidgin-English, until he receives further instructions [p. 365].

The natives of Lake Kutubu describe the "personal leavings" magic as *fanabu*. Some contact symbol of the intended victim, for example, a morsel of chewed or spat-out sugar cane, is introduced into the sorcerer's bamboo tube. Various magical substances are already in the tube, such as the minute hairs scraped from the shoots of bamboo or the juices of a decomposing corpse. The personal leavings, as already indicated, are stowed in a bamboo with these substances, and on top of them is placed some *yekako* (magic poison). The victim sickens and will die unless the sorcerer relents and empties the mixture out. It is not clear what *yekako* is; possibly it is a poisonous fungus (Williams, 1941, p. 381).

At Maloita the sorcerer steals some of the food remains of his victim, recites a spell over them, and then calls upon a spirit-familiar to eat them. This being is the height of a child, very bent and shriveled, with enormous quantities of long grizzled hair. Once the spirit has consumed the morsels of food, the victim inevitably dies (Hogbin, 1935, p. 20).

At Lesu the spell is made over the remains of some food which the man has half eaten. The same spell will be effective if made over the man's feces. It is for this reason as well as for cleanliness that, at the end of a feast, the remains of food are always thrown into the sea, and great precautions are taken never to leave feces where anyone will see it (Powdermaker, 1933, pp. 303-304).

Why should a man be identical with the scrap of food he has left over? For this assumption clearly underlies these forms of magic, because whatever is done to the leftover takes effect on the man who ate the bird or fish.

The first food we eat is mother's milk. In this situation the principle of sympathy is valid, and it is the bond which unites the mother and child.

ANAL MAGIC

We have seen above that magic really becomes "autarchic" as a countermove against the frustrating object, and that the erotogenic zones or qualities of the body are the weapons used in this countermove. Defecation certainly involves pain and relief; we thus find it as one of the means of warding off the evil eye or witchcraft.

A sterile woman, according to Serbian beliefs, has been influenced by the evil eye. To counteract this, she puts the excrement of a pig, or of a black hen hatched before St. George's Day, into her shoes. In labor pains, a woman swallows excrement in order to facilitate delivery.

The uses of excrement and the reference to St. George's Day indicate that we are dealing here not only with the pleasure aspect of defecation and with the rectum as an erotogenic zone but also with an unconscious fantasy. Defecation and delivery are identified; the child will come out as easily as the feces.

In Scotland a calf will be protected against the evil eye if some of its mother's dung is put into its mouth (Seligmann, 1910, p. 219). The witch cannot "eat" the child with her evil eye because the child is eating the witch (bad mother, excrement).

The cat is a frequent witch symbol in European folklore. Thus, for example, if the people of Hegyhát (Hungary) think that a child has been overlooked by the evil eye, they put coals in half a glass of water; then they dip their hands into the glass of water, and with this water they wash a cat's rectum. The child drinks some of this water, and the remainder is poured on the lintel (Nagy, 1892, p. 69).

If the cat is a witch, the tom-cat must be a wizard, that is, the father. But in other cases the major emphasis is clearly on that which is regarded as dirty but which was originally considered magically valuable because of its erogenous quality. In Göcsej (Hungary), the evil eye cannot hurt anyone who keeps his own navel string under his pillow, or they put the excrement of pigs into the first water with which the child is washed. Water taken from a pig trough is another common defense against magic. In Nyirmegges (Hungary), the child who is suffering from fright is made to drink foal dung in a glass of water (Luby de Benedekfalva, 1941, p. 116).

There seems to be an intimate association between witches and excrement. Some Indian witches are believed to learn their craft by eating filth. Interestingly enough, these women are always scrupulously clean and lovely in their personal appearance (Crooke, 1896, pp. 275-276).

On the Walpurgisnacht the German-speaking people of Czechoslovakia believe that the dung heap must be guarded against witches. If the witches manage to pour the fluids exuded by a corpse on the dung heap, the cows will lose their milk. Cow dung which is stolen by the witches gives them power over all the cows in the barn for an entire year. The symbolic equation of feces and food (milk) is quite obvious.

In Siklód (Hungary), the witches cannot steal the cow's milk if a newborn calf is pulled three times through a woman's underwear. Besides, nothing should leave the house for three days at this time, and no dung should be cleaned out from under the cow. All this helps the cow to keep her "luck" (Hegyi, 1937, p. 472).

Oldfield (1865) informs us that the Watchandie of Western Australia regard the anus as the main source of magical power (p. 235).

We have already noted that in Göcsej the *apotropaion* is

either one's own navel string or feces. It should be noted that anal magic is more "autarchic" than oral or genital magic, because the oral is directed toward the nipple, the penis toward the vagina. And, as we have also shown above, identification likewise enters into the complex of anal or fecal magic in the form of playing the role of the mother who is delivered of a (dead) sibling.

The role of excrement is even more marked in *black magic*. This is not surprising, especially since we know that there is such a thing as the *anal-sadistic* phase of the libido.

Evans-Pritchard (1937) writes: "Azande believe that witchcraft is a substance in the body of witches . . . When people cut open the belly they have only to pierce it and witchcraft-substance bursts through with a pop . . . I believe it to be the *small intestine in certain digestive periods*" (pp. 21-22; italics added).

Among the Pangwe, the *evu* (killing magic) is something similar. It is found in the upper part of the stomach, wanders about in the body, and causes disease of all kinds. If it goes into the head, it can also cause death. A woman may have her *evu* in the vulva; the result is a *penis captivus*. The remedy is to pour blood into her mouth or vagina (Tessmann, 1913, pp. 128-130).

According to the Bavili, the *ndongo* (evil power) lives in the stomach. When a corpse has been wrapped up, the *ndongo* fights its way out with a fearful expression, burning a hole through the wrappings (Dennett, 1906, pp. 83-84).

The transition from the oral to the excremental is frequently made. The reason for this is obvious: food becomes feces in the intestines. Both represent "body contents," that is, good or bad body contents.

The medicinal use of excrement has a long history in Europe. In 1533, for instance, Christian Petersen prescribed the following bath as a specific for aches and pains: Gather the dung of cows, horses, cats, and chickens; mix it all with vinegar and stale beer; warm it; sit in a bath tub and bake yourself in this mixture. If somebody's stomach is loose, he should take the excrement of white dogs that eat only bones. It should be pulverized, boiled in sweet milk, and given to the sick person as a drink. In a medical book of the next century, human excrement is called the "golden plaster." A pharmacopeia of Jean de Renou, published in 1608, observes that the excreta of all sorts of animals have specific healing powers; and the apothecary is advised to keep in stock the dung of goats, dogs, storks, peacocks, pigeons, and so on (Hovorka and Kronfeld, 1908, p. 247).

All this goes back to Greek and Roman sources. Pliny the Elder's *Naturalis Historia* contains an endless array of medicines based on the magical properties of excrement. Goats' dung against the evil eye; hens' dung for a heartburn; donkeys' feces as a cure for the ears; and the like.

Paullini, in his famous *Dreck Apotheke* and in his *Philosophischer Feyerabend* of 1700, defends the medical use of excrement:

It does not matter whether we use the word excrement or dirt or earth. It all amounts to the same thing. Human beings come from the earth, and the earth is our universal mother. Everything grows in her and goes back to the earth. Decomposition or putrefaction is life.

God is always and will be the old potter who day by day forms things. How do we obtain health and how do we restore it? With medicines made of roots, herbs, animal and mineral substances. But if you look into the origin of all this you have excrement and nothing else. Anybody who despises excrement despises his own origin.[9]

We find here that the magical value of excrement is based on the infantile anal birth theory and, as we have already

---

9 *Editor's note:* The source of this quotation, according to Róheim's manuscript, is *Der Unrat in Sitte, Brauch, Glauben und Gewohnheitsrecht der Völker* (Leipzig, 1912, p. 437). The book being unavailable, it has not been possible to verify this reference.

noted, that excrement also represents the essence of the mother, that is, the "good body contents."

A patient of mine (somewhat schizoid, whose analysis consists mostly of images produced on the analytic couch) frequently sees himself on the toilet defecating. What comes out is his younger brother. The fantasy goes on. He tries to kill his little brother, that is, flush the toilet; but the feces-child bites his buttocks. Sometimes the fantasy is this: Lots of little people are coming out of the excrement. He also sees the blackbirds of the nursery rhyme coming out of a pie, or black cats coming out of a horse which he has cut up.

One of his recurrent fantasies is that of "clothes on the line." He sees his mother hanging clothes (sometimes clean, sometimes dirty) on a line in their backyard, and he says: "I see a child defecating, then I am that child and I eat my own excrement."

He repeatedly produces the "cliff scene." Somebody pushes a covered wagon over a cliff, or galloping horses pull the wagon over the cliff. The "covered wagon" always referred to his mother when she was pregnant with his brother. The wagon falls, and a horse defecates into the chasm. He sees "something" (himself) peering into the wagon, and then he proclaims the following discovery: "Evacuation is the integrated vacuity."

Vacuity is a swollen but empty belly. By defecating a child, he evacuates his brothers, that is, he *makes mother's belly empty*. In his childhood he had rejected food, which was the same kind of behavior (his belly is empty = mother's belly is empty). The best thing to do would be to help all the excrement within him in the competition with his pregnant mother.

He visualized himself as a baby on a pot. He defecates gold coins and shows them proudly to his father. His father tastes one and throws it away, saying, "This is shitty."

Dream

President Roosevelt is going to speak in a hole. It is really a hall under the ground. I have a front seat, blocking the view from the others.

Associations

Senator Borah, boring from within. I see a penis coming out, an arm coming out.

Interpretation

He is outside. He wants to bore in, where all the good things are (good body contents = embryo, feces, penis).

After the interpretation he says: "Just before going to sleep, I had a very lively vision. It was like a hallucination. I saw a witch; it looked like my mother; it looked like you [i.e., the analyst]; it was ready to attack me per rectum with a soap suppository." This is the body-destruction fantasy in *talio* form, as *retribution*.

After this he sees a series of fantasies about feces or urine as fire, as destructive forces emanating from him. He sees what he calls "eyes," a demon looking at him. The "eyes" become a vagina, a penis, a breast; then semen is ejaculated from the penis, and feces come from the rectum.

This can be compared in European folklore with excrement or the phallos (cf. below) as countermagic against the evil eye. The libidinal-aggressive organs or substances coming at him from the "eyes" or "demon" are now in reverse; originally they went from the subject to the object.

Frustrating situations are the starting point, the beginning, of independence. A minimal degree of inevitable frustration is enough to achieve this result. Body-destruction fantasies are followed by the corresponding *talio* anxiety. The child's (not the mother's) insides will be empty, scooped out. Withholding the excrement or swallowing them means a reassurance against this anxiety.

The role of excrement in magic is similar to that of all other execretions and secretions. Frustration occurs inevitably in the dual-unity, or mother-child, situation. This frustration is countered by an erogenous zone; the defecating child is the mother; the excrement, the child. With this identification and change of roles, the object-seeking trend also sets in, with the emphasis either on the libido or the destrudo.

PHALLIC MAGIC

Paramount in many ways is the role of the phallos, of erection, as the supreme form of magic.[10]

The phallos was the main amulet against the evil eye or fascination—therefore the Romans called it the *fascinum*. In Lavinium, the town of the *lares* (household gods), a month was dedicated to the phallic god *Liber,* and the phallos or *fascinum* was carried through the market and back again to the temple of the god. The phallos was the final answer to all hostile magic, to envy, and to the evil eye (Preller, 1858, pp. 441-442). Priapos, the god, was represented as a red pole with an erect phallos; and it was his primary function to protect gardens against the evil eye. Threatening an eye, the phallos appears frequently on reliefs (Seligmann, 1910, pp. 188-200). Graves are also protected by Priapos (Roscher, 1902-1909, pp. 2967-2990).

The answer to the evil eye in Sicily, in Greece, and in Russia consists in touching one's own genitals. In Calabria, they press the penis firmly and shake it (Seligmann, 1910, p. 202).

Modern amulets also emphasize the phallos. In Italy, straightforward phallic amulets are frequently made of bronze, with the closed fist and the thumb protruding between the fore and middle fingers (Elworthy, 1895, pp. 149-

[10] We omit urethral magic because it follows the same pattern. For data cf. Róheim (1921).

154). This gesture occurs also in real life and is correctly interpreted by Seligmann as a combination of penis (thumb) and vagina, in other words, as coitus. The gesture is called the "fig," both in Greek and in Latin, and this also means the *cunnus*. In Greek the gesture was also called "to hit the *cunnus*" (Seligmann, 1910, pp. 183-184); and in German and Hungarian "to show the fig" (Tolnai, 1904). In Otranto the same gesture is called *fava* and refers to the glans penis (Seligmann, 1910, p. 184).

If we review all the charms used in Italy against the evil eye—coral, mother-of-pearl, or silver horns, nickel hands, mother-of-pearl or nickel hunchbacks, skulls, fish, flasks, keys, rings with the device of a skull, boars' tusks, and so on (Harrison, 1907, p. 189; Belluci, 1907; and Hildburgh, 1951, pp. 446-447)—we could probably show that they all represent either the penis or the vagina, or a combination of both. In Scotland we have the Sheila-na-gig, depicting a woman with exposed vulva, which was put on churches to ward off evil or to promote fertility (Murray, 1934, p. 99; 1936).

Coitus as a means of promoting the fertility of fields or cattle is too well known to require detailed discussion. Yugoslav farmers have intercourse with their wives in the stables at Christmas amidst the cattle. It is believed that this will induce the animals to do likewise and that the result will be many calves, lambs, and so on. In Dalmatia they say, "The way we embrace, cattle will do likewise" (Schneeweis, 1925, p. 120).

During the midsummer festival of Vedic times a priest and a prostitute reviled each other and then had intercourse in order to promote the fertility of the year. In other versions of the same ritual an Aryan and an aboriginal fight for a round piece of leather (a symbol of the sun), and a man and woman have intercourse within a fenced area (Schroeder, 1908, pp. 161-162; 1916, pp. 325-326).

We could continue to enumerate cases of this type, but it

is not necessary.[11] It should be noted, however, that in some instances ceremonial coitus is either a breaking of taboos or a means of allaying anxiety.

Berndt (1951) describes the *kunapipi,* which is the central mystery of the natives of Arnhem Land. Ritual copulation is termed *ka'rangara;* it is associated with special forms of dancing by men and women on the sacred grounds. At Yirkalla it is called *djambinba,* meaning "the working," since the natives use the word *djama* ("work") *when referring to the act of coitus.*[12] In this context there are both the exchanges of wives and the dances that represent coitus.

These dances are performed in a crescent-shaped trench called *kanala* or *ba'uma.* The trench may signify the following: the track mark of the female snake Julunggul; the mark left by her fall after she swallowed the Wauwalak (mythical sisters who are the most important mythological beings of this area); the crescent-shaped position in which the Wauwalak rested (slept) in their hut before the snake swallowed them; the clitoris of the Wauwalak; and its real "inside" meaning, the uterus of the Wauwalak. A smaller trench, called the "younger hole," is also dug and symbolizes the uterus of the younger sister.

When the crescent-shaped trench is completed, snake-totem dancers or actors approach it. Two male actors, one representing a man and the other a woman, perform the "mating dance." As Berndt (1951) describes it:

> The "man" has an erect bark penis and moves in pursuit of the "woman," who is desirous of coitus; they move towards the trench and dance around it, and at its entrance they simulate sexual intercourse. The Mother is said to be present in the *ba'uma,* and her *life-giving powers are made*

---

[11] Cf. Frazer (1911b, pp. 98ff.). See also the various volumes of the publication *Anthropophyteia,* edited in Vienna by F. S. Krauss.

[12] My Aranda informants at Hermannsburg called ritual in general *urkabuma.* This is the English *work,* transformed into an Aranda word.

operative by the sexual actions of the two dancers. ("The
acting of coitus by the totemites is like the uterus being
fertilized":[13] *the Mother is having sexual intercourse so*
that she may produce) [p. 43].

After this, two men represent male and female wagtails
having intercourse; then they act out the coitus of rock
pythons.

We can better understand the meaning of this behavior by
comparing it with the description given by Warner (1937).
The natives told him:

> The wet and the dry seasons are caused by the snakes.
> During the wet the snakes curl up and have sexual inter-
> course; the Great Father Snake does the same. Then they
> come out of the water and want to lay their eggs. This
> brings on the dry season so that they can have such a place.
> [One of the clan leaders explained the relationship be-
> tween real and mythical snakes:] The children are little
> Muits (mythical snakes). They live here on the earth or
> with their father in the sky or with him in the waters down
> below the earth. Their children are true wirtits (i.e., real
> snakes). It is the little Muits (mythical snakes) who swallow
> a man or woman when they do some unclean thing such as
> a woman's getting into a canoe while menstruating. It is
> Muit (the snake father, the rainbow) who makes the rain
> [p. 384].
> [Another explanation is:] The cycle of the seasons with
> the growth and decay of vegetation, copulation, birth and
> death of animals as well as man, it is all the fault of those
> two Wawilak sisters. "If they hadn't done wrong in their
> own country and copulated with Dua Wongar (an inces-
> tuous act) and then come down to the Liaalaomir country
> and menstruated and made that snake wild (angry)," this
> cycle would never have occurred. "Everyone and all the
> plants and animals would have walked about by them-
> selves." There would have been no copulation between the
> sexes and no children and no change [p. 385].

[13] *Ipsissima verba* of the natives. My italics.

When Berndt's informant talks about "the Mother" who brings forth everything because of the coitus dance, we have the positive aspect of the whole complex; that is, the result is regarded as something desirable, something that should be achieved through the ritual.

The magical character of the whole performance is clear. Human beings do something (the coitus dance); therefore, the animals and the world in general do the same. We note also that there is an identification with the past, because the ritual is a repetition of events which happened in mythological times. What makes the world revolve, the seasons change, men and women copulate, and so on? *It is incestuous libido, the symbolic coitus with the mother.* The performance is certainly magical, but at the same time it is obviously a sublimation.

That it is really incest that keeps the world going is proved by the ceremonial exchange of wives which takes place at the same time. There is a ceremonial exchange of wives between cross-cousins who are otherwise taboo to each other (Berndt, 1951, pp. 48-49).[14]

Warner (1937) writes:

The cycle of songs sung and the dance, first of the male of the species, then of the female, and finally their offspring, are symbolical of reproduction [p. 297].

[However, there is another aspect to these magical dances, as Warner notes:] . . . a single man filled with sexual desire and looking for a mate is danced. Then a man representing a woman, also sexually hungry and looking for a mate is danced. And finally the two together perform a dance; meeting at the entrance of the kartdjur (trench), they simulate copulation but do not enter the "well". . . . The kartdjur is that head inside the woman's vagina. It is the same as her marn-bu (clitoris). The crescent shape is

[14] Cf. Howitt (1904, pp. 276-277) on the exchange of wives to dispell the anxiety caused by the Aurora Australis.

the way the two women laid down in the house before the snake swallowed them [p. 302].

Why can they dance in the trench that represents the clitoris (this is the more common interpretation) but not in the well? In order to answer this question we must go back to the myth. We cite only that part of the myth where one of the two Wawilak sisters has angered the Great Snake by polluting his well with her menstrual blood. The Snake rises and starts a rain which threatens to flood the earth. The two sisters build a hut and go to sleep, but the flood still keeps coming. They keep singing and dancing to stop the flood. But it is in vain, for finally the great serpent swallows them (Warner, pp. 252-254).

We see now why the coitus dancers do not enter the "well." Residing in the water holes or "wells" of the clans are the unborn spirits of children, and also the totemic ancestors themselves and the dead members of the clan (Warner, pp. 448-450). It is quite clear that the totemic water hole is the womb. The coitus dance is performed *at* the entrance of the womb. The mythical dance was danced to *delay* the swallowing (or uterine regression). This is the significance of the basic dream—it is a genital defense mechanism against sleep or uterine regression (Róheim, 1951; 1953, Chap. 1).

As I have shown previously (1925b, p. 297; 1945b, p. 125) the various rites for multiplying the totemic animal are all abbreviated symbols of coitus. Scattering sand, throwing, blood letting, and especially blood letting from the subincised penis—they all amount to the same thing. We now see quite clearly what I suspected a quarter of a century ago, namely, that the real *magic* in the multiplication of the totemic animal is the repressed oedipal libido.

Black or hostile magic is predominantly phallic in Australia. Among the natives of Ooldea, if a woman refuses to have intercourse with a man who desires her, he may use the object called *tulu*. The tapering end of this object is said to be "like a penis." The man pushes the *tulu* downward into sand upon which the woman has urinated. This damp sand represents her vulva. The power of the *tulu* pierces the woman's uterus (Berndt and Berndt, 1943, pp. 124-125).

The famous "pointing bone" is the outstanding example of phallic (anal) aggression. If a man has been "boned," his dream will show it. First he sees a crack, an opening in the ground, and then two or three men walking toward him within the opening. When they are near they draw a bone out of their own body. It comes from the flesh between the scrotum and the rectum. The sorcerer, before he actually "bones" his victim, makes him fall asleep by strewing in the air some semen or excrement which he has taken from his own penis or rectum. The man who uses the bone holds it under his penis, as if a second penis were protruding from him.

The Pindupi refer to black magic in general as *erati,* and a special type is described as *kujur-punganyi* ("bad make"). Several men hold a string or pointing bone with both hands and, bending down, point backward, passing the magical bone just beside the penis. The victim is asleep, and the bone goes straight into his scrotum.

Women also make evil magic through the agency of their imaginary penis. Luritja women cut their pubic hair and make thereof a long string. They take a kangaroo bone and draw blood from their vagina. The string becomes a snake which penetrates into the heart of their victims (Róheim, 1950, pp. 129-133).

IDENTIFICATION

In psychoanalytic literature magic or magic gesture has come to signify imitation, or identification, or the playing of a role (Bergler, 1945a, 1945b). Frequently, the magician takes the part of a mythical hero. Thus, on Normanby Island, the leader of the *kune* (canoe expedition) performs the magic in the role of Kasabwaibwaileta, the mythical originator of the whole institution. The incantation itself is very often of the epic formula type. The idea is that a recitation of events which occurred in the mythical past will inevitably cause these events to recur.

Normanby Island magic is based in general on a mythical precedent, and in the incantation there is at least an allusion to the mythical past. The following is an epic incantation connected with love magic:

> Sine Gaga Loyloy[15]
> On the shore of Gabuwana
> You and your own brother
> He saw your vagina
> He insisted, he begged
> He desired you
> Sister, let us do wrong
> They did wrong, it was done
> Married women and girls
> For them I drink water
> O, woman who lives beyond the ocean
> I slept with her, I left her
> Now she cries for me, she sobs for me
> Sister, let us do wrong
> Girls with desirable breasts
> For them I drink the salt water.

[Now the girl is speaking:]

> Where is a fine man
> What did you do to me
> Your mother shouts for you in vain
> My tears they are for you
> Brother, let us do wrong
> We have done wrong, it's done.

This incantation is based on the incestuous myth of Tau-hau, with the dialogue having allegedly taken place between

15 The name of a woman.

Tauhau and his sister. In the love magic which is based on this myth, human beings or events follow a mythical or divine prototype. The man drinks salt water, chews half a coconut, and, after speaking the incantation *into* the other half, gives it to the girl to chew. He will thus be successful in obtaining the girl's love, just as Tauhau had intercourse with his sister in the mythical past. That is, love and love magic are based on the rediscovery of the incestuous love object of infancy.

In European magic this is called an *epical incantation*. Perhaps the best-known example is the famous Merseburg incantation about Balder and Odin and Balder's horse, where a divine prototype exists for healing a wound (Mansikka, 1909, p. 258).

Ancient Egyptian elements survived in the incantations which were in use in the Fayum in the eighth century A.D. For example, a child has a pain in the stomach, and the relevant incantation recounts how Horus, suffering from a pain in the navel, was cured by Isis, his mother (Erman and Krebs, 1899, pp. 257-258). In a papyrus dated toward the end of the New Empire we find the narrative of how Ra was bitten by a serpent and healed by Isis. For a long time this was a specific against snake bite (Roeder, 1915, pp. 138-141). In Babylonia the retelling of how the gods conquered the seven mythical devils served as magic against eclipses or torrential rains (Jastrow, 1905, pp. 361-363). Likewise, sacred names may be invoked; and, as in Vedic India, a narrative account of the desired result produces the effect, just as the mentioning of the name would (Oldenberg, 1894, p. 516).

Innumerable variants of the epical incantation are known in European folklore. The following, for example, is recited to extinguish a fire:

> Jesus Christ traveled and he met a fire. Fire, be extinguished, don't go any further [Köhler, 1867, pp. 403-404; Seyfarth, 1913].
>
> [Or compare the Finnish formula:] In ancient times

Kuume locked up the Moon. She locked up the Moon and hid the Sun. Kave liberated the Moon from the yard, from the inside of an iron barn; and from a hill of steel she liberated the Sun. In the same way I liberated this person from the evil words of the villagers, from the words of the bearded ones, from the magic of long-haired ones, from the magical arts of women, from the curses of dirty prostitutes. I liberated him by permission of the Creator. Just as the Son of the Sun was liberated when the Daughter of the Sun liberated him, this man shall be free now that I liberate him [Lönrott, 1880, p. 92; see also Abercromby, 1898, pp. 133-134; Christiansen, 1914; and Hästesko, 1914].

According to Koch-Grünberg (1914), the Taulipang of Guiana have elaborate epical incantations. They say the following, for example, if somebody has worms or if they wish to protect a corpse from worms:

A young man of the ancestors was suffering from worms. I shall clean his stomach so he never has pains. Just like this the people of the present time, these children of our days [p. 373].

If the parents of a newborn child want to eat fish, they recite the following incantation to prevent the child from getting a stomach-ache and diarrhea:

The great beaver had a newborn son. A week after the birth she went fishing and caught two little fish. Then she met two little beavers. They asked the big beaver, "Why didn't you catch the fish with a spear?" The beaver replied, "Because then the child would get diarrhea and die." The two other beavers said, "How is it that we never have diarrhea among our newborn children when we kill fish? The way we kill fish, you can do it too; it won't hurt the child" [p. 374].

[The meeting, like the dialogue, is repeated with a number of water-dwellers, who add:] I eat this fish with this pepper and this salt. With this pepper I drive disease away, so that disease should never come to our son [pp. 375-377].

This is the way the people of today should talk when they have little children and want to eat fish. For a week after the birth they eat only small fish.[16]

According to the Takelma Indians, various spirits have their medicine songs, and these are efficacious in countering the sorcerer's magic. These songs are mythical narratives. For instance, they recount how a great misfortune befell a shaman of yore, and they thereby project the same misfortune on the contemporary shaman:

> When this great world was first set, at that time the Old Rock Woman was told, "Thou shalt be a shaman wisher" (or "poisoner"); "if an evil-minded shaman devours people, thou shalt sing for that.".... And then she sang for the shaman, whereupon the shaman died [Sapir, 1907, p. 46; 1909, pp. 171-173].

The Koryak tell the following tale in order to put an end to rain or a snowstorm:

> In order to cause rain on earth, Universe attaches his wife's vulva to a drum, which he beats with his penis: and and the liquid which is squirted out from the vulva falls down on the earth as rain. In order to put an end to the incessant rain, Big-Raven and his son Eme'mqut turn into ravens and fly up to heaven. They cause the deity and his wife to fall asleep, and carefully dry their privates by the fire [Jochelson, 1905, pp. 26-27].

The same is true among the Chukchee, where the "Raven Incantation," a narrative tale, is used as an epical prototype (Bogoras, 1907, p. 478). Folk tales in general, if told at a certain time, are also supposed to serve as fertility charms or incantations (Frazer, 1911c, pp. 384-386; Shortland, 1882, p. 7; and Parkinson, 1907, p. 198).

The Yabim of New Guinea, for example, believe that they get more taro by telling the following story:

16 The forbidden fish represents the child. Fish in the water = embryo in the womb.

Once a man worked in his field, and he complained that he had no taro shoots. Two pigeons flew from Poum; they had eaten a lot of taro. They sat on a tree in the field and vomited all the taro. So he had plenty of taro shoots; he could even sell some [Neuhauss, 1911, p. 333].

The Yabim achieve a victory in war by telling a narrative about a victorious warrior. Similarly, every myth of the Kai ends with the formula, "Plenty of shoots and fruit," and some versions add, "So be it certainly."

There are also other forms of identification. The desired result is achieved by representing it as occurring to the magician himself or to an object that represents the magician. The Mara of Northern Australia have special rain makers. After various incantations, including the drinking of water and spitting, the magician throws water all over himself (Spencer and Gillen, 1904, pp. 313-314). A Wotjobaluk rain maker dips his own hair into the water (Howitt, 1904, p. 398). This type of behavior is especially notable in the *intichiuma* rites, or increase ceremonies, in which the totem animal is magically multiplied.

At Malupiti (Kangaroo Hole), the Pitjentara perform a ritual to multiply kangaroos. The men are decorated with bird-down; the women, with white paint and ochre. The men imitate kangaroos playing in the grass; as a result it is expected that the kangaroos will multiply. In the ritual of the emu totem, it is important for the participants to imitate the manner in which the emus stretch their necks and how they drink at the pools. At the rain ceremony the performers represent the gathering rain clouds.[17]

The identification with water is the outstanding feature of the Vedic rain-making ceremony. The candidate who is learning the incantation has to touch water three times a day, and he has to wear black clothes and eat black food

17 From my own field notes.

(black clouds). If it rains he must sit in the rain, and whenever he crosses water he must be sure to touch it (Oldenberg, 1894, p. 420).

In Eastern Europe this kind of rain making takes an interesting form, with water being poured over a little girl. In Rumania, for example, a naked gypsy girl is covered with leaves, weeds, and flowers, and she goes through the village. The people drench her with water at each doorway. She is accompanied by a large number of people, who sing:

> Paparuda-ruda,
> Come and wet us,
> That rain may fall,
> With water pails:
> To make the corn grow
> As high as hedges . . .
> [Beza, 1928, pp. 27-28].

In Bulgarian, *peperuda* means "butterfly." In one district the girl must be an orphan. She is decorated with bushes and plants, and two desiccated frogs hang from her ears. The songs emphasize poverty and implore heaven for water. One song in particular asks the deity to provide plenty of rain, especially for the orphans, who have no mother or father to take care of them. Finally, the frogs are buried.

The Arabs of Moab dress a dummy as a woman and call it the "Mother of the Rain." They carry it in processions and sing:

> O, Mother of the Rain, O Immortal, moisten our sleeping seeds.
> Moisten the sleeping seeds of the sheikh, who is ever generous
> She is gone, the Mother of the Rain, to bring the storm; when she comes back, the crops are as high as the walls.
> She is gone, the Mother of the Rain, to bring the winds; when she comes back, the plantations have attained the height of lances.

> She is gone, the Mother of the Rain, to bring back the
> thunders; when she comes back, the crops are as high
> as camels [Jaussen, 1908, pp. 326-328].

The frequency with which children are drenched with
water in these rites is possibly explicable on the assumption
that the rain is a mother's gift (milk) to the child. Shedden-
Ralston (1872) suggests that Dodola, which is the name of the
girl in the Slavic rain-making rites, may be derived in Russian
from *doit*—"to give milk" (p. 229).

In Armenia the effigy is called "Drenched Mother." They
ask, "What does Drenched Mother want?" The answer is,
"She wants wheat in her bins, she wants bread on her bread
hooks, and she wants rain from God!" Then they pour water
on the dummy from the roofs, and the rich people give
presents to the children (Frazer, 1911a, p. 276).[18]

This is reminiscent of the "magic gestures" described by
Bergler (1945b). The fluid is poured on the mother: this is
how bountiful *she should be*. Proof: it is the children who get
the presents.

Identification comes closest to reality in the dual-unity or
child-mother relationship. We sometimes speak of dual unity
and sometimes of the oral phase. Actually both mean the
same thing. In the first instance, what we emphasize is the
subject-object relationship; in the second, the libidinal zone
through which the relationship takes place.

It must be obvious, therefore, that we grow up via *magic*.
We pass through the pregenital to the genital phases of organization, and concurrently our mastery of our own body and
of the environment increases. This is our own "magic," and
it is analogous in some ways to the invocation of his own
luonto ("nature") by the Finnish wizard.

At the same time we also grow up by identification or
introjection. Boys play at being men, girls at being mothers.

---

18 Frazer is quoting here from the MS. of J. Rendel Harris. Frazer also
quotes some of the aforementioned data.

A series of introjections take place; and these, together with what is innate in us, condition the final shape of our personality. *Persona* means "mask" (Mauss, 1938, p. 274), the mask used by actors whereby they are transformed into the god or hero they represent. The Australian native who is decorated with the body marks of a mythical hero has identified himself with that particular "eternal one of the dream." Toward the end of the *kunapipi* ritual, the "Old Woman" is supposed to enter the ceremonial grounds. When the men eat the food given to them, *she also eats it*; and then, in return for the food, she vomits up the novices whom she still has in her belly (uterus) (Berndt, 1951, p. 160).

The child deals with the threat of object loss either by identification or by calling on the sources of pleasure within its own body. Magic may thus be oral, anal, urethral, narcissistic, or phallic. It is our great reservoir of strength against frustration and defeat and against the superego. While the magical omnipotence fantasy of the child means growing up, magic in the hands of an adult means a regression to an infantile fantasy. The individual is talking to the world outside: "If you frustrate me, I can still find pleasure in my own body." The ego talks to the enemy within the gates: "I refuse to give up my desires." To anxiety we say: "I have lived and overcome frustrations so far; I mean to win my battles in the future."

Magic, in its late development, reverts to its origins. One of its earliest sources is the hallucinatory wish fulfillment of the infant; and in the Middle Ages magic becomes the art of creating an illusion or delusion.

Faust, the famous sorcerer, finds himself without any money. So he transforms three bunches of straw into three fat hogs and sells them to a peasant. But beware of letting the hogs touch water, he says. When they lie down in the mud, however, the illusion ceases and there they are, back in the shape of straw (Kiesewetter, 1921, pp. 226-227). The sor-

cerer comes to an inn and produces fish and wine out of
nothing for the guests. Then a group of students are trying
to fight each other with drawn swords. He deludes them so
that they cannot see each other. He sees a priest carrying a
prayer book and he makes him believe that what he has in
his hand is not a prayer book but a pack of cards (Kiesewetter,
1921, pp. 228-229). Here, by imperceptible transitions, the
magic of folklore becomes the parlor magic of modern times.

A Silesian *Gaukler* was giving a performance in which a
cock walked up and down with a straw in its mouth. The
audience, believing the piece of straw to be a beam of wood,
was impressed and amazed. A girl who was fortunate enough
to have a four-leafed clover in her basket recognized the
deceit and told the people. The magician took his revenge.
By means of his magic art he made her believe that the room
was full of water; she lifted her skirts up high, and everyone
laughed at her (Kühnau, 1913, pp. 230-231). Similar stories
are told about a Hungarian magician of the Faust type; likewise, the art of Prospero and Ariel is essentially the art of
creating an illusion.

We grow up through magic and in magic, and we can never
outgrow the illusion of magic. Our first response to the frustrations of reality is magic; and without this belief in ourselves, in our own specific ability or magic, we cannot hold
our own against the environment and against the superego.

The infant does not know the limits of its power. It learns
in time to recognize the parents as those who determine its
fate, but in magic it denies this dependency. The ultimate
denial of dependency comes from the all-powerful sorcerer
who acts out the role which he once attributed to the projected images. Greatness is also based on identification. As
opposed to the lay world, the magician plays the part of the
ego ideal or the superego. Thus the wonderful Wizard of Oz
can easily confer absent qualities on the cowardly lion and
on the others, because the very absence of these qualities is

due to the superego. It is the superego that tells the ego, "You are a coward, or have no heart or brain." But if the superego is won over, all is well again.

Magic is also a revolt against the gods. The sorcerer is the son who claims equal powers with his father, and, like the giants of Pentheus' blood, *he stands against God, against the Thunder* (Harrison, 1912, p. 434). The analyst, in giving interpretations, actually (but only temporarily) takes the side of the primary process; and that which has been distorted by secondary elaboration is restored and made conscious. Repression is undone; concept and libido are reconnected. We actually can move Acheron against the Gods. And, in analyzing others, we are fighting their superego and our own. For this is dream interpretation (and Freud's motto): *Flectere si neque superos Acheronta movebo!*

In magic, mankind is fighting for freedom. Fromm (1941), taking a more optimistic view of human development, believes that mankind, like a child, emerges from the stage of dependency on the mother to an ever-increasing degree of individuation and freedom (p. 24). If the biogenetic law of Haeckel were valid, this would be correct. But, since we are prone to an ever-increasing degree of foetalization, the opposite is true. We are neither as free nor as "adult" as our stone-age ancestors (Róheim, 1950, Chap. 10; Carter, 1953, p. 340).

Gesell (1940) indicates that, in a functional sense, the infant after birth remains a part of the mother. It is fed, carried, and cared for in every respect by the mother. In time, the child slowly learns to "grasp" other objects and gives up "grasping" the mother. As Hermann (1936) has shown, the primary reaction of the child consists in clinging to the mother, thus attempting to cancel the separation that has taken place in the act of birth. These attempts are naturally futile in the long run. The mother becomes less and less yielding, the child more and more frustrated. But the process of growth is at work, and the child becomes more and more capable of fending for itself. At the same time, there is a withdrawal of the libido from the object-erotic to the narcissistic position.

Gesell (1940) points out:

> The 28-week-old infant is relatively self-contained . . . Having acquired such a creditable command of eyes, head, mouth, arms and hands, he cannot give too much attention to onlookers! He takes keen delight in the exercise of his newly attained neuro-motor abilities . . . If he were too socially compliant he would refer and defer his activity too much to others. He can consolidate and correlate his developmental gains to better advantage by this independence. In his self-sufficiency he reminds us somewhat of the 18-month runabout who also is especially fond of his own devices. The most conspicuous difference in these two age levels is postural: 28 weeks is sedentary; 18 months is ambulatory; but both are much preoccupied with private enterprise for sound developmental reasons [pp. 23-24].

Through a series of oscillations from the narcissistic to the object-erotic positions, the child grows up. The two-year-old oscillates between independence and self-containedness:

> His "negativisms" and ambiguities are due to the same factors which create confusion in the use and application of pronouns. He has not yet made complete distinction between himself and others. But his dramatic play is much more elaborate than at the age of 18 months; it penetrates further into his cultural environment. Whether boy or girl, the 2-year-old is especially prone to dramatize the mother-baby relationship through dolls and otherwise. In a dim way he is beginning to understand this relationship which means that he himself is becoming somewhat detached from his mother [p. 40].

THEORIES

In pre-Freudian times, anthropologists understood the meaning of magic but not its ontogenetic background. Marett, as we shall note presently, came very close to the core of the problem. All that we must add to Marett's insight is that the efficacy of magic originates in the first year of life (oral phase), when the infant's gestures, like its crying, are really effective (Ferenczi's omnipotence of gestures).

Vierkandt (1907) took the reflex action as his starting point, while Preuss (1904, 1905) emphasized everything that emanates from the body. But it was Marett (1914) who noted that in magic a subjective effect is equated with an actual influence on the environment: "The inwardness of such *mana* or magical power we have seen reason to regard as derived by the magician from a more or less intuitive perception of his projective act of will as the force which occultly transmutes his pretence into ulterior reality" (p. 59).

A decade or two earlier, Brinton (1897) wrote the following about magic: "A study of its aspect in savage life shows that it arises from the perception of the latent activity of the sub-consciousness, from the strange sense of activity, will and power, which, under favorable conditions of concentration (suggestion), it imparts to the more or less conscious Self" (pp. 59-60).

It is a familiar fact that we dislike change. The result is that we abreact our anxieties in ritual. It is generally known, since van Gennep (1909), that transition rites are among the most universal forms of ritual. Birth, the transitions from infancy to childhood and from puberty to manhood, marriage, death—all these are marked by rites. Similarly, as I have shown elsewhere (Róheim, 1942), the crossing of a river, a frontier, or the like, tends to repeat the drama of separation from the mother and of reunion with a mother substitute. It is, in other words, akin to the process of growing up.

As Hermann (1936) has emphasized, when "graspings" are transformed into "seekings," that is, when mother-directed trends become "away-from-the-mother" trends, then it is the narcissistic cathexis which bridges over the intermediary period in the individual's life. The growing child leaves the mother, but the cathexis remains narcissistic until he finds a sweetheart or a wife. The individual withdraws the cathexis from the object world and invests it in his own body, but only to send it out again toward the object world. In other words, we see (a) oral dependency, (b) growth, (c) genital primacy.

As we have already noted above, Fromm believes that growing up is a process of individuation and that mankind is also growing up in this sense. That is, moving from a condition in which the individual is very limited by society to one in which the individual is free and self-reliant.[19] This may appear true if we look at that section of European history from the Middle Ages to the nineteenth century. But if the testimony of anthropology indicates anything, it shows that primitive man is free, untrammeled, and truly self-reliant in comparison with Medieval or Modern Man.

I shall never forget the Pitjentara children, who, at the age of eight or ten, went roaming about the desert and were practically self-supporting. A boy, with his keen eyes and his spear, can catch what he needs in small fry and keep going from morning until evening. Even an adult male cannot do very much more. The outstanding characteristic of primitive economies is the absence of a true differentiation of labor. An incipient or rudimentary division of labor may exist along sexual or age lines, and there may be some incipient and part-time specialization in matters of ritual and magic. But true specialization is lacking. This means that every individual is technically a master of the whole culture or, where certain modest qualifications are necessary, of almost the whole

---

[19] Fromm, who avoids thinking in terms of libido displacements, quotes *A High Wind in Jamaica*, by R. Hughes, in order to illustrate the psychology of individuation. A ten-year-old child suddenly becomes aware of her individuality: "The contact of her face and the warm bare hollow of her shoulder gave her a comfortable thrill, as if it was the caress of some kind friend" (Fromm, 1941, p. 28).

culture. In other words, each individual is really self-reliant and grown up.

We, however, do not grow up as simply as that. The "intro-jected object" is not only something we assimilate (and thereby increase our powers), it is also something in us that says "No" to whatever we are trying to achieve. Nor is it necessary to belabor the point that the very marked speciali-zation and division of labor which are characteristic of com-plex societies do not make for any blithe self-reliance.

THE SUPEREGO

The road that leads to *mana* (magical power) is frequently that of asceticism and self-torture.

The Yogi, according to the Kshurika-Upanishad, must re-nounce not only the external world but also his own body. The separation from his own body takes place by means of a successive *cutting off* of the parts of the body, with the *manas* (will, desire) being the knife used in these proceedings. This is achieved by the concentration of cathexis on certain parts of the body, with these being gradually separated from the ego and relinquished. The aim of the entire process is to break through the cycle of reincarnation (Deussen, 1905, p. 633).

The practice of austerities is the means of gaining power for the ultimate union with the infinite. When we read the regulations which are recommended by the Yoga for the acquisition of the highest degree of omnipotence, we observe at once that they amount to a complete frustration—that is, to the great triumph of the superego or destrudo. Eros, how-ever, is sometimes mobilized against destrudo, as the follow-ing feat will indicate. Oman (1908) writes:

> . . . the Yogi Haridas, after voluntarily falling into a self-induced trance in the presence of the Maharaja Ranjít Singh, of the Punjab, and his court, was carefully buried outside the city of Lahore. For forty days strict watch was

kept over the grave, and, at the expiration of that time, the
Yogi was exhumed, cold, stiff, and unconscious; but was
gradually restored to animation by applying warmth to the
head and friction to the body, while forcing air gently into
the lungs [p. 17].

[We are confronted here with a philosophy in which all
human faculties are regarded as evil and must be killed:]
If in this state you have any consciousness of seeing the
Infinite Spirit, cancel that consciousness also. For who is it
that sees, and what is it that sees, and what is it that is
seen? In fact, empty yourself from the consciousness of
wisdom and duality; you must become the Infinite Spirit
without the idea of becoming the Infinite Spirit [p. 18].

It is important to note that all this asceticism, all these
austerities, are really a form of self-punishment in which the
object world, a source of pleasure, is being taken away from
the ego by the superego. Alexander (1923), who discussed
these phenomena from the viewpoint of regression, emphasized the parallel between these ascetic practices and melancholia (p. 40).

The origin of penance and austerity from the superego, in
this case from the primitive, preoedipal superego, becomes
quite clear in the example which follows. Baba Farid, a
modern Mussulman saint of India, resolved to fast for twelve
years. He satisfied his appetite merely by gnawing on a piece
of wood which was shaped like a piece of bread. Apparently,
when he returned home after an absence of twelve years, his
mother still considered him a glutton, because he had kept
the thought of bread before him. He took this to heart and
left again for a period of penance, this time living only on
the leaves of trees. His mother reproached him again, this
time for having deprived the trees of their hair. So he went
away for a third period of penance and suspended himself
head downward in a well, without partaking of food of any
kind and without even moistening his lips with a drop of
water. As he hung in the well, the birds fell upon the flesh

of his body, and the only favor which he asked was that his eyes might be spared. This devotion was finally accepted by Allah (Oman, 1907, p. 313).

The whole doctrine, which considers duality as the fundamental evil and omnipotence as the final goal, is completely intelligible from the viewpoint of the fundamental dual unity of mother and child, with separation being the original frustration. The archaic superego or mother image is then introjected as the "bad mother" and begins to kill the subject. This is the austerity phase; while the communion with the infinite in the Yoga, the union with Atman, the attainment of absolute omnipotence, is the fantasy reparation after the phase of absolute self- (and object-) destruction.

Similar phenomena, with destrudo and libido in succession, or melancholia and mania, are typical of many magical rites. Catlin, for example, tells us about the "mystery" or "medicine" of the North American Indians. The mystery bag or medicine bundle is the key to the Indian's life and character. These bags are made from the skins of animals, birds, or reptiles, and are often stuffed with moss or grass. The Indian pays homage to this bag and looks to it for safety and protection during his entire life. Catlin (1859) writes:

> The manner in which this curious and important article is instituted is this: a boy, at the age of fourteen or fifteen years, is said to be making or "forming his medicine," when he wanders away from his father's lodge and absents himself for the space of two or three, and sometimes even four or five days; lying on the ground in some remote or secluded spot, crying to the Great Spirit, and fasting the whole time. During this period of peril and abstinence, when he falls asleep, the first animal, bird, or reptile, of which he dreams (or pretends to have dreamed, perhaps), he considers the Great Spirit has designated for his mysterious protector through life [p. 71].

Then he kills the appropriate animal or bird, procures its skin for his medicine bundle, and regards the animal-spirit

in question as his protector or guardian. The Indian considers the medicine bundle as the bearer of his luck and
power; to lose it would mean to be degraded in the eyes of
other people.

Prince Wied-Neuwied (1841) describes how the Mandans
call upon their guardian spirits. They fast and do penance
for a number of days, and they cut off the joints of their
fingers. They lament, howl, and cry to the Master of Life or
to the First Man to give them a guardian spirit (p. 166).

The point to the whole complex of seeking the guardian
spirit is obvious, namely, that melancholia, followed by mania
or euphoria, is the basis for a normal adjustment. In this
connection Loskiel (1794) writes: "An Indian is *dispirited*,
and considers himself as forsaken by God, till he has received
a tutelar spirit in a dream; but those who have been thus
favored, are *full of courage, and proud of their powerful ally*"
(p. 40).[20]

Heckewelder, according to Frazer (1910), has described the
sequence of melancholia and mania among the Delawares:

> When a boy is to be thus initiated, he is put under an
> alternate course of physic and fasting, either taking no food
> whatever, or swallowing the most powerful and nauseous
> medicines, and occasionally he is made to drink decoctions
> of an intoxicating nature, until his mind becomes suffi-
> ciently bewildered, so that he sees visions and has extraor-
> dinary dreams, for which, of course, he has been prepared
> beforehand. He will fancy himself flying through the air,
> walking under ground, stepping from one ridge or hill to
> the other across the valley beneath, fighting and conquering
> giants and monsters and defeating whole hosts by his single
> arm . . . When a boy has been initiated, a name is given to
> him analogous to the visions he has seen, and to the destiny
> that is supposed to be prepared for him. The boy, imagin-
> ing all that happened to him while under perturbation to
> have been real, sets out in the world with lofty notions of

[20] My italics. Cf. Frazer (1910, pp. 391-401).

himself, and animated with courage for the most desperate undertakings [p. 395].

It must be emphasized that *the omnipotence which is achieved in magic is a rejoinder to the aggression of the superego. The superego, the introject of primary, oral, object frustration, is represented in rites with a strong emphasis on oral frustration and on an inward turning of aggression. The countermove to this aggression is the additional "mana" which is derived from this period of deprivation.*

In Goethe's *Faust* we find a graphic representation of the relatedness of magic and the superego. It will be recalled that Faust is not in a happy mood when he resorts to magic:

> Then, too, I've neither lands nor gold,
> Nor the world's least pomp nor honor hold—
> No dog would endure such a curst existence.
> Wherefore, from Magic I seek assistance,
> That many a secret perchance I reach
> Through spirit-power and spirit-speech,
> And thus the bitter task forego
> Of saying the things I do not know,—
> That I may detect the inmost force
> Which binds the world, and guides its course;
> Its germs, productive powers explore,
> And rummage in empty words no more!
> [Taylor, 1930, pp. 19-20].

The German has *Kraft und Samen* (semen) where we read "germs" in the English translation. At any rate, the drive is clearly toward the object world:

> Thee, boundless Nature, how make thee my own?
> Where you, ye breasts? Founts of all being, shining,
> Whereon hang Heaven's and Earth's desire,
> Whereto our withered hearts aspire,—
> Ye flow, ye feed: and I am vainly pining? [p. 22].

The suicide scene (superego) follows; and then, instead of Faust's killing himself, Mephisto helps him to fall in love and to seduce Margaret.

The problem is clarified by our data from Normanby Island (Róheim, 1950, Chap. 3), where the following situation exists. The ideal of the group, the personality which everyone is supposed to emulate, is the *esa-esa* (the rich man, chief, or famous man). Functionally, however, what is an *esa-esa?* He is primarily a person who never becomes angry and who always gives things to everyone, expecting nothing in return. The main field of activity for the *esa-esa* is the food-distribution ceremony, the *sagari* (the feast for ancestors), and the *mwadare* (the feast for in-laws). One must have lots of yams in order to be an *esa-esa,* and these cannot be had without yam magic. The number of incantations used for the garden and the yams is endless, and nobody denies knowing many of them. Moreover, the data I gathered indicate that the behavior of the *esa-esa* is really an ideal which has been patterned on the mother imago; but we can leave this aspect of the problem in abeyance for the present.

The *esa-esa* is also the leader of the *kune,* the famous inter-island trade or barter expedition first described by Malinowski in the *Argonauts of the Western Pacific.* Since the *esa-esa* has two functions (to direct the food-distribution ceremony, and to lead the *kune*), I questioned the people about the purposes and motives of the *esa-esa.* In each case the answer was: He does it for *his name*—that is, for reputation or glory. (*Esa-esa* is the "rich man," and *kana hesana* is "his name.") Further questions revealed another remarkable fact, namely, that both functions of the *esa-esa* are extremely dangerous. For example, the leader of the *kune* expedition is expected to die within a year. Why? Because all the witches are trying to kill him. These witches are "the mothers," and it is also they who wreck the boat of the travelers and eat its occupants. Great success means great danger. Since there is danger in success, the *to-kune* (leader of the *kune* expedition) does not behave like the mother who gives things but like the child who cries (sings incantations) in order to receive gifts and love.

One day I asked Sawaitoja for the incantation which is used in rain making. He said that he could not give it to me now, because he was preparing his *sagari*. All the other *esa-esas* were doing their best to spoil his feast by making rain. If it would rain, the roads would be muddy and nobody would come to his feast, and that would be a terrible shame.

On another occasion I was told that all *esa-esas* are also *barau* (sorcerers). Why? Because all the sorcerers are making magic to destroy them; and the mere fact that they survive is proof positive that they must be sorcerers themselves. *The fear of success*, which is a typical manifestation of the super-ego, is quite clear in all these instances.

We should add, however, that the natives are very far from being free givers (*esa-esa*). The ideal is only a camouflage; they believe in it, but it is the very opposite of the truth. They are really both *gewana* (demanding) and *ose* (stingy), but they will not admit to either of these traits.

The food-distribution ceremony requires that a house be filled with yams and that these be distributed at the feast to guests and in-laws. The necessary incantations revolve in general around two themes. The first is: What presumption on their part to imagine that they can fill the yam house! The second is: Ill-wishers are making magic to prevent them from filling the yam house, and then there won't be enough yams for the guests!

In the incantations connected with gardening, the yam is equated with the "body contents" of a pregnant woman. These incantations reveal the aggression behind the whole *esa-esa* complex. We have discussed elsewhere the oral traumas that habitually occur in this area (Róheim, 1948, 1950). The answer to these oral traumas is the body-destruction fantasy. They do not want to fill the mother's body (the house) with "good body contents." What they really wish is to tear everything out of the mother. They deny this, however, in the great restitution fantasy of filling the house.

In giving a feast, a man is demonstrating that he is grown up, that he is capable of giving (not only of receiving) gifts. The food-distribution ceremony itself frequently originates in a domestic quarrel or in curses exchanged between two groups. For example, a husband will say to his wife, "You thick vagina." This is a formal offense. In order to appease the wife and her clan, the husband and his clan will start making gardens for a food-distribution ceremony which will be given in honor of the wife and her clan. In general, presents and ceremonies are vindications of one's honor, that is, accusations that have been refuted. Thus, Bulema's people said that Padede never worked, that he only sang on the road. To refute this, Padede raised a pig and gave it to them, and he called the pig To-Wari-Keda-Keda (Singing on the road). The purpose of such a gift, which is a *refuted reproach,* is to make the recipient feel so embarrassed and guilty that he will reciprocate and wipe out the debt by a countergift, a food-distribution ceremony.

Tubuyay's mother, for example, raised a pig for her uncle. It came about in this way. He had to paddle far to visit her, and he always used to say:

> I paddled through the ocean *(Yahwaura)* just to see you. I nearly died with fatigue, but you have no pig for me!

At Gagayowana, when they made the *mwadare* ceremony in honor of Daiko, the following remarks were made by her sister-in-law, To-Dimurey:

> Close the house now,[21] I am going to give my brother a piece of my mind. He always used to tell me, "I walked up the path in hot weather to work in your garden on the slope of the hill and on the seashore. And what about you, you are not making a *mwadare* for my wife."

21 The house has been filled with yams.

Magiseura, a sister of To-Dimurey, added, quoting Daiko:

Has my daughter no father and therefore no aunts, so that there is nobody to make a *mwadare* for her?

These were Daiko's words, Daiko's reproaches, now being refuted by the *mwadare* (Róheim, 1932).

When a husband quarrels with his wife and then wants to make up for it by a gift, it is evident that he is reproaching himself for his aggressions, or, in other words, that he is placating his superego by the gift. When one in-law group reproaches the other for being slow in making a feast, it is equally clear that they are really belittling them—doubting their ability to do so and therefore questioning their rank and status as adults.

Now this is exactly the function of the superego in its relation to the ego. The superego treats the ego the way an adult treats a child. The ego is spurred to deny this charge by working (ego function) and by giving things, that is, by assuming the role of the adult who takes care of the child. The ego is continually trying to deny the criticisms which emanate from its own superego. But success can only be temporary, since the superego is a force within. The superego says, "You must be like father," that is, you must be a grownup. But it also says, "You are not allowed to be like father,"[22] and that is why we can never grow up.

Growing up, like the success of an *esa-esa* at a feast, gives rise to anxiety. Thus, when Bebe, an *esa-esa,* is at the very height of his triumph, he is afraid that he will be killed by other sorcerers because of the great glory he achieved at his feast. Bebe shows me a model of the ceremonial house and says: "I am only a little child; if I were really a great person, this *duguma* [house model] would be ever so small." He is here manifesting the curious antithesis between the desire to grow up and the fear of growing up.

[22] Cf. Freud (1923, p. 378).

Human beings are never satisfied, they are always trying to do something else or be something else. *This tension between superego and ego is a basic factor in our fate. It is evident that this is the underlying explanation of all competitive forms of society. The ego is trying to prove to the superego that it is grown up by finding others whom it can look down on and treat as a child.*[23]

The structure of the whole complex is this: (1) oral trauma; (2) body-destruction fantasy; (3) the body-destruction fantasy is turned against the ego and becomes the archaic superego; (4) actual magic and magical attitudes or unconscious magic,[24] to cover up the aggression and to appease the superego: "We are not dangerous warriors or sorcerers (men), we are all good mothers or children."

In analyzing the concept of the *esa-esa,* which is intimately interlocked with magic, we have found something new. Hitherto, we have discussed magic as a reaction to the frustrating object, as a reaction to the introject or superego, with the libido (or, in more general terms, the potentialities of the body) moving toward a reconquest of the object world. But the behavior and attitudes of the *esa-esa* constitute a more complicated structure. The *esa-esa* denies or camouflages his aggressions, and at the same time he bribes or deludes his superego by a misleading show of kindness. An *esa-esa* knows a great deal of garden magic; therefore, if you are an *esa-esa,* if you behave like an *esa-esa,* you will inevitably have many yams in your garden. This link in the chain is latent and must be inferred from the fact that the *esa-esa* also expects and receives many countergifts, that is, plenty of yams. But every *esa-esa* is also a *barau* (sorcerer) and the male *par excellence,*

---

23 We are here discussing unconscious motivation. Socioeconomic and historical factors are relevant and form a frame of reference. Cf. Róheim (1950, p. 376).

24 I prefer these expressions to Bergler's "magical gesture" because the latter suggests gesture language.

with male aggression being camouflaged as maternal kindness and generosity.

THE COUVADE

Similarly, the custom of the couvade is a magic ritual directed against one's own aggressions. The father may go through an elaborate pretense of lying-in, very much in the manner of a parturient woman, and/or he may abstain from certain acts that would injure the child.

A French explorer witnessed a childbirth among the Galibi Indians of South America:

> The mother uttered no sound, and at daybreak M. Voisin watched her go to the riverside with her infant. Here she first washed herself, then threw the child several times into the water ... The husband meantime remained in his hammock, acting the invalid, and on his wife's return to the hut he received with the greatest seriousness all the attentions she lavished upon him [Dawson (1929, pp. 96-97), quoting Maurel (1884).]

The following occurs among the Erukala-Vandu of Southern India:

> Directly the woman feels the birth-pangs, she informs her husband, who immediately takes some of her clothes, puts them on, places on his forehead the mark the women usually place on theirs, retires into a dark room where there is only a dim lamp, and lies down on the bed, covering himself with a long cloth. When the child is born, it is washed and placed on the cot beside the father. Assafoetida, jaggery, and other articles are then given, not to the mother, but to the father [Cain, 1874, p. 151; see also Crawley, 1927, p. 180, and Webster, 1942, p. 79].

Among the Miao-tse, an aboriginal tribe in China, the father takes the mother's place in bed as soon as the mother is strong enough to rise. It is he who collects the congratulations, and he who exhibits his offspring (Tylor, 1878, p. 300).

The evidence cited indicates that there is no such thing as

a father; only a mother, or two mothers.[25] There are two reasons for this denial of fatherhood: (a) it is dangerous to be a father; (b) fathers are dangerous.

The abstentions which are variably associated with the couvade in different cultures are worthy of study. Among the Caribs of the West Indies, the mother returned to work shortly after childbirth. Then the father started complaining and took to his hammock. He was visited as if he were very sick. He spent five days without eating or drinking and abstained "from everything else for a whole month." During this time he ate only the inside of the cassava. When the forty days were up, he invited his friends and relatives to a gathering, at which time they hacked his skin with agouti teeth and drew blood from all parts of his body and then increased the pain by washing the wounds with a peppery infusion. For six months the father ate neither bird nor fish. To do so would have injured the child's stomach, and the child could have been like the animal the father had eaten; for example, deaf and stupid like a turtle (Dutertre, 1667, p. 371; Rochefort, 1681, pp. 550-551).

In this case, as Reik (1919) noted, we see an abreaction of oedipal revolt—the father has to be punished for becoming a father. But in many other instances we find that the father's passivity is a kind of obsessional undoing or denial of his desire to injure or kill the child.

The spirit of the infant is supposed to follow the father wherever he goes; therefore, if the father uses an axe or cutlass in the forest, he could easily cut the child, or an arrow could pierce the spirit and thus kill the child (Karsten, 1926, p. 448). Among the Canelos Indians, the father does not go hunting; if he shoots a bird, he may be shooting his young

[25] This is almost the opposite of the old view according to which the couvade marks the transition from "matriarchal" to "patriarchal" society. Cf. Bachofen (1861, pp. 17, 255).

infant. And if he uses his forest knife, he may also run the risk of killing his child.

As indicated, the psychological principles involved in such behavior are quite clear.

NEUROSIS AND MAGIC

The sketchy material that we now present from a few case histories is intended to show the neurotic and normal functions of magic in our lives. The thesis to be expounded here is that we find the magical attitude or behavior in every neurosis. Indeed, it is an important part of every neurosis— and, even if we scratch only the surface, of every personality.

The cases I am about to describe are quite commonplace in every respect, and I suggest that the same approach could be applied to every neurosis.

The patient is a European professor who cannot find employment in this country and cannot publish anything. His father showed the habitual behavior which is found in a father of that social class in Europe. He would always insist that his son bring home the best marks from school, but at the same time he would discourage all initiative. "You are too young for that"; "You don't understand"; "Maybe later, when you grow up." This was the attitude his father always took. The mother was a devout Catholic, a woman with a rigid personality. She suppressed all the loving and tender emotions which she felt toward her son and believed that her sole responsibility was to be a strict disciplinarian, in which attitude she was supported by a grandmother and a host of aunts.

When the boy started going to elementary school he made friends with one of his schoolmates and initiated him into the mystery of his daydreams. The friend did not keep these secrets but told them to the whole class. The result was that the patient became the butt, physically and psychologically, of his classmates. Some years later he seems to have made some attempts at sexual play with his sister and/or a female cousin, for which he was severely reprimanded. His mother died, and his father remarried. This took place at about the time when he was a freshman at the university. His stepmother was a girl of approximately his own age, and he was playfully in love with her. She reciprocated his love. In fact, when the father had hesitated about marrying her, she had even told him, "If you don't marry me, your son will." The young man had also had a completely innocent love affair with a much older woman, the wife of his father's colleague, and her jealousy prevented him for some years from getting very far with girls of his own age.

Now what is the situation that developed on this basis? Well, he was a good boy, as his father and mother wanted him to be—that is, he continued to study all the time. He took one diploma or degree after the other, but that was the total extent of his life. He had many ideas, a wide knowledge, a great desire to express himself; but he never did anything about it. He did not indulge in daydreams, but he showed a refusal to grow up. Obviously, there was no point in growing up, he felt. Especially when, after his mother's death, he had grown to manhood and felt that it was his turn to marry, it was again his father who became the young husband. He was not worried about spending his financial resources because he felt that his parents were bound to take care of him. Also, because he was such a good boy, he felt that his stepmother would appreciate and love him.

If he were a sorcerer in a primitive culture, he would at this phase be wearing his clothes like a child and performing an incantation, saying, "I am a good boy"; and the aim of the performance would be to make his stepmother love him.

In the course of the analysis he developed another kind of magic. He would not do anything to find a job; instead, he carried on many and successful love affairs. The aim of this coitus magic was to fight his superego; and he firmly believed that he would be successful in life if he were merely a good lover. His love affairs were like the bugle calls that made the walls of Jericho crumble. In fact, the motto of his activities might well have been:

> Bella gerant alii,
> Tu felix Austria, nube
> Quodque aliis Mars
> Dat tibi regna Venus.

In one of his dreams he finds himself walking up a stairway in a church. The stairway leads past many niches with saints in them, and there is a main altar at the top. His associations show that the church is really a brothel and that the niches are the rooms of the prostitutes. He associates pictures with the main altar: one is the Madonna with the young Jesus; the other is Abraham, sacrificing Isaac.

At about this time he had been talking about the various young women with whom he was having an affair, or with whom he would like to have an affair. He can make love, his fear of women is over; but he cannot risk the conflict with his father (Abraham killing Isaac), and all men represent his father. The coitus magic is also aimed at correcting the past, by making up for the platonic nature of his love affair with the older woman who was so jealous of him.

Coitus is, of course, the supreme magic against the superego. When, as in European folklore, intercourse is performed on the fields to obtain a good harvest, this is not merely because of the analogy between human fertility and fertility in general. It is also because the harvest means success. And success is what the superego is out to prevent. In the same way the patient is fighting his own superego by asserting his right to love. Yet he is carefully avoiding reality, which to him means challenging the father in earnest.

The patient reports the following dream:

I am in an apartment; one room seems to have the same tapestry as the other, even the corridors are the same as the rooms. I find a desk and see a letter; it seems to be addressed to me. It is not, however, but I read it nevertheless, although furtively. It is to my friend, N.N., whose desk it is lying on. But it is from my wife, asking him about my address. He comes in and says that three or four dollars are missing. It must be connected with a pair of shoes he sold, but he never got the money for it. Is it possible that he sold them and was so drunk that he did not know what he was doing? And that somebody took the shoes without paying? He shows a pair of shoes to a crowd of people, but they all deny that anything like that could have happened.

The uniformity of the tapestry motif reminds him of an umbrella which he bought yesterday while he was with his girl friend. It was decorated with triangles which did not fit properly. The umbrella was irregular. Reading a letter which was not intended for him means that he is prying into secrets of a sexual nature which the analyst is withholding from him. He identifies his friend N.N. first with the analyst, then with himself. The letter is not addressed to him, but it is about him. He associates the selling of shoes when drunk with the fact that his girl friend is not sure about having had sexual intercourse with another man when she was drunk recently. Three and four refer to the male and female genital organs. The shoes remind him of children's shoes, of his own and his sister's. After they had been outgrown, the shoes were gilded and made into ash trays.

Now we know what the patient's dream is all about. Is it possible that there is unconscious material here which the analyst, or rather he himself, is withholding? Did he have, or try to have, intercourse with his sister and does not know anything about it? The crowd, that is, public opinion, denies the possibility of such a thing. Yet it is clear that this must have been the case. The worry about one triangle not fitting into the other shows what happened. His penis was too big to enter the little girl's vagina. Now he has an obsession, all the decorations on the tapestry must fit exactly. If he manages to make them fit, he will have managed to achieve the unfinished task of having intercourse with his sister. Hence, also, the role of coitus magic as a weapon against the superego. This is especially striking if we remember the connection between the unfinished task and the superego. (The superego formulae are, "You can't do it!" and "Don't dare to do it!")

He falls in love with a girl during the analysis and thinks of marrying her. He fears, however, that something will go wrong with the marriage. (This is a countermove of the superego.) He also has a mistress now and feels duty-bound to continue with her. It is clear that the superego has deprived the id of its weapon; coitus is now a duty, not a successful revolt. It is the type of behavior that constituted his first type of magic in childhood. The first type of magic means "I am a good boy"; it denies masturbation, adjusts to the parents and to the superego, and refuses to acknowledge sexuality. The second type of magic revolts against the superego, denies failure with his sister, and solves all of life's problems on the basis of sexuality.

The next case is that of a doctor undergoing a training analysis in Budapest. His father was a noncommissioned officer in the cavalry, who, after being discharged from the army, went into business and made a lot of money. The patient got the best possible education, and he was always successful in his love life and in his profession.

The first girl who refused to become his mistress created a crisis in his life. He even offered to marry her, and she agreed to this, but then she changed her mind and married another man. The result was a complete breakdown. He refused to work, and his whole personality regressed from the phallic to the anal-sadistic level. He gradually picked himself up again and resumed his studies. A few years after this he had an affair with a woman who was his mother's age. She always remained the ideal woman for him, and he always held her up in this light to his many mistresses and later to his wife.

He had one symptom derived from childhood which would crop up in situations of anxiety. He was not able to breathe deeply when he was in a room, and he feared that this would kill him. His personality was that of a perfectionist. This manifested itself in the following ways:

(a) His work—he was actually very efficient.

(b) His car—he was always planning to buy a new car or to add a new gadget to the old car. His car had to be better than anyone else's, and he became very depressed if one of the new gadgets became widely available. This was true of any other object he owned, and he would send a thing back to the store if he found a scratch on it or any slight detail that was wrong.

(c) His son—a little boy of three at the time of the analysis; very bright and strongly attached to his father. But his father always expected him to accomplish things that were far above his age level.

(d) Finally, his wife—he was extremely critical of her and threatened to send her home for anything that did not suit him.

This whole structure of perfectionism was a gigantic and rather successful attempt to deny castration anxiety. The car, the camera, the radio—they all represented his penis. And always getting the latest model meant that there was nothing wrong with his penis.

The usual way to describe a neurotic symptom is to say that something *means* something else (latent content). But if we look at the following sequence closely, we see that this expression is inadequate: if his car is perfect, his penis will be perfect. That is, by always buying better and better cars he is *performing magic* to maintain his penis in perpetual erection. If there is a scratch or scar on one of his gadgets, his penis is not intact; in other words, the magic will fail since it is performed by a castrated penis symbol.

The meaning of the scar is made quite clear by the events that took place after his son's circumcision. He imagined that there was a slight scar on the surface of the glans penis. He was not at all certain, but to doubt was enough. He did not like the infant any more. The son as a penis symbol, as a defense against all his castration anxiety, had lost its value. When later a daughter was born, his dreams revealed a strong degree of castration anxiety.

His wife was a woman who looked rather masculine, and this was the quality in her to which he objected all the time. But this was a reaction formation. The real trouble was her femininity—that she had a vagina but no penis. His whole life was really a system of magic. The magic was performed to ward off the superego, that is, his father. Whatever he achieved, it was done so that his father would not criticize him or cut his allowance (castrate him).

In a dream he is flying high to win the love of a girl, but the girl prefers an insignificant old man. The old man is his father; how can his mother prefer the father to the son?

His conscious ego ideal is the scientist; in the preconscious, the rich man; but in the unconscious his penis is in permanent erection.

There were three traumatic situations in his childhood. He appears to have seen the black pubic hair and the vagina of a woman who squatted down to urinate or defecate. This was associated with his gypsy nurse who, of course, dealt in all kinds of magic and became identical with the black vagina. Another childhood incident was repressed, but it was remembered in the analysis. He must have been about three years old when a circumcision ceremony was performed in his house. His father was holding the baby (a cousin), and the baby was wailing loudly and bleeding. Another incident illuminates the origins of his claustrophobia. He was saying his prayers in Hebrew, and his mother was holding the book to see if he knew the lesson. He became so frightened that he rushed through the text, and his mother had to run out of the house with him because he showed symptoms of choking.

He was afraid of God—because God is omniscient and would know that he had masturbated. Such an unclean person would not be allowed to pronounce the holy words; in fact, the holy words could choke him. Having seen what he had seen, there was reason enough for him to suspect that his penis was in danger and that his father or the God-Father was the aggressor.

The first sight of the vagina would tend to confirm the dread that some beings have no penis, that it must have been cut off. Moreover, the sight excited him sexually and made his penis erect, and he was thus exposed to the castrating father. All of his neurotic symptoms aimed at the same thing: to ward off castration anxiety. The result was that his personality was an unconscious representation of a permanent erection.

We can begin the description of the next case with a dream:

I am on my way to Europe in a Cunard Line ship. I meet my friend, David N., on the ship and he tells me he is not a musician any more, he just does it for fun. He has a cabin on the ship with N., and they play together. The ship docks somewhere half-way and I am afraid that I shall be left behind. Then I go around on the shore and see all the ocean-going ships together. I wonder, how they can all be together in such a small space? Then I find out that they are only models, toys.

Then I am in an army camp, but reclining on my cot while the others are going on with their drill. I know I am in the army by mistake and that I will be going home soon. The captain comes and tells me, although reluctantly, that I will be the last man to be called in the whole country. Now I can go home.

The day stimulus for this dream is the fact that the patient has obtained a job and will have to do regular work. The captain looks like his father and like the analyst. He does not like the job (army discipline); and in the dream he says that it is simply a misunderstanding, that there is no need for him to work. He must also pay for his analysis if he works. David, the musician, reminds him of the David in the Bible—who killed Goliath. The models of the ships remind him of a painter's models and of the analyst's wife. The ship to Europe, like the Cunard Line, remind him of the fact that he teaches music; they also remind him of the analysis. The fear that the ship will leave him behind means that perhaps he can stop being analyzed and stop doing any regular work. Then he says that his wife was telling fortunes the other day. The cards showed that they were about to get plenty of money; so why work?

Music always meant emotional expression to him. It had brought him success in the past and must bring it again. He had been a child prodigy, and as such he had enjoyed a privileged position in the family. David's roommate reminds him of his sister. He is not compelled to grow up; rather, he simply continues the childish sex play he once had with his sister. The ship models are fantasies of ships or of women.

His music, developed of the child's crying, is his magic. Then why isn't he successful in his music, why can't he make a living out of it? The reasons are aggression and guilt feelings. His music is both crying and defecation. He defecates his rival siblings, that is, he takes his mother's place in giving birth to them, but they are stillborn (feces). This is the reason for his guilt feelings and his lack of success. Once again we see that the superego wrenches magic out of the hands of the ego and turns it against the ego.

Although he revolts against the idea of systematic employment, he really desires a permanent job and security. At the same time he does everything possible to prevent himself from getting a job. The reason is that the job (with its permanent supply of milk) represents his mother. But his mother is a bad mother. That is, he has made her a bad mother in order to defend himself against his oedipal wishes. His attitude about not growing up is also a kind of magic, his aim being to induce his mother to take care of him as if he were still a child.

In one of his fantasies he dances gleefully around a toadstool which is much taller than he is. The little imp runs around the toadstool and sings, "This is all my own! Nobody can have it!"

The toadstool is a mushroom which gives poison instead of nourishment—it is a symbol of the "bad mother." He had to share the real mother with his siblings; but the bad mother, his neurosis, is all his own.

In the two cases which follow we are also dealing with magic. In one, the magic is successful; but in the other, we are able to note the reasons for its failure.

The first patient is a married woman with a talent for painting. When she was a child her family had migrated from Russia and lived in a small town in the Mid-West. It was one of the very few Jewish families in the neighborhood. Since it was an otherworldly and devoutly orthodox family, the patient's mother forbade her and the other children to eat what the Christian children offered them. The result was that social contacts were somewhat complicated. The mother was a depressed person who continuously complained about her husband or poverty or poor health. She kept saying that her one goal in life was to sacrifice herself for her children.

The patient and her sister played various anal-sexual games, such as being teacher and pupil, beating each other's buttocks, and giving each other enemas. She always envisaged herself in a profession that meant a maximum of self-sacrifice. She wanted to be a nurse in a hospital, a technician in a laboratory, and the like. Incidentally, they were professions which she strenuously disliked.

She had always been very gifted as a painter, and this was the only thing that really gave her any pleasure. That is, with the exception of her sexual life, which had always been a series of triumphs for her. She was very beautiful and had always had a whole cortege of men in love with her. In her temperament and sexual life she was more like her outgoing father, but she had obsessional thoughts which were clearly derived from her mother's depressions. For example, when she was on the beach or at a picnic or a party, she always thought: (a) Things are sure to go wrong; (b) Things could be better.

Her art was the battlefield between sublimation and the superego (Róheim, 1943a). Although (rather, *because*) it gave her so much pleasure, she kept delaying it and would invent a thousand reasons for doing something else. One day she said that she would not paint any more because it was impossible to get the paint off the brushes and that this would clog the sink. She must wait until after the analysis and then take another apartment.

The analysis revealed that her painting had an anal meaning (smearing) for her, and that the brush was a penis. She had many Lesbian dreams, mostly with herself in the active role. Her first reaction to this awareness was: "Well, then I should not paint, I don't want to be a Lesbian." In addition to sublimating her masculinity, painting had another function for her—it permitted her to project parts of herself onto the canvas. While in real life she was a happily married woman, on the canvas she appeared as a prostitute, as old, poor, or sick, and as a bad character. She always wanted to destroy these paintings because they were too *revealing*.

During the analysis she devoted more and more time to painting, but the number of her pictures did not increase. For one thing, the pictures she had painted last month were no good, they did not represent her any more. She would also cover one picture with another and thus destroy what she had created. A painting of a young girl would later become a house or a part of the beach or a still life—it was always only one canvas.

Analysis finally convinced her that her problem derived from the introjected mother, and she eliminated these difficulties. As in the previous case of the musician, we note that *magic and sublimation are here identical.*[26]

The next case deals with a magician who fails. The patient, an obsessional neurotic, has been in analysis with various analysts in Austria and Germany for fifteen years intermittently before coming to me in Budapest. The two defense mechanisms of undoing and isolation go right through his entire life. He keeps repeating two formulae: (a) I won't be able to stand it; (b) We have not cleared up matters as yet, we are not such good friends as that. The patient is the youngest of four children. In the background we have a kindly father and a rather obsessional mother who favored the three older sisters.

The patient's first formula refers to all sorts of things but primarily to his anxiety about not being able to withhold his feces and messing his underwear. The manifold difficulties that arise from this formula are quite amazing. For example, renting an apartment is a problem to him. He cannot live in a fashionable part of the city because the catastrophe of soiling his drawers is much worse if it were to occur in a fashionable place than in the slums. But he cannot live in the

26 In passing, I am reminded of a similar case. The patient is a middle-aged woman who teaches science at a college. She has a very obvious "writer's block," and this prevents her from making much progress in her profession. Her parents were shopkeepers, very practical-minded people for whom money was the only thing that mattered. (The patient had been a daydreamer and an avid reader in her childhood.) She does not write because what she prefers to write is fiction, not science. But fiction means an open avowal of masturbation. And she is afraid of publishing anything which she does write; it might be criticized.

slums either—because he is a man with an artistic temperament who prides himself on being well-dressed and has considerable means. The next difficulty arises in connection with the floor. If his apartment is not on the ground floor, what will happen if he wants to go to the toilet while ascending or descending the stairs? He can ring at one of the apartments between the ground floor and his apartment and say that he must go to the toilet. But suppose a lady comes to the door when he rings? Or suppose the apartment is very elegant, high class? The next difficulty is in regard to the distance between his apartment and the tram stop. If there is a public toilet on the street, or if the distance is not more than one hundred yards, it is all right. Once, when he rented a villa in the suburbs, he had his wife buy him a bicycle so that he could cover the ground more quickly between his house and the tram stop. The tramcar itself posed another problem. It was satisfactory for a short distance in town, but he refused to use tramcars that take people to the Danube beaches near Budapest—the distance was too long and he might not be able to endure it.

He could not go to a fashionable summer resort near Budapest, where some of his friends had a house, because on the way up the hill in the tramcar he might meet a pretty young debutante or a virgin[27] and in that moment he might feel an irresistible urge to defecate; and then what would happen?

Another fantasy was of this sort. He would be drafted into the army and he would be arrested as a communist; or if the communists were victorious, as a capitalist. In either case, he would be required to wait, and they would not permit him to go to the toilet while he was waiting. War would not matter, and he would go straight to the trenches. Once there, it would not be of any consequence when and where he defecated.

27 Debutante, virgin, pretty, beautiful—all these factors tended to make matters worse.

Another and less important subdivision of these obsessive ideas was the fear that he would feel an irresistible urge to kill his wife or daughter and that he simply would not be able to keep from doing it.

The patient's second formula, "We have not cleared up matters as yet," and so forth, refers at present to his wife, but originally it referred to his father. He was his father's favorite, and his father indulged him in every possible way. He had endless talks with his father, or at least he tried to have them; but this bewildered and alarmed his father very much, and the upshot of it all was a feeling on the part of the son that something was wrong between them.

The one great event in his life, the turning point for the worse, was World War I. His father being in combat, the family moved to the country and lived in a cramped apartment with relatives. He was taken from a fashionable school to a less fashionable one; and, instead of his father, who was a spendthrift and a very easygoing person, he now had to deal with an uncle who was stingy, hard-working, severe, and puritanical.

The uncle was always watching him and asking him if he had masturbated. One day, after he had been swimming and boating with his uncle, he developed an edema on his penis. He regarded this as the consequence of his masturbation and responded immediately with depersonalization. There was a veil between him and the world, and the whole world seemed different. It was at this time that his neurosis began to get progressively worse.

Analysis revealed quite clearly the situation or scene toward which his neurosis was regressing. It was the following: a series of frequently repeated enemas which he had experienced in infancy and childhood. His mother was always concerned about the children's defecation, and the slightest delay would be enough reason for an enema. In addition to the mother, there were also three sisters in the family and a nurse and governess. The children always teased each other and giggled, betting that the one who had received the enema would not be able to withhold the feces until he or she reached the toilet. This never happened, but it was always a humiliating prospect, what with the irresistible urge from within and the triumphant expectation of the sisters that he would be put to shame (castration). It is quite clear that he had regressed to this anal scene as a result of his castration anxiety and masturbation.

Another one of his obsessions was connected with his wife's infidelity. In fact, their entire relationship was very peculiar. She was a rich, young, society girl with a great deal of masculinity in her personality and appearance. He was a poor student with a romantic and neurotic outlook on life. She wooed him and induced him to have an affair with her. He kept telling her that he did not care for her, that her nose was too big, and that she should have an affair with somebody else. But when that finally happened, his desperation knew no bounds and he made up his mind to marry her immediately, for fear of losing her completely. In time he ceased abusing her for having a large nose; instead he kept calling her a prostitute.

She was required to tell him all the details of the affair again and again and also that she was sorry for what she had done, and that she had changed and would never do a thing like that again. When he had worked her up to the proper pitch of excitement, he was satisfied and all was well for a time. The curious thing, however, was that his desire to have these talks with her seemed to increase as the years passed. Apart from this obsession, he was not jealous; he said that he would not mind if she were to have an affair *now*, but it was the affair in the past that he could not forgive.

Analysis revealed the significance of the affair for him: it was the primal scene, in which he identified himself with both his mother and father.

He had been brought up in an exceedingly prudish and feminine atmosphere, where the adventurous and Don Juan-esque father (who was generally in Austria or Germany, ostensibly for business) was an outsider. The son, too, was an outsider. He grew up among five females, and he had to leave the room when they undressed. He had some sexual play with one of his sisters, inserting a pencil or a finger into her anus. They went to the toilet together in order to do this. Although these episodes were not repressed, his general attitude was that women are *much superior* to men and he had a male "inferiority complex," though not a vagina envy.

His conflict was the conflict between his male instinctual urges and his tendency to identify himself with the female members of his family, especially with his mother and one of his sisters, because they meant home. Loss of his home coincided with his prepubertal castration trauma (the edema), and thus he regressed to the position in which he was in the bathroom and getting all the attention of his mother and sisters.

Now his whole life was devoted to the task of undoing. No "enema situation," no urge to defecate; but he stayed near the toilet—that is, at home—most of the time. He could sometimes go hiking if he took along an object (a cloak) that symbolized home. He played the role of his mother in his married life and always stayed at home, while his wife played the role of the breadwinner, the father. His sexual potency was unimpaired, and it seems that he had sacrificed maleness in personality or character development to be able to retain it in his sexual life.

He also sacrificed the real love object. The young women whom he really loved were all modeled along the lines of his beautiful sister; they were all blondes and all very delicate, coy, and shy. These were the girls he was afraid to meet in fear of being shamed before them by a need to rush to the toilet. His wife represented his father, and his sexual life with her was merely a veiled form of homosexuality. He had really given up his youthful sexual adventures with his sister because he was fearful of his father, with whom he was now having sexual intercourse in the guise of his wife. He hated her because she was so masculine, yet this was the reason he had married her. He had actually given up his maleness in order to obtain security; and, however much he might occasionally desire an extramarital affair, this was the one thing he would not do. As long as he remained faithful to his wife, it did not matter that he was being kept by her.

Psychoanalytic interpretations were obnoxious to him. He objected to them, he said, because they mixed things with each other, and the main thing in his life was to keep things separate, isolated. Mixing things together referred to my giving interpretations of his ethical or aesthetic ideas; for him this meant mixing the sublime and the dirty. As we have said before, this protest against mixing, against union, was the main trend of his neurosis and the great ideal to which he had dedicated his entire life.

What he desired fundamentally was to soil or attack his sisters with his feces, and all his obsessions revolved around the one idea of avoiding this. But this isolation is also a reaction formation, an exaggerated acceptance of the situation that prevailed in the nursery, when he and his "sordid" desires were kept separate from his sisters. He has accepted the infantile prohibitions but he overdoes them. He has now made up his mind to go on being a child and to depend on his wife. Yet he finds her quite unattractive. Her voice is too loud, there is too much of her in general, and she is not to come into his room. He keeps asserting his independence and pushing her away; at the same time he will not let her go.

In the course of his analysis he recognizes that he ought to do something about earning money. Suddenly he starts inventing things, and all these inventions symbolize one thing: an object that hangs on the other, that is attached to the other in such a way as to deny this hanging or make it invisible. These were advertisements for show windows; photos suspended on walls without frames; and the like. If he could have sold these inventions, he might have made the decisive step from child to father. But the very attempt also contained the negative, the clinging and dependence.[28]

The real magic is found in what he denies. He wishes, through the magic of his excrement, to destroy all the beautiful virgins who reject him; they are but so many re-editions of his sister. He had never had intercourse with one of his great and ideal loves, but the victory of his magic would have been achieved if he could have seduced one of them and then told the whole world about it. And his eternal discussion of his wife's affair—it was never quite certain whether this had even happened—was a reliving of the primal scene.

His fantasies are so powerful that he is not sure he might not act them out. The real triumph would be to cover his sister with feces, to master the traumatic situation of the enema with his omnipotent excrement. He is a sorcerer who is afraid to be one; the superego has blocked the path to adult life.

Magic, as we find it in neurosis, frequently appears in a negative form, as aggression turned against the ego. A young girl once exclaimed excitedly during the analytic hour, "I ought to cut my tongue out, and that would castrate all the men." When we sometimes say that in melancholia and its milder forms the object is introjected and the aggression turned against the ego, it is really the object which is meant. What we are really saying is that this is a form of magic to destroy the object. This roundabout quality is characteristic of many forms of magic.

We started this study with the *ilpindja,* or love magic, of the Central Australians. This form of behavior seems "autarchic" because the man is "singing" himself, is projecting

28 This analysis was interrupted when I left Budapest.

duplicates of himself; but ultimately it all aims at the woman whom he desires. We might say that in magic the cathexis (libido or destrudo) is withdrawn from the object to the subject and then reprojected to the object. This is the feeling (desire, emotion, and so on) which rules reality.

In two situations this attitude is not far removed from reality. The child's feelings usually call forth the corresponding action in the mother in the oral or mother-child situation. This is also true in the male-female situation: libido creates libido. These two situations, one with the mother and the other with the partner in love, are the two most powerful levels of emotion. We perceive also that magic, both conscious and unconscious, operates very much along the lines that I have described in my book, *The Origin and Function of Culture*—it oscillates between narcissism and object cathexis.

We have discussed the relationship between magic and play. Karl Gross interpreted the play activities of young animals and human beings as *Vorübungen,* as preparatory activities or a kind of play through which we grow up. If we look upon growing up or upon personality or character from the psychoanalytic point of view, we notice that here, too, there is a gradual transition from organic pleasure (plus identification with—or against—others) to a kind of adjustment to reality. An anal character means anal libido (smearing, coprophagy), plus reaction formations (constipation, cleanliness, pedantic order). All these activities with feces were magical at first, they were valuable gifts to the object; then they become a revolt against the object to gain more attention. And finally there is the behavior that deals with reality or with the choice of a profession on the basis of excremental magic. The same could be said for the other types of personality (oral, anal, urethral, or phallic-genital).

We all have a character, that is, a personality, and we all tend to repeat certain reactions and to believe that our way is the right way, that it will ward off danger and achieve happiness. This is certainly unconscious magic, relying on a specific formula developed in childhood. The repetition compulsion keeps us true to ourselves and prevents the loss of our infantile introjects or love objects.

But this is not all. What about defense mechanisms? (Since personality is certainly a private defense mechanism, the next sentences have, in a certain sense, already been said.) We have observed how reaction formation and the turning against the ego fit into the pattern of magic. Projection and introjection, like aggression turned inward, show the same tendency to deal with the environment (object) "as if" it were part of the subject. Isolation seems to aim at the opposite goal: to set up a frontier. Denial, repression, and also projection: we think that we can get rid of something within us by pretending that it is not there.

We might, therefore, identify the unconscious part of the ego with magic. In fact, if the ego directs id strivings toward the environment, we may say that this very function of the ego is exactly what we mean by magic. Since we are a species with a delayed infancy, since magic originates in the dual-unity situation, and since our basic anxiety is separation anxiety, it follows that all our strivings (magic) aim at a reunion with the object.

To quote Freud (1923): "Furthermore the question might be asked—and the problem would merit detailed research—whether this is not the general mechanism of sublimation, by which, through the intermediary of the ego, sexual object-libido is transformed into narcissistic libido and then redirected toward a new goal?" (p. 374).

Following Freud's (1911, p. 409) definition of the pleasure principle as wish fulfillment in imagination, and of the reality principle as the ability to weight the pros and cons of a situation, we must postulate a third or *magical principle* that deals with the world outside as if it were governed by our wishes or drives or emotions. We hasten to remark that this attitude, while completely unrealistic because it is an archaism, because it reacts to the world *as if* the world were the dual unity of child and mother, is at the same time the only way in which we can achieve something in reality. Certainly, if we do not believe that we *can* get what we want, even that we can get it *because* we want it, we could not get it simply on the basis of realistic action. *We might therefore say that mankind functions mainly according to the magical principle.* The ego as a battlefield of id and superego implies this. It would be wrong, therefore, to say that the goal of analysis is to eliminate magical thinking. We cannot transform a species with a prolonged infancy into a calculating machine. Unconsciously, we always believe that victories can be achieved on the basis of past victories and that the world will take the mother's place.

If, nevertheless, we regard the patient's magic as part of his neurosis, or even as the essential part, we must differentiate three types of magical thinking. Magic in its first or original form is the basic element in thought, the initial phase of any activity. We have the desire, we act on it; we make yam magic, and then we cultivate a garden. Magic in schizophrenia (see Part II) is a different thing. The ego could not integrate or, which amounts to the same thing, there is no ego. Dual unity and the world are destroyed, and what we observe is an attempt at restitution. But only the first step is made (imagination magic), and action does not follow. This type of magic, a thin veil for defeat, is also an important factor in neurosis. In the third type of magic we find a rigid personality ("This is the way to do things, and this is the only way") which may impede adjustment. We see that the turning against the ego, or the appeasing of superego pressure, is an essential element in this type of personality (masochism).

Our first type of magic is what we usually call sublimation. The object-directed trend (libido or destrudo) is withdrawn from the object to the ego (secondary narcissism), but to form intermediate objects (culture) and thereby to master reality with our own magic (Róheim, 1943b).

Not only the people who write books or compose music or paint pictures, that is, the people in the so-called creative professions, but, to a certain degree, *everyone* practices magic or sublimation or the counterphobic attitude, that is, everyone who believes that he does his work well. If people have the opposite attitude ("inferiority complex"), the superego is triumphant and their magic is defeated.

When we see the Central Australians representing their mythological ancestors (the sources of genitality, magic, and culture) in ceremonies that renew life periodically, it is obvious that we are here dealing with magic and that it is what we describe as sublimation. But how are we to explain the fact that the primitives pierce their veins and pour blood on a rock in order to make rain or kangaroos? Although we may form similar mental associations, we certainly do not act on this basis or believe that self-torture will influence the physical environment.

Is it that the primitives have magic and that we have the unconscious magic which is personality? This is not correct, since members of a nonliterate tribe also have personalities, though these may not be as differentiated from each other as in a modern city.

The answer is that, with our increased mastery of reality, we have found out that we cannot make rain or sunshine by immersing ourselves in water or by keeping dry. Why don't the primitives find out? Well, there is always an answer, namely, that somebody is making countermagic.[29] What has happened in the history of mankind is that, with the increasing domination of the superego, the priest has ousted the magician, sacrifice replaced magical ritual.

Prayer replaces spell, and all power is vested in the gods.

[29] Unlike the magician, the scientist cannot explain his errors or failures in this way.

The belief in our own magic has become repressed but returns from repression in those hazy beginnings of science that gradually evolve out of magic. In this sense, therefore, Frazer is correct, and the shamans and sorcerers *are* our ancestors. They are the forerunners of science because they believe that man can pit his powers against the world.

Why is it that primitives act out their magic? It may perhaps be that they have a greater tendency to dramatize, to act out, than we have. But we must recognize that magic, whether it is conscious or unconscious, is the ever-present matrix of our actions. As Frazer has said, and perhaps even to a greater degree than he believed, this is the truly catholic creed: *quod semper, quod ubique, quod ab omnibus creditum est.*

BIBLIOGRAPHY

Abercromby, J. (1898), *The Pre- and Proto-Historic Finns,* Volume 2. London: David Nutt.

Abraham, K. (1916), Untersuchungen über die früheste prägenitale Entwicklungsstufe der Libido. *Internationale Zeitschrift für Psychoanalyse, 4*:71-97.

Alexander, F. (1923), Der biologische Sinn psychischer Vorgänge. *Imago, 9*:35-57.

Bachofen, J. J. (1861), *Das Mutterrecht.* Basel: B. Schwabe, 1897.

Bartsch, K. (1880), *Sagen, Märchen und Gebräuche aus Meklenburg,* Volume 2. Vienna: Wilhelm Braumüller.

Belluci, G. (1907), *Il Feticismo primitivo in Italia.* Perugia: Unione Tipografica Cooperativa.

Bergler, E. (1945a), Thirty Some Years after Ferenczi's "Stages in the Development of the Sense of Reality." *Psychoanalytic Review, 32*:125-145.

—— (1945b), The Problem of "Magic Gestures." *Psychiatric Quarterly, 19*:295-310.

—— and Eidelberg, L. (1933), Der Mammakomplex des Mannes. *Internationale Zeitschrift für Psychoanalyse, 19*:547-583.

Berndt, R. M. (1951), *Kunapipi.* New York: International Universities Press.

—— and Berndt, C. (1943), A Preliminary Report on Field Work in the Ooldea Region, Western South Australia. *Oceania, 14*:124-158.

Beza, M. (1928), *Paganism in Roumanian Folklore*. New York: Dutton.

Blackwood, B. (1935), *Both Sides of Buka Passage*. Oxford: Clarendon Press.

Bogoras, W. (1907), *The Chukchee*. Memoir No. 7. New York: American Museum of Natural History.

Brinton, D. G. (1897), *Religions of Primitive Peoples*. New York: Putnam.

Cain, J. (1874), The Couvade or "Hatching." *The Indian Antiquary*, 3:151.

Callaway, H. (1870), *The Religious System of the Amazulu*. London: Trübner

Carter, G. S. (1953), The Theory of Evolution and the Evolution of Man. *Anthropology Today*, 327-341. Chicago: University of Chicago Press.

Catlin, G. (1859), *Letters and Notes on the Manners, Customs, and Condition of the North American Indians*. One-volume edition. Philadelphia: J. W. Bradley.

Christiansen, R. T. (1914), Die finnischen und nordischen Varianten des zweiten Merseburger Spruches. *F. F. Communications, 18*.

Crawley, A. E. (1927), *The Mystic Rose*, Volume 2. New York: Boni and Liveright.

Crooke, W. (1896), *The Popular Religion and Folk-Lore of Northern India*, Volume 2. London: Constable.

Curtin, J. (1890), *Myths and Folk-Tales of the Russians, Western Slavs, and Magyars*. Boston: Little, Brown.

Dawson, W. R. (1929), *The Custom of Couvade*. Manchester: Manchester University Press.

Dennett, R. E. (1906), *At the Back of the Black Man's Mind*. London: Macmillan.

Deussen, P. (1897), *Sechzig Upanishad's des Veda*. Leipzig: F. A. Brockhaus.

Dutertre, R. P. (1667), *Histoire generale des Antilles*, Volume 2. Paris: T. Iolly.

Elworthy, F. T. (1895), *The Evil Eye*. London: John Murray.

Erman, A. and Krebs, F. (1899), *Aus den Papyrus der Königlichen Museen*. Berlin: W. Spiemann.

Evans-Pritchard, E. E. (1937), *Witchcraft, Oracles and Magic among the Azande*. Oxford: Clarendon Press.

Eyre, E. J. (1845), *Journals of Expeditions of Discovery into Central Australia*, Volume 2. London: Boone.

Frazer, J. G. (1910), *Totemism and Exogamy*, Volume 3. London: Macmillan.

—— (1911a), *The Golden Bough*, Volume 1: *The Magic Art and the Evolution of Kings*. London: Macmillan.

—— (1911b), *ibid.*, Volume 2. London: Macmillan.

—— (1911c), *ibid.*, Volume 3: *Taboo and the Perils of the Soul.* London: Macmillan.
Freud, S. (1911), Formulierungen über die zwei Prinzipien des psychischen Geschehens. *Gesammelte Schriften,* 5:409-417. Vienna: Internationaler Psychoanalytischer Verlag, 1924.
—— (1923), Das Ich und das Es. *Gesammelte Schriften,* 6:351-405. Vienna: Internationaler Psychoanalytischer Verlag, 1924.
Frobenius, L. (1910), Kulturtypen aus dem Westsudan. *Petermanns Mitteilungen,* 35:1-125.
Fromm, E. (1941), *Escape from Freedom.* New York: Rinehart.
Gesell, A. (1940): *The First Five Years of Life.* New York: Harper.
Grubb, W. B. (1911), *An Unknown People in an Unknown Land.* London: Seeley.
Harrison, J. E. (1912), *Themis.* Cambridge: Cambridge University Press.
Harrison, M. C. (1907), Serpent-Procession at Cocullo. *Folk-Lore, 18*:187-191.
Hästesko, F. A. (1914), Motivverzeichnis west-finnischer Zaubersprüche. *F. F. Communications, 19.*
Hegyi, J. (1937), Siklódi hiedelmek. *Ethnographia, 48*:472-474.
Hermann, I. (1936), Sich-Anklammern—Auf-Suche-Gehen. *Internationale Zeitschrift für Psychoanalyse, 22*:349-370.
Hildburgh, W. L. (1951), Some Spanish Amulets Connected with Lactation. *Folk-Lore, 62*:430-448.
Hogbin, H. I. (1935), Sorcery and Administration. *Oceania, 6*:1-32.
Hollis, A. C. (1905), *The Masai.* Oxford: Clarendon Press.
Hovorka, O. von and Kronfeld, A. (1908), *Vergleichende Volksmedizin,* Volume 1. Stuttgart: Strecker und Schröder.
Howitt, A. W. (1904), *The Native Tribes of South-East Australia.* London: Macmillan.
Jacobs, J. (1892), *English Fairy Tales.* London: D. Nutt.
Jakab, J. (1895), Szatmármegyei babonák. *Ethnographia, 6*:410-416.
Jastrow, M. (1905), *Die Religion Babyloniens und Assyriens,* Volume 1. Giessen: J. Ricker'sche Verlagsbuchhandlung.
Jaussen, A. (1908), *Coutumes des Arabes au pays de Moab.* Paris: J. Gabalda.
Jekels, L. and Bergler, E. (1949), Transference and Love. *Psychoanalytic Quarterly, 18*:325-350.
Jespersen, O. (1922), *Language: Its Nature, Development, and Origin.* London: George Allen and Unwin, 1949.
Jochelson, W. (1905), *The Koryak.* Memoir No. 10. New York: American Museum of Natural History.
Junod, H. A. (1912), *The Life of a South African Tribe,* Volume 1. London: D. Nutt.
—— (1913), *ibid.*, Volume 2. London: Macmillan.

Kaberry, P. M. (1939), *Aboriginal Woman, Sacred and Profane*. London: Routledge.

—— (1941), The Abelam Tribe, Sepik District, New Guinea: A Preliminary Report. *Oceania, 11*:233-258, 345-367.

Karsten, R. (1926), *The Civilization of the South American Indians*. New York: Knopf.

Kiesewetter, C. (1921), *Faust in der Geschichte und Tradition*, Volume 1. Berlin: H. Barsdorf.

Koch-Grünberg, T. (1914), Zaubersprüche der Taulipáng-Indianer. *Archiv für Anthropologie, 41*:371-382.

Köhler, J. A. E. (1867), *Volksbrauch, Aberglauben, Sagen im Voigtlande*. Leipzig: Fr. Fleischer.

Kühnau, R. (1913), *Schlesische Sagen*, Volume 3. Leipzig: B. G. Teubner.

Landtman, G. (1927), *The Kiwai Papuans of British New Guinea*. London: Macmillan.

Langloh Parker, K. (1905), *The Euahlayi Tribe*. London: Constable.

Lönnrot, E. (1880), *Suomen kansan muinaisia loitsurunoja*. Helsinki: Suom. kirj. Seuran.

Loskiel, G. H. (1794), *History of the Mission of the United Brethren among the Indians in North America*, Volume 1. London: The Brethren's Society for the Furtherance of the Gospel.

Luby de Benedekfalva, M. (1941), Treatment of Hungarian Peasant Children. *Folk-Lore, 52*:101-119.

Lys, C. de (1948), *A Treasury of American Superstitions*. New York: Philosophical Library.

MacGregor, A. (1901), *Highland Superstitions*. London: Gibbings.

Malinowski, B. (1935), *Coral Gardens and their Magic*, Volume 2. London: George Allen and Unwin.

Mansikka, V. J. (1909), *Über Russische Zauberformeln*. Helsinki: Suomalaisen Tiedeakatemian Kustantama.

Marett, R. R. (1914), *The Threshold of Religion*. New York: Macmillan.

Maurel, Dr. (1884), De la couvade. *Bulletins de la Société d'Anthropologie de Paris*. Series 3, 7:542-550.

Mauss, M. (1938), Une catégorie de l'esprit humain. *Journal of the Royal Anthropological Institute, 68*:263-281.

McConnel, U. H. (1935), Myths of the Wikmunkan and Wiknatara Tribes. *Oceania, 6*:66-93.

McDonald, A. (1872), Mode of Preparing the Dead among the Natives of the Upper Mary River, Queensland. *Journal of the Royal Anthropological Institute, 2*:176-179.

Murray, M. A. (1934), Female Fertility Figures. *Journal of the Royal Anthropological Institute, 64*:93-100.

—— (1936), A "Sheila-na-gig" Figure at South Tawton. *Man, 36*:184.

Nagy, J. (1892), Hegyhát vidéki babonák. *Ethnographia, 3*:64-73.

Neuhauss, R. (1911), *Deutsch Neu-Guinea*, Volume 3. Berlin: D. Reimer.

Oldenberg, H. (1894), *Die Religion des Veda*. Berlin: Wilhelm Hertz.

Oldfield, A. (1865), The Aborigines of Australia. *Transactions of the Ethnological Society of London*, New Series, *3*:215-298.

Oman, J. C. (1907), *The Brahmans, Theists, and Muslims of India*. London: T. Fisher Unwin.

—— (1908), *Cults, Customs, and Superstitions of India*. London: T. Fisher Unwin.

Parkinson, R. G. (1907), *Dreissig Jahre in der Südsee*. Stuttgart: Strecker und Schröder.

Paton, W. R. (1907), Folk-Medicine, Nursery-Lore, etc., from the Aegean Islands. *Folk-Lore, 18*:329-331.

Piaget, J. (1929), *The Child's Conception of the World*. New York: Harcourt, Brace.

Powdermaker, H. (1933), *Life in Lesu*. New York: Norton.

Preller, L. (1858), *Römische Mythologie*. Berlin: Weidmannsche Buchhandlung.

Preuss, K. T. (1904), Der Ursprung der Religion und Kunst. *Globus, 86*:321-327.

—— (1905), *ibid. Globus, 87*:333-337, 380-384, 394-400, 413-419.

Reik, T. (1919), *Probleme der Religionpsychologie*. Vienna: Internationaler Psychoanalytischer Verlag.

Rochefort, C. de (1681), *Histoire naturelle et morale des Iles Antilles de l'Amerique*. Rotterdam: Reinier Leers.

Roeder, G. (1915), *Urkunden zur Religion des Alten Ägypten*. Jena: Eugen Diederichs.

Róheim, G. (1914), *A varázserö fogalmánuk eredete*. Budapest: Posner.

—— (1921), Das Selbst. *Imago, 7*:1-39, 142-179, 310-348, 453-504.

—— (1923), Nach dem Tode des Urvaters. *Imago, 9*:83-121.

—— (1925a), Love Magic. *Magyar Néphit és Népszokások*. Budapest: Atheneum.

—— (1925b), *Australian Totemism*. London: George Allen and Unwin.

—— (1932), Psychoanalysis of Primitive Cultural Types. *International Journal of Psychoanalysis, 13*:1-224.

—— (1942), Transition Rites. *Psychoanalytic Quarterly, 11*:336-374.

—— (1943a), Sublimation. *Psychoanalytic Quarterly, 12*:338-352.

—— (1943b), *The Origin and Function of Culture*. New York: Nervous and Mental Disease Monographs.

—— (1945a), *War, Crime and the Covenant*. Monticello, N.Y.: Medical Journal Press.

—— (1945b), *The Eternal Ones of the Dream*. New York: International Universities Press.

—— (1948), Witches of Normanby Island. *Oceania, 18*:279-308.

—— (1950), *Psychoanalysis and Anthropology*. New York: International Universities Press.

—— (1951), Mythology of Arnhem Land. *American Imago, 8*:181-187.

—— (1952), The Evil Eye. *American Imago, 9*:351-363.

—— (1953), *The Gates of the Dream.* New York: International Universities Press.

—— (1954), Some Aspects of Semitic Monotheism. *Psychoanalysis and the Social Sciences, 4*:169-222. New York: International Universities Press.

Roscher, W. H. (1902-1909), *Ausführliches Lexikon der Griechischen und Römischen Mythologie.* Leipzig: Teubner.

Sapir, E. (1907), Religious Ideas of the Takelma Indians of Southwestern Oregon. *Journal of American Folk-Lore, 20*:33-49.

—— (1909), Takelma Texts. *University of Pennsylvania Anthropological Publications, 2*:1-267.

Schneeweis, E. (1925), *Die Weinachtsbräuche der Serbkroaten.* Ergänzungsband 15 zur *Wiener Zeitschrift für Volkskunde.*

Schroeder, L. (1908), *Mysterium und Mimus in Rigveda.* Leipzig: H. Haessel.

—— (1916), *Arische Religion,* Volume 2. Leipzig: H. Haessel.

Schulenburg, W. (1882), *Wendisches Volkstum in Sage, Brauch und Sitte.* Leipzig: Otto Harrassowitz, 1934.

Seligman, C. G. and Seligman, B. Z. (1932), *Pagan Tribes of the Nilotic Sudan.* London: Routledge.

Seligmann, S. (1910), *Der böse Blick und Verwandtes,* Volume 2. Berlin: H. Barsdorf.

Seyfarth, C. (1913), *Aberglaube und Zauberei in der Volksmedizin Sachsens.* Leipzig: W. Heims.

Shedden-Ralston, W. R. S. (1872), *The Songs of the Russian People.* London: Ellis and Green.

Shortland, E. (1882), *Maori Religion and Mythology.* London: Longmans, Green.

Skeat, W. W. (1900), *Malay Magic.* London: Macmillan.

Spencer, B. (1914), *Native Tribes of the Northern Territory of Australia.* London: Macmillan.

—— and Gillen, F. J. (1899), *The Native Tribes of Central Australia.* London: Macmillan.

—— (1904), *The Northern Tribes of Central Australia.* London: Macmillan.

Spielrein, S. (1922), Die Entstehung der kindlichen Worte Papa und Mama. *Imago, 8*:345-367.

Steinmetz, R. S. (1896), Endokannibalismus. *Mittheilungen der Anthropologischen Gesellschaft in Wien, 26*:1-60.

Taplin, G. (1874), *The Narrinyeri.* Adelaide: J. T. Shawyer.

Taylor, B., trans. (1930), *Faust* (Goethe). Modern Readers' Series. New York: Macmillan.

Tessmann, G. (1913), *Die Pangwe,* Volume 2. Berlin: Ernst Wasmuth.

Tolnai, V. (1904), Fügét mutat. *Ethnographia, 15*:28-31.

Tylor, E. B. (1878), *Researches into the Early History of Mankind.* Third edition. London: John Murray.

van Gennep, A. (1909), *Les rites de passage.* Paris: E. Nourry.

Vierkandt, A. (1907), Die Anfänge der Religion und Zauberei. *Globus,* 92:21-25.

Warner, W. L. (1937), *A Black Civilization.* New York: Harper.

Webster, H. (1942), *Taboo.* Stanford: Stanford University Press.

Werner, A. (1906), *The Natives of British Central Africa.* London: Constable.

Whiting, J. W. M. (1941), *Becoming a Kwoma.* New Haven: Yale University Press.

Wied-Neuwied, M. A. P. (1841), *Reise in das innere Nord-America,* Volume 2. Coblenz: J. Hoelscher

Williams, F. E. (1928), *Orokaiva Magic.* London: Oxford University Press.

—— (1930), *Orokaiva Society.* London: Oxford University Press.

—— (1941), Native Tribes of Lake Kutubu, Papua. *Oceania, 11*:121-157, 259-294, 374-401.

Williamson, R. W. (1912), *The Mafulu: Mountain People of British New Guinea.* London: Macmillan.

Wirz, P. (1922), *Die Marind-anim von Holländisch-Süd-Neu-Guinea,* Volume 1. Hamburg: L. Friederichsen.

—— (1925), *ibid.,* Volume 2. Hamburg: L. Friederichsen.

Wuttke, A. (1900), *Der deutsche Volksaberglaube der Gegenwart.* Third edition. Berlin: Wiegandt und Grieben.

PART II

Fantasies and Dreams in Schizophrenia

CHAPTER ONE

Introduction

At the conclusion of Part I, in which I attempted a broad and schematic survey of the origin and function of magic, I promised to undertake a more intensive discussion of the relationship between magic and schizophrenia. It is that problem to which I address myself now.

Being a more specialized approach to the psychology of magic, this study will permit me to amplify certain aspects of my previous arguments, especially those dealing with orality and magic. Apart from some prefatory remarks on the general theory of schizophrenia, particularly of the oral trauma, the bulk of the present discussion will be concerned primarily with the fantasies and dreams of a male schizophrenic whom I observed for approximately eighteen months at the Worcester State Hospital in 1938-1939. I have made some brief references to this patient in several previous publications (Bergler and Róheim, 1946, pp. 192-194; Róheim, 1952, pp. 82-87), but without the elaboration which the case merits.

Schizophrenia is, of course, a complex problem, and I intend to explore only a few of its many ramifications. Although this study will be primarily concerned with the mechanisms of schizophrenic fantasy rather than with the etiology of the ailment, it is important to point out at the start that opinions differ about the origin or cause of schizophrenia. As Balint

(1942) has noted, there are two possible answers to this problem:

> (a) Schizophrenia is an almost physical (anatomical) process, which often affects the central systems of perceptions, causing hallucinations thereby. (b) Schizophrenia is mainly a psychological process which attacks the integrating functions of the ego [p. 212].

It may be that schizophrenia is the culmination of a series of circumstances which are both physiological and psychological. In fact, many students trace the ailment to the operation of certain psychogenic precipitating causes on a generic constitutional predisposition. The causes of schizophrenia, however, whether physiological, psychological, or both, have only a secondary bearing on this study. We are concerned primarily, not with the etiology of schizophrenia, but with the mechanisms of schizophrenic fantasy and with their relation to magic.

It is fully in keeping with the psychoanalytic tradition that we use our knowledge of schizophrenia in order to gain further insight into the meaning of magic. Schizophrenics themselves state in so many words that they are practicing magic or are being influenced by the magic of others, and they frequently believe that their wishes are omnipotent and that they can influence other people either by their generic powers of will or by particular words or actions.

For example, B.G., a twenty-five-year-old schizophrenic at the Worcester State Hospital, told me that it was his job to keep the sun in its place. He looked out of the window at the sun and indicated with his hands that he was "making a ball of meat." He blew "buoyancy" into it and lifted it up into the air. He explained: "You have to keep it up there with your will power. Otherwise it will fall down." He had been compelled to make a new sun recently because, as he put it, the sun was "torn to pieces and bleeding." Making a pushing gesture with his hand, he said: "To make a new sun, I just have to push my hand like this. I can do things just by concentrating and thinking. For instance, I can make a pair of golden eyeglasses come out of your eyeglass case." He sat very stiffly and then opened my eyeglass case, waiting for the golden eyeglasses to emerge. After a while he said: "They can't come out because somebody is sitting on my head with her fanny. When I am alone I can do anything just by thinking of it . . . I can make holes in people with the tubes I have, but I can also give them a completely new body or a new head just by thinking about it."

On another occasion he told me that he had been curing people with his "radium tube": "I put a lens into the tube. It is like a phosphorous ball, with rays. Then I look at a person and make him a new head. I can make your head nice and round and normal. Or I can make a new body or a new kidney or heart for someone. I have recently been curing officers' wives in China. In this case I hid the tubes and used only my head, because I did not want the officers to find the tubes on me. I keep the whole world well by using the radium tube." Then he jumped out of his seat and began to perform various gymnastic exercises. These were calculated to show how well he felt and consequently how well the whole world must feel as a result.

Returning to his seat, he attempted to communicate his therapeutic method to me. He advised me to proceed as follows: I was to put my soul (in the shape of a miniature human being) before me on the table; by thinking of my soul, I could make it feel good; and after putting my soul back, my entire body would feel good. He himself, he explained, was trying to make the whole world feel good. Unfortunately, he was impeded in this work by Catholics, lunatics, and a goddess, and he first had to shake them off because they clung to him.

His therapeutic "radium tubes" do not require any extended interpretation. If the tubes are understood as penis symbols, their meaning becomes quite clear.

Y.Z., another patient at the Worcester State Hospital, spent most of his time performing magic. The nature of this magic was quite obvious—it was a coitus fantasy against castration anxiety. His primary function in life, as he saw it, was to restore people who had been *multilated* (a neologism and evidently a condensation of *multiply* and *mutilate*). People were being multilated all the time and were appealing to him for help. As he expressed it:

> The people who are after the others put them in rocks or make the rocks freeze around them, and then they use the multilated ones as slaves to make gold. The sun, moon, and trees all must have people to make them and to keep them from freezing in the winter. These are the people who live in tombs and in statues, and it is they who make the seeds sprout. Otherwise the seeds would never sprout into corn.
>
> My real father was President of the United States nine thousand years ago. My other father, the one into whose family I was born, was a general and also lived several thousand years ago.
>
> No man is allowed to have a child with his own wife. He would be killed in every civilized country if he did this. The people who have the privilege to make children are those who have their *state right* or *ritual state right*. This means that they can *stay* the children, keep and hold them. I have this privilege, and a gang has been trying to take it away from me, while another gang is after my money. I can make a child with any woman in the United States at any moment, and they send children to me from Europe so that I should *stay* them.
>
> They have tried to multilate me and to kill me by sending two thousand people in a rock who were afflicted with pneumonia and full of phlegm to infect me. This is done by contact, by binding them together and then they would be bound to me. I wiped them all off my skin with a brush in a bath, and by sheer force I liberated them from the rock and liberated myself. Once I had to fight a congress

of the whole universe; they were all bound to me and I had to brush them off.

Apart from the obvious genital significance of *staying* (erection) and *multilation* (castration), the magic in this case has a feature in common with the case which will be discussed below in considerably greater detail: The emphasis on clinging or binding or sticking to someone or something, and on those who hinder the patient's magical activities by clinging to him.

A twenty-five-year-old woman, whom I analyzed many years ago, told me that she had a secret magic power. If she went through the motions of sucking, then anyone toward whom these motions of her lips were directed would inevitably fall in love with her. We shall have more to say about such behavior, but for the present it may be noted that in this case the erotogenic zone underlying the magic is obviously oral.

Schilder (1928) has contended that the locus (or fixation point) of schizophrenic magic is to be found in the realm of narcissism. But he adds:

We know nothing of the specific experiences of the schizophrenic at this level of development . . . The magical phase of her psychosis might be looked upon as typical of the psychology of narcissism. The ego aims to affect life exclusively through wishing. Thought itself is compelling and action becomes superfluous. At the same time the will is apperceived as a physical totality, is thought of in physical terms, only that every part of this totality has the same magical characteristics as the whole [p. 87].

In discussing the magic which is manifested in the symptomatology of schizophrenia, Schilder notes:

The cases reported here show with great clarity that the magical is greatly surcharged with the sexual. To affect, to influence, means, on this level of development, to influence sexually. Tausk has shown that in schizophrenia the influencing mechanism is nothing else than the body, and in the last analysis, the genitals of one thus influenced . . . One patient felt herself influenced by a Phoenix, a bastard who had no genitals, or only a shrunken penis. The patient, however, called herself a bastard and claimed to derive from this characteristic her witchcraft [p. 89].

Schizophrenia means split-mindedness, duality of purpose, lack of integration. Thus, a fifty-five-year-old laborer, born in Hungary but residing in the United States, complained bitterly that whenever he wanted to drink a glass of water, the baby in him protested violently or wanted another glass for itself. (His name was John, and he called the baby Little John.) It was impossible for him to buy one necktie because the baby always wanted one too. He felt an urgent need to get rid of the baby, and he would frequently tell the baby (with great emphasis and in the manner of an adult) that it should go out. He spoke in English; the baby answered in Hungarian, in a whining and pitiful voice, explaining that a baby could not live without its mother, and that if it went out into the world there would be nobody to feed it and there would be no bed to sleep in. The disputation between him and the baby went on endlessly. It is quite clear that he was both adult and baby and that the baby did not wish to come out of the womb. In this case contact with reality has ceased.

But with other patients, who are partly schizoid and partly schizophrenic, we find the duality only in the form of eternal self-criticism and doubt. This corresponds more or less to the usual struggle between the superego and the ego, but in an obsessional form.

In schizophrenia the contradicting voices are obvious superego representatives. Thus the patients find themselves being "criticized" by the hospital attendants, the doctors, the police, or simply by "the voices." They hear the voices say, sometimes in an ironical manner, "Now she is dressing," or "Now she is combing her hair." This criticism is at times quite sound, and the patient himself may describe the voices as "the voice of conscience." If he is in a mood of revolt, the patient may call the voices "a scolding devil." The patient may also hear voices that contradict each other, or he may recognize a voice as that of his mother (Bleuler, 1911, p. 98).

Learning becomes almost impossible because every sentence is questioned or every action undergoes severe criticism. As Bleuler (1912) has pointed out:

> The patient cannot do exactly what he wishes to do. In the stage between thought and expression an inhibition, a contrary impulse, can make the action impossible. So we see patients who rush to take a proffered bit of food, stop half way between the plate and mouth, and finally refuse the morsel; with every act the same results follow. If they start to shake hands: at any point the action may not only stop but the hand, as the result of a contrary impulse, may be placed behind the back [p. 4].

The negative impulse is frequently projected into the environment and may appear as a hallucination:

> A catatonic, for example, who will say something, hears his neighbor command, "Hold your mouth." Another, who will eat, the voices forbid, or say it would not be right; if he does not eat, it is again not right; he asks despairingly, what in heaven's name he may do. If one requests such a patient to eat, stand up, he does not do it . . . Afterwards he complains that he gets nothing to eat, that the physician compels him to lie in bed, forbids him to walk [p. 6].

Another way of expressing this split-mindedness is to call it a lack of integration. It is thus obvious that the patient, lacking this integration around a focus, is prone to fleeting identifications with his environment.

Kempf (1920) was told by a female patient: "When you speak I think I speak. I am trying to do everything" (pp. 639-640). She believed that she was everybody. On one occasion she said with great anxiety: "Today the nurse threw the cat out and I thought it meant me" (p. 640). She also begged to have the hot-air baths discontinued:

The hot-air cabinet, she said, was a "hot box" in which she was to be suspended and drawn up in a fetal position and to float "on her side" in her own urine and feces and would be "whirled around and around." She would be cut open and worms put into her, snakes would crawl through her, old rags would be sewed up in her, and she would be smothered. The walls of the hot box would contract around her and she would get smaller and smaller.

She also dreamed at this time about being smothered in a "hot box," and a little white girl having her mouth open for sexual intercourse. The infantile determinant for oral eroticism (nursing) is obvious in the little white girl and the affective regression.

During the most vivid period of her intra-uterine fancies she had to be dressed and fed. She would curl up under a blanket, and paying no attention to anyone, would laugh and giggle to herself for hours at a time.

While in this state she happened to see a cat eat the umbilical cords of its young. She worried about the cat eating its young and worked herself into a panic about having eaten her baby [pp. 641-642].

Bleuler (1911) has described these identifications as *transitivism:*

Not infrequently, a part of the personality detaches itself and is then attached to another person . . . Whatever the patient does or hallucinates, is an experience of another person [p. 145].

For example, a patient used to declare that her hands were full of holes and that she was half-blind. As time passed she said that the attendant's hands were full of holes and that the attendant was half-blind. Other patients said that their relatives were psychotic and were confined in institutions. One patient struck himself twenty times and believed that he was beating his enemies. Another screamed and declared that it was his neighbor who screamed. Still another struck the attendant on the head and then started to cry, "Oh, my poor little head" (*ibid.,* p. 145).

This proneness to identification is seemingly in contrast to another schizophrenic trait, the lack of transference and the rigidly inflexible attitude of the patient. The schizophrenic reacts with anxiety whenever attempts are made to influence him. This is so because a lack of *ego boundaries* or the imperfect development of ego boundaries makes it impossible for him to set limits to the process of identification. Thus, shortly before starting the analysis, a schizoid patient dreamed: "I have a little dog and they want to take it away from me." He believed that the analyst was a kind of wizard who would perform tricks to which he would not be adequate. The little dog was his own little dog, whom he regarded as queer like himself. The dog was his disease, his personality, and his penis.

The phase in which the patient is being passively subjected to magic or magicians is more frequent than the active or megalomanic phase. Schreber (1903), for example, was subject to all kinds of miracles and induced to lust by divine rays or "afflicted souls" *(geprüften Seelen)* (p. 137). In this whole complex the separation of some divine nerves from the main mass of nerves played a very significant role *(ibid.,* p. 206) and may be compared with my observations above about clinging and separation. As Schreber explained it: "The swinging of human nerves takes place in accordance with a certain regular rhythm" *(ibid.,* p. 137, n,).

The schizophrenic is a martyr—he is persecuted by mysterious gangs. In modern life these gangs may be Masons, Jews, Catholics, Communists, or whatever you will; but the interesting thing is that the patient frequently identifies himself with his own persecutors.

The persecutors and "influencers" work through electricity or magic. In some instances the doctor stabs the patient's eyes with a "knife-voice." Or the patients are being cut to pieces or electrified, or machines are being installed in their heads. Thus a female patient is informed that her flesh would make delicious veal chops for hungry wolves. Some patients declare that their intestines have been twisted, or that elephants and other beasts live in their bodies. A female patient believes that human beings live in her fingers and that these miniature people want to kill her or suck her blood. Similarly, some patients feel that they are being deprived of their strength or beauty, which is given to someone else (Bleuler, 1911, pp. 118-119). Schizophrenics frequently affirm that they are being beaten or burned, that their heads are being turned backward, that their legs are being made shorter, and that their eyes are being pulled out (with the empty sockets being visible in a mirror). Food disappears from their stomachs; their testicles are swollen; any and every organ has been removed, inverted, or cut to pieces; or their lungs are inflated because a fat gentleman has been sucked into the body via the genitals (*ibid.*, p. 101).

All this sounds exactly like primitive magic. These are the things that a normal primitive fears; these are the things he believes that a sorcerer can do to him. One of the most common forms of magical persecution, both among psychotics and primitives, is the idea that they are being poisoned—that is, that the food they eat has a supernaturally destructive quality. One patient, who was jealous of a woman physician (that is, in love with her), believed that she was being poisoned by her; but in this case the poison was not in the food, it was the doctor's "poisoned words." Another patient had quarreled with her daughter; she later came to believe that her daughter had salt in her mouth and projected it as a poison into the patient's food. Another patient was afraid of milk because of the poison in it (*ibid.*, p. 433).

Kempf (1920) has described a patient who tried to prove that his body was capable of overcoming any deleterious substance that might be introduced into it: "He ate all sorts of leaves and seeds, and finally produced a climax by drinking sewer water from a ravine because it was 'full of germs.' " (p.

596). The patient would also eat sand to "scour" himself out; or he would submerge himself completely in the tub, drink inordinate quantities of water, and then exclaim enthusiastically that he was able to force the water directly through his bowels while he was thus submerged.

Though the cases cited above are subject to several interpretations, it is my opinion that an oral trauma plays a significant role in the etiology of schizophrenia. The case of N.N., a hebephrenic at the Worcester State Hospital, will, I think, confirm this opinion. Before turning to a detailed study of this case, I wish to note that my assumptions about the importance of the oral trauma in schizophrenia have been supported by several other psychotics whom I interviewed at the Worcester State Hospital. For example, the patient F.M. complained constantly that spirits were eating his flesh and that he needed more milk. Previously, he said, he had been in a hospital where he fasted and was unable to speak. F.K., another patient, regarded "dope" as the magical substance which was responsible for his desire to masturbate. People or devils put this dope into his food. He claimed that when he was three years old his parents had shown him a boiled lobster and told him that they could not do such a thing to him. This fantasy can be interpreted only as a negation of early anxieties about being eaten, with these in turn being derived from oral aggression. He also spoke about invisible people who spat at him every time he ate an orange, and of an invisible lactic acid that was put into his milk. X.H., another patient, said frequently that "concentration is due to starvation."

Some very interesting data on oral frustration, aggression, and anxiety are contained in a study of schizophrenic dreams by Boss (1938). One of his patients, a woman in an advanced state of schizophrenia, dreamed that she ate her mother (p. 475). Another patient dreamed (two months before the onset of a catatonia) that she was locked up in a big tower which was full of water. In this tower she suffered starvation, became quite emaciated, and finally died (*ibid.*, p. 482). Shortly before another onset of catatonia the same patient dreamed that she was sinking into the sea and that crocodiles were gathering around her. They bit her to pieces until only her head remained, and then that disappeared in a burst of flames (*ibid.*, p. 482).

One of Boss's hebephrenic patients dreamed (after three years of illness) that a cow was about to be slaughtered. She rushed to rescue the animal; but, getting stuck in the dirt, she could not get into the barn and was laughed at by her nurse maid. (Before her illness the same patient had dreamed that she was taking care of her little brother in the cradle because her mother had dismissed the nurse maid.) In the ninth year of her disease she dreamed that she was walking through a swamp with her mother. She was suddenly possessed by a fit of rage, and she pushed her mother into the swamp, severed her legs, and pulled off her skin (*ibid.*, pp. 465-466). These dreams reveal that the cow is the mother and that her aggression against the mother's body is connected with sibling rivalry (the brother in the cradle).

Gruhle (1932) has quoted the poem of a schizophrenic patient in which hunger is described as the ultimate source of all things:

> Hunger, that is the soul.—
> Because knowledge
> Of misery
> Is the great wisdom
> Of what life is,
> Of what is called life [p. 164].

A case history described by Levin (1930) is especially instructive. The father was a quiet, submissive man; the mother, young and energetic. The patient ascribed his troubles to an incident which occurred six years before he came under psychiatric observation. He had been eating a sour tomato when his mother called him. Being in a hurry to run to his mother, he hastily swallowed a piece of the tomato, which lodged in his throat and momentarily choked him. At that very moment he suddenly recalled having read of people who were choked to death in this fashion, and he became panicky. From that time on he experienced repeated attacks of anxiety whenever he ate solid food. Two years after the episode with the tomato he sat down to a meal and found that he had to adjust his chair to the table for a full minute before he could begin to eat comfortably. Such behavior always took place when he was hungry or when there was something especially good to eat, that is, whenever he was in a hurry to eat. This "table phenomenon" was very similar to the performance of an act of *sacrifice* and was intended to appease someone (pp. 955-957).

A schizophrenic child with an eating inhibition equated his toys with food and clothing. Instead of the oral trauma he sometimes spoke of his loss of clothing. The equation of food and clothing is a phenomenon which we shall observe again in our detailed examination of the case of N.N.

It is the exaggerated importance of the oral zone which explains the fact that schizophrenics have a marked tendency to identify *word* and *object* or to use words in a magical way. As Freud (1915) discovered, the role of words in schizophrenia is similar to that of the images in a dream:

> If we ask ourselves what it is that gives the character of strangeness to the substitute-formation and the symptom in schizophrenia, we come at last to understand that it is the predominance of the word-relation over that of the thing [p. 133].

In schizophrenia the objects have become decathected, but the cathexis is retained with the words that represent the objects.

There is an obvious similarity here between the process of repression and the schizophrenic process. But there is also an obvious contrast. In both cases we are able to observe a flight reaction of the ego. However, schizophrenia is peculiar in that the cathexis is not withdrawn from the word concept (that is, from those concepts which form the preconscious). On the contrary, the cathexis seems to become intensified. The only possible explanation appears to be that this part of the process is not an aspect of the disease but is a *renewed attempt to recathect the lost object* (Freud, 1915, pp. 135-136).

Katan (1939) has achieved further insight into the role of words in schizophrenia. Katan demonstrates the manner in which his schizophrenic patients play with words, and he shows that in each case the word has something to do with a danger situation. The result is that contact with the word is the same as contact with the danger that the word represents (pp. 355-356).

Katan believes—especially in the struggle against the danger situation which takes place in mania—that primary organic processes are utilized and displaced into the sphere of the psyche. In melancholia and schizophrenia, however, it becomes impossible to recathect the object concepts because the danger situation cannot be dealt with realistically. Depression is thus an attempt to prevent the acting out of aggressive impulses. Or as Katan (1939) writes:

> According to my view the new method of mastering the danger is the main point. A delusion is an attempt to master once more the danger which caused the severance of relations with the external world . . . It is clear that in the attempt at restitution the secondary process is no longer at the disposal of the ego, which is forced to adhere to the primary process. How the renewed cathexis of the danger situation proceeds in connection with the mastery of that situation has to be considered in each case separately [p. 358].

The psychosis is thus a renewed attempt to cope with the original danger that caused the patient to sever his ties with reality. In this renewed attempt the ego, as indicated, has lost control over the secondary process and has only the primary process at its disposal.

The main preoccupation of one of Katan's patients was to avoid losing his own strength and to appropriate the powers of others. He made waving motions with his hands in the direction of his own body in order to reincorporate all the precious substances he had lost. Or he stood for a long time at a place where a person in authority had previously been standing—in order to gain possession of that person's magical powers. The same patient would pronounce only half of important words (*ibid.*, p. 359). Katan's explanation of this verbal behavior is not quite clear; he interprets it as indicating that the patient is showing "a mastery of the castration danger inherent in the way in which he pronounced a word" (*ibid.*, p. 359). To me it would seem that the patient is afraid to lose the powerful word (castration anxiety) by pronouncing it, that is, by letting it out; and he therefore keeps a part of the word for himself. In other words, he castrates the word and keeps half for himself.

This patient is more fully described by Katan (1940) in a German version of the same paper. The analysis of the fantasy words and of the magical substances which the patient is thereby manipulating indicates that the three magical elements are urine, excrement, and semen. Similarly, a female patient suddenly declared after months of silence that she did not talk because people might say that she was urinating (*ibid.*, p. 145).

Katan's hypothesis is that the words have been reconnected with concepts which otherwise remain unconscious. This is an attempted "restitution." Thus, symbols are used abundantly by schizophrenics, but not in the way they are used in a dream or in a neurosis. The neurotic does not know the connection between a symbol and the symbolized content; and when this connection is made conscious during the analysis, he regards the symbol as the *representative* of that content.

For the schizophrenic, however, word and object, symbol and content, are the same thing. For example, a schizophrenic patient told Katan that she could not talk to him any more because he had made an "obscene gesture." He had rumpled his hair with his hand, and to her this was the same thing as if he had been masturbating (*ibid.*, p. 146). In her mind his head and genitals were identical.

One may postulate the return of repressed elements into consciousness; but Katan rejects such an explanation because, if it were true, there would no longer be a symbol. It seems rather that the symbol previously used by the defense mechanisms now serves the opposite purpose: it is an attempt at restitution (*ibid.*, p. 147). Katan regards mania as a defense against melancholia and schizophrenia and as an attempt at restitution.

In mania the word has the character of the object, and the object is the nipple. Katan thinks that urethral, in addition to oral, factors also play a decisive role (*ibid.*, p. 157). A manic-depressive patient said to Katan (1940):

> It does not matter what I say but how I say it. By pronouncing the words they become different. It comes from above (shows her head). Then it goes all sorts of ways down, then it goes back into my throat, and when I have said it, the core of it is out. It is shrunken, the juice is out, it is dry [p. 158].

Just before this remark she had been talking about a child at the nipple, so that the identity of word and nipple was quite obvious.

Before we quote the views of other authors who have also emphasized the importance of the oral zone in schizophrenia, we wish to note another important analogy between schizophrenia and magic: the tendency to use *symbols*. For example, a maid servant declares that her master has used magic to make her fall in love with him. He used a "magic wand" or a "snake," she says, illustrating with her finger the position of an erect penis. While discussing her master's magic, she goes into convulsive coitus movements and has an orgasm. This orgastic attack occurred for the first time when she saw an actor play the role of a teacher in the theater (she had had an affair with a teacher); she felt her legs pulled apart, she was lifted up, and she experienced an orgasm. She suffers these attacks whenever she sees a brush with a long handle, and once they occurred when she had to press hard while defecating. She is also afraid to release her feces into the toilet bowl because it might be a child (Bleuler, 1919, p. 428).

Another case described by Bleuler shows the identification of the word with the body content (as emphasized by Katan) or the symbolic significance of poetry. When the patient is in love with her physician she gives him poems wrapped in many layers of paper—in the center of it all she puts her pubic hairs, menstrual blood, and occasionally a little feces (*ibid.*, pp. 411-412). Another patient complains that the doctor's eyes have been stabbing her like a knife, and that this form of sexual intercourse is responsible for the pains in her genitals (*ibid.*, p. 413).

To be burned is the same thing as to have intercourse. Thus a woman accuses a boarder of wanting to set her house on fire and of wanting to have an affair with her (*ibid.*, p. 417). Mouth and vagina are also equated. The physician tries to pour some milk for a patient, and she protests: "Yes, but you can't marry me" (*ibid.*, p. 424). (It may be noted parenthetically that most of this behavior is mirrored in the magic of primitive and folk societies—for example, in much "love magic.")

Schizophrenia, therefore, is a psychosis which may be taken as representative of the dual unity or oral phase of organization. The patient represents two persons (mother and child), identifies himself in fantasy with the various persons and objects in his environment (empathy of mother and child), with oral symptoms playing a conspicuous part in the disease. The word becomes a symbol of the nipple, and the patient coins words of his own, words of magical power (Jung's *Machtwörter*).

Tausk was the first to explain the "magical" element in schizophrenia on the basis of the oral phase and the dual-unity organization (though the latter name was not yet invented). In a memorable contribution to psychoanalytic theory Tausk (1919) has described and explained the "influencing machine" that persecutes the schizophrenic:

> The main effects of the influencing machine are the following:
>
> 1. It makes the patients see pictures. When this is the case, the machine is generally a magic lantern or cinematograph. The pictures are seen on a single plane, on walls or window-panes, and unlike typical visual hallucinations are not three-dimensional.
>
> 2. It produces, as well as removes, thoughts and feelings by means of waves or rays or mysterious forces which the patient's knowledge of physics is inadequate to explain . . .
>
> 3. It produces motor phenomena in the body, erections and seminal emissions, that are intended to deprive the patient of his male potency and weaken him. This is accomplished either by means of suggestion or by air-currents, electricity, magnetism, or X-rays.
>
> 4. It creates sensations that in part cannot be described, because they are strange to the patient himself, and that in part are sensed as electrical, magnetic, or due to air-currents.
>
> 5. It is also responsible for other occurrences in the patient's body, such as cutaneous eruptions, abscesses, and other pathological processes.
>
> The machine serves to persecute the patient and is operated by enemies [pp. 54-55].

The remarkable thing, however, is that many patients have the same complaints without the "influencing machine."

They do not believe that they are being influenced by something foreign, but they complain of a feeling of inner estrangement—they seem "foreign" to themselves (*ibid.*, pp. 55-56). Intermediate between those who are persecuted by the "influencing machine" and those who have the same symptoms without ascribing them as yet to any external machine or persecutors, are those who operate their own influencing machines from within. One such patient said that he himself produced the electric current that ran through him, "declaring with pride that that was his power" (*ibid.*, p. 57).

Another schizophrenic patient, a woman of thirty-one and formerly a student of philosophy, declared that she had been under the influence of an electric machine for a period of six and a half years. The machine resembled her own body, but with certain differences. The torso was in the shape of a lid, resembling the lid of a coffin, and lined with silk or velvet. She said at first that the limbs were natural human members like her own; then she described them as arms and legs which were merely drawn on the lid in two dimensions. She was not clear about the head of the machine. At any rate, though she did not know how the machine was connected to her or how it was operated, she was certain that it influenced her. Whatever was done to the machine—she would feel in the corresponding part of her body. If the machine were struck, she would feel the pain. If the genitalia of the machine were manipulated, she would feel a sexual sensation. The machine was manipulated by a rejected suitor, a college professor, whose aim was to make her accept him (*ibid.*, pp. 62-63).

The fact that the limbs are clearly visible at first and then become mere images is part of a general process of distortion —the machine loses all human characteristics and slowly becomes a typical and unintelligible instrument for persecution. The loss of ego boundaries is a characteristic feature of schizophrenia. Patients complain that people know their thoughts, that their ideas are not safely enclosed in their own

heads but enter into the minds of other people. This is true
if it is applied to the life of an infant. The parents know
instinctively whatever the child describes. The influence
exerted by other people means that the child cannot do anything alone; it receives everything from others—the use of its
limbs, language, and ideas. In a discussion Freud once remarked that *learning to talk* was the factual basis of a patient's
statement that his thoughts were made by others. The regressive nature of the whole process is clearly shown, for example,
in the remarks made by one of Tausk's patients:

> I feel that I am constantly becoming younger and smaller.
> Now I am four years old. Shortly, I shall get into diapers
> and then back into mother (*ibid.,* p. 75, n.).

Tausk has also indicated an identification with the patient's mother during pregnancy. This, therefore, is the second meaning of the influencing machine: the coffin and the
lid are symbols of the mother's womb during pregnancy, and,
as many dreams indicate, the woman without a head is the
mother (*ibid.,* pp. 64-65, n.; 83-84).

Machines occur also in the dreams of our "normal" patients. The following dream of a mildly neurotic man is worth
quoting in this connection:

> I live in a big house which is similar to the elementary
> school I went to. I am going home, and I try to go up in an
> elevator. I can't go up because the door is blocked by
> women who are holding some sort of a defense meeting.
> Then I go to another elevator. This is a mixture between
> a self-service elevator and a regular one with service. This
> elevator has thirty-two squares or numbers on the floor.
> Whenever one of these lights up it stops on the corre-
> sponding floor. I have to think of the floor I live on very
> quickly, just when the elevator is there, and then it stops
> at that floor. However, I cannot think so quickly, so it does
> not stop but goes up and down very rapidly.

The elevator reminds him of a gambling machine, an adding machine, and his financial difficulties. The women with "defense work" who block the passage are all those women who have refused to have intercourse with him. The number thirty-two reminds him that there are thirty-two ounces in a quart of milk. Then he recalls some men who were discussing their ages and weights the night before. The elevator which goes up and down reminds him of a scale for weighing babies.

The second elevator—with its associations about milk and the weighing of babies—is his own mother. His mother was always full of anxiety, and she probably held him in a tense and nervous manner (as we can infer from the baby on the scale, the dreamer in the elevator, and the rapid movements up and down). The elevator is partly a service elevator, where somebody else lifts him, that is, the mother; and partly an elevator with a self-starter, which means that he has to use his own autoerotic magic to counteract his mother's insecurity. The thinking which is supposed to stabilize the elevator means the same thing.

We have here, in the dream of a normal person, a machine that is both a symbol of the mother and of the man's own eroticism (milk equals oral, elevator equals erection). But in this case, even though it is a dream, it is the dreamer, the ego, who has (or tries to obtain) mastery over the machine!

Bychowski (1930) has described the case of a thirty-five-year-old workman who complained that people were contracting his head and sucking it until it was dry and festered. They did this because they were hungry. Whenever anybody "squeezed up" his head in this fashion he felt it in his mouth, he declared, going through the motions of suction.

> Similarly his hands would be made feeble and dry: people made the muscles contract. A thin person, he thought, would drain a fat one dry. Someone passing by would bend his head back and thus "squeeze" the patient together . . . He said he felt hunger in his hands, for they became weak,

and that his head was hungry and therefore was drained dry... Women wished to be plump and beautiful, and therefore they sucked at him and by means of their heads and their teeth made him contract... He ought to eat more in order to strengthen his penis, and especially he ought to drink more milk. Milk was good for one. (Here he pointed to his breast.) [pp. 332-333.]

When he himself engaged in any oral activity, though always involuntarily, he, unlike his persecutors, received only harm from it. His magical sucking at passers-by resulted only in a mouth full of pain and pus (*ibid.*, p. 333).

The child, the patient said, was harmless. He himself felt as a child does, he was conscious of his parents' every movement and his body had grown small like a child..."They make me like a child by sucking at me. It is my family who destroys me and turns me into a thirteen-year-old boy. It is my mother who crumbles me to pieces, so that her breasts may grow large and she may be better able to nurse the child. By destroying me she herself goes on growing larger" [p. 334]...
The patient's libido had evidently undergone fixation at the oral level, oral sadism being a particularly noticeable feature. In correspondence with this fixation, his ego—the sum of his conscious personality—was in part held fast on the level of the sucking infant [p. 335].

The patient's ideas of persecution, as Bychowski indicates, all have reference to the mother. It is she who is "sucked dry" by the child. The patient, having identified himself with the maternal breast, was now himself subject to all those oral-sadistic attacks which he had once launched against his mother. His persecutors suck substance out of him even by the way they move their hands (we can see the picture of the infant grasping and pressing and trying to extract more milk). The patient reacted to every oral frustration by introjection and identification. Every new frustration now became an attempt to deprive him or the mother's breast (the two now amounted to the same thing) of milk (*ibid.*, pp. 335-337).

Westerman Holstijn (1934) has discussed the question of oral eroticism in the various delusional psychoses. Eating, drinking, and other oral functions are often prominent in the delusions, and the persecution itself is generally conceived as a cannibalistic threat.

Often the patients declare that they themselves eat other people, or parts of other people, that they come across sperma, blood or fragments of bodies in their food, and frequently hallucinatory voices accuse them of cunnilingus or fellatio, of cannibalistic or gastronomic tendencies. A considerable part of their delusion may be summed up in the formula: *they eat and are eaten.* Generally, too, it is plain that it is their homosexual objects whom they eat or by whom they are eaten [pp. 161-162].

Westerman Holstijn notes that gastronomy is often really oralonomy. (One may add parenthetically that the expression "cock sucker" is certainly the most common derogatory epithet among the patients in a mental hospital.) At any rate, these patients are being poisoned, and people spit at them or put their tongues out at them. Their persecutors appear most typically in cafes and restaurants; and patients of this sort attempt to sublimate their oral drives by studying philology or by inaugurating food reforms (*ibid.,* p. 162).

Westerman Holstijn quotes numerous cases from nonpsychoanalytic literature in which the oral trauma is emphasized; and, like Katan, he discusses schizophrenia in conjunction with the manic-depressive psychoses, since both ailments are similar in regard to the heightening of oral eroticism and the situation of the ego ideal. Persons in the pyknic group, according to Westerman Holstijn, generally display a predilection for good food and drink, and they make use of the mouth more than other people, both in eating and drinking and in talking and chatting (p. 170). He quotes the cases of two female patients, both showing:

(1) An identification of the subject with her mother and a homosexual object-fixation to her; (2) a tendency towards eating a part of the mother's body; (3) the idea that certain persons, who were mother-substitutes, ate parts of the patient's body; (4) the situation of the infant at the mother's breast, as a background to these fantasies of eating [p. 173].

[Westerman Holstijn adds incisively:] The withdrawal of the mother's breast (termed by Stärcke, "the primal castration") produces a condition of excitation in the mouth and evokes a reinforced tendency to employ that organ against the mother's body, or possibly the subject's own (in the shape of sucking or biting the fingers). No doubt this oral excitation lays the foundation for the later feelings of being poisoned. As Kempf and others have found, to imagine oneself poisoned is certainly a symbolic expression for being libidinally stimulated or excited in the mouth. The word *venenum* = poison is indeed derived from Venus and originally meant a love-philtre [p. 174].

Westerman Holstijn does not assert that the oral fixation is the only cause of the delusion of persecution. The other possibility is that a conflict arises for which no solution can be found, with the result that regression takes place to the oral phase (*ibid.*, p. 175).

Hajdu-Gimes (1940) has developed a theory of schizophrenia on the basis of a specific parental situation and the oral trauma:

In four cases of schizophrenia I found identical environmental constellation. All four patients are women. In course of many years' analysis of each of them I succeeded in penetrating fairly deep into their inner problems. Common features of their environmental constellations were: the cold, rigorous, sadistically aggressive mother, the soft, indifferent, passive father. Furthermore, in all four cases I could trace back to a period of starvation during infancy, partly in consequence of insufficient lactation, partly on account of the mother's cruelty and lack of devotion. The privation during infancy as well as the anger-conditions aroused by it might have led to an introjection of the external evils, while the fear of them made the child think that its mother was a vicious hostile person [p. 423].

Hajdu-Gimes assumes that the infant, if it has to endure hunger and tension situations frequently and without relief, will go through a development in which the tendency to hallucinate gratification and to deny reality becomes stiffened into a reflex. Reality, if it has proved too frustrating at the outset, may cause a fear of any tension and a mistrust of one's power to eliminate tension (*ibid.*, pp. 427-428).

We cannot do better than cite the following words from one of Hajdu-Gimes' case histories:

> The patient was the only child of the family. As an infant she went through a starvation period of three months due to insufficient lactation. The mother had not wanted the child, had felt its presence as an intrusion into her life, and had even spoken about that to the child when it was quite young . . . From her childhood she had but one pleasant memory: *her nurse who gave her the food with two spoons* [p. 436].

This patient continually wanted to drink milk, asked the analyst to nurse her, talked in a childlike manner, and sat in the analyst's lap (*ibid.*, p. 438).

In summary, it may be noted that four basic types of schizophrenic fantasy have been delineated:

1. The magic power to make or restore things and to influence people, with these magic powers emanating from within.

2. The subjection to magic influences from outside, with these influences generally operating through the mouth.

3. A strong tendency to identify with other people or with objects in the environment.

4. The patient's belief that he is really two persons who are incompletely united.

Two people in one! This dichotomy is reflected not only

in the very name of the disease (*schizo*phrenia) but also in the fact that the patient actually represents two persons, namely, mother and child. We have noted that the schizophrenic feels an infantile empathy with the mother (or, which is the same, with the various persons and objects in his environment), and it is thus to be expected that oral symptoms should so frequently characterize the disease. The concept of dual unity clarifies the split in the personality, the identification with others, and the predominance of magic in schizophrenic fantasy. This magic is oral magic—the denial of infantile dependency.

We shall presently observe, and in considerable detail, that the theory of dual unity illuminates the narcissistic aspects of schizophrenic fantasy. For the moment, however, it must be emphasized that *schizophrenia is the magical psychosis par excellence and that it lends significant confirmation to our assumption that many types of magic derive from the oral or dual-unity phase of psychic organization.*

CHAPTER TWO

Fantasies and Dreams of a Schizophrenic Patient

As indicated above, I observed a male hebephrenic for approximately a year and a half in 1938-1939. He was a white, native-born American, unmarried, and about thirty-two years old when I first saw him. He had been gainfully employed until the onset of his psychosis.

I first saw the patient some five years after he had been institutionalized. The following remarks, taken verbatim from the records of the Worcester State Hospital, served as my introduction to the patient:

Name: N.N.
March 30, 1934
This patient was today transferred to the Research Service for special study. He is pleasant, co-operative, productive of speech, fairly neat and tidy in appearance, has been on parole, and has been working in the Occupational Therapy Shop.

April 2-4, 1934. Mental Status:
Behavior and Attitude: This patient has been interviewed and observed during the present three days on many occasions. During this period he has been co-operative on tests and on interviews. He is fairly neat and tidy in appearance, although his hair is usually tousled, his clothes wrinkled, and he has food stains on his clothes. Although he has parole, he has not used his parole privileges during the present three days. He spends most of his time in the ward, except when he leaves it to go to the cafeteria or for some test. He is quiet, sits about a good deal of the time by himself, as though not interested in what is going on

around him and as though somewhat preoccupied. When approached, he is quite friendly and pleasant and smiles very readily. He tends to laugh and smile a good deal more than seems warranted, and at times his smiling and laughing approach the point of silliness.

Stream of Talk: For the most part the patient seems to need stimulation before he will talk very much, but he does exhibit some spontaneous talk, although usually after he has been interrogated by someone for a time. He replies promptly to questions. Some of his replies are relevant. His speech is intelligible and coherent, but is very rambling and disconnected. He tends to begin discussing one subject and usually ends up by discussing some topic very remote from the original one.

Affect and Mood: Patient is pleasant in manner, smiles very readily, seems quite contented with himself, and at times giggles and laughs in a rather silly fashion. He expresses a great many bizarre and delusional ideas, and discusses the hallucinations he experiences without displaying the affect appropriate to the particular delusion or hallucination. He complains of various bodily ailments, but without displaying the affect one would expect with such complaints.

Content of Thought: The patient expresses many delusional ideas, many of them of a rather bizarre nature and frequently somatic in character. At the first interview the examiner had with him while on the ward, the patient very readily and spontaneously discussed one of his somatic delusions. At subsequent interviews this same delusion was again discussed, and has also been discussed with other physicians. Pointing to a small brown area along the edge of his right jaw, he explained that a "phaeton-beetle-lion-bug" had stung him in that spot, that this had been about ten years ago, that it had affected his jaw, so that his face is thin, and that it caused some disturbance in the bone. At the first prolonged interview in the examiner's office, the patient was asked to relate the events leading up to the onset of his present illness and his hospitalization here. His speech, however, was so rambling and disconnected that it was difficult to follow, and therefore, he was asked direct questions concerning the events of the remote past, such as age, date of birth, etc. Although he gave the correct replies to these questions, yet he always qualified his responses by stating that he was not sure that he has been born on such and such a day, or that his name is N.N., or that his parents are his parents. He seemed to have the feeling that there are two N.N.'s, and that he is foiled in all his attempts to get work by this other N.N., who usually gets the job. He stated that he felt that everyone was against him, that "the other fellow" interfered with him in every way, even with his girls.

When asked how he knew about there being another N.N. just like himself, he replied, "All my life I've trained myself to be—you know what I mean—a service man, all my life I've trained myself to trail things." Then he stated that he had looked it up and found there were other N.N.'s in another city. He seemed to feel some resentment against his younger brother, stated that his younger brother would get more things from his family than he did. He said that, when at the dinner table at home, he would get a hint in some way or another that the family did not seem to want him there. He said that this made him feel that there is something wrong some place. He says he is in doubt as to what has happened to the other seven siblings of the family, who are supposed to be dead. He says he thinks they may be alive, or that they may have been away somewhere. He asserted that by and by he would learn who he is. He was asked, "Who are your enemies?" He replied: "I don't know them by name. I couldn't select to say. I don't know them by name. You know what I mean. Sometimes I've just got the feeling that they are." He then gave a somewhat rambling account of getting into trouble whenever he tried to handle money, that usually the trouble was with governments. He then stated spontaneously that one of his great troubles at home had been his tendency to dream. He then related the following dream:

About October, 1933, when he was in bed one night and asleep, he dreamed of going across a field, dressed only in a loin cloth, made from the skin of a black-spotted leopard and accompanied by a pet lion which walked at his right side. He stopped part way across the field to sit down and rest. When he was sitting down he looked up in the sky above him and saw a big eagle. Suddenly an angel whose face seemed to be familiar appeared out of the sky to his left and behind him. The face of this angel resembled that of an aunt of his or a girl friend he had known or "someone like that." Then another figure appeared off to the left side—a huge black figure like death, with a cloak on. Then straight ahead of him he saw a mountain which seemed to go up in the sky, and on top of the mountain, like a sunset, was a big orange sun. The eagle and angel seemed to guide him forward, the eagle in advance of him, the angel beside him, telling him to go ahead. When the angel told him to go ahead, the figure of death seemed to swing around behind him and to follow him.

When asked what he thought about this dream, he said that he thinks that the figures of the dream have been with him in the waking state ever since and have at times protected him from danger. When questioned concerning any accidents he may have had, he stated that a wagon had run across his abdomen when he was four years old and he intimated that he had been in two or three accidents since that time and that he had again suffered some injury to his abdomen.

Memory: Patient gave the date of his birth and his place of birth correctly, but he immediately stated that he was not at all certain that he had been born on this date or in this place. He then went into an explanation of how he had been puzzled about this matter, and according to his birth certificate, the authenticity of which he doubted, he should be almost twenty-eight years old now. But when he tried to figure out his age by adding the number of years he had lived in certain places, it seemed as though he should be thirty-three years old now. He asked the examiner to help him solve this difficulty. He stated that his father, who is about fifty years old, is not in good health, because his back hurts. He said that his mother is about fifty-two or fifty-three years old, and that she is not in good health, since she has rheumatism. He says that he has one brother and one sister living. His sister is thirty years old, and she attends high school. The sister named F. died when she was about sixteen years old. According to the patient, she died from a carcinoma of the stomach. He says that there were

six other children in the family, that some were said to have
died in infancy or shortly after birth, but that he does not
know about the others, who may still be alive. Later on
during the course of the interview the patient expressed
doubt about the death of these six siblings, saying that for
all he knew they may have been sent away by his supposed
parents.

December 4, 1934.

Since the time of the discontinuation of the medication
the patient has become somewhat morose. He began to
express his aggressive tendencies somewhat more freely
than before. When the nurses asked him to do some errands
he became quite cross. He told the examiner that at
Thanksgiving time something will happen to him, because
at Thanksgiving time something always happens to him.
(The day after Thanksgiving he was found in a state of
panic, which foreshadowed that new unconscious material
was breaking through, and he made enormous efforts to
repress it. In the next days, however, his resistance was
overcome and he began to produce new material.) He loses
more and more contact with reality and becomes less and
less critical. His conflict takes on cosmic dimensions. He
gave up the idea that he might be a crown prince, and now
believes that he is Satan and more powerful than God. He
has ideas about ruling the universe. He has begun to build
up a cosmology. There are four gods, he says. The first is
Satan, the deceiver. The second is God, the creator. The
third is Satra, the law or love, and the fourth is the Devil,
who rules hell. He hears hallucinating voices during the
interviews. His previous neurological symptoms, like past-
pointing to the left, are now much more pronounced. It is
also noteworthy that the acute manifestations of the patient's illness had their onset at Thanksgiving time.

January 26, 1935.

The patient lately tends to speak about sexual matters,
but he is extremely repressed on the subject. He has begun
to build up a delusion that he was married several times.
He also has some rather vague incestuous fantasies. He
thinks that his younger sister, now dead, was perhaps not
his sister but his wife. Once he said that it seemed to him

that at one time he was the head of the family, and his father and younger brother forced him out. He is very hostile toward his father and his brother.

July 25, 1935.

Patient was returned from a visit by his father, who reports that during the past few days he has begun talking in a rambling fashion, accusing his brother of beating up a girl. The patient believes that this girl loves him and that the brother has injured her. He used a good deal of foul language and at times was excited. The father reports that the patient has been taking his thyroid medication regularly during this period. When seen on the ward, the patient was disturbed at needing to remain in the hospital and accused his father of not carrying out his promise to take him back home. He offered no physical resistance to being taken back to the ward. The father wishes a report by letter in two weeks on how the patient is adjusting.

January 4, 1936.
Therapeutic Note:

Patient was recently at home on a visit. He was found to be quite aggressive toward his brother, and most of the interview was taken up with his statements in this regard. He claimed that while at home they kept him in bed, that they didn't want him to go out and enjoy himself, and that they prevented him from attending motion picture shows. He claimed that his brother attacked him and that his brother wanted to take away his Christmas presents, his clothes, and his food. Because he (the patient) was sick, his brother also got sick. He does not think his parents want him with them. His brother doesn't like him. If the patient speaks to a girl, his brother will make an effort to take her away from him. He accused his brother of spitting in his face at a meal and then coming around the table and committing sodomy on him. He claimed that his brother has also tried to do that when he was in bed. He is at times afraid that he may hit his brother or shoot him. He also claimed that his brother can hit him in the back of the neck with his teeth. Patient claimed that he has a photographic machine which takes pictures of people eating. He expressed many ideas about people trying to deprive him of food. He spoke of his skull having been removed and said that his brother now has this skull and that his own skull is made of wood. He spoke about the fact that if he receives an injury it shows up on his brother.

The hospital records just quoted constituted my introduction to N.N. I interviewed him three times a week for approximately eighteen months. Psychoanalytic therapy was not attempted. In fact, the patient was quite beyond the point at which he could understand psychoanalytic interpretations, let alone be influenced by them. The interviews were for purposes of research, and my notes were taken immediately after each session.

Before summarizing these interviews, I wish to note that the stream of the patient's talk constituted real free association. It was interesting to observe how all the themes interlocked, mutually illustrating and explaining each other. The type of presentation that I shall use is one that may be called the "folklore method," that is, the use of variants. The difference is that in European folklore the versions of a tale have diffused from Scandinavia to the South Seas and have been obtained from hundreds of informants. Here, of course, the variants of the same recurring themes were supplied by the same informant but at different times. These themes include: food, the patient's name, "bugs" and other supernatural beings, teeth, and so on. Some repetition occurs in my summary of the interviews, but infinitely less than if a straight chronological presentation were attempted.

There seems to be little doubt that the patient attributed his difficulties to an oral trauma or early starvation experiences. Food, as will be evident below, was a recurring theme in most of the interviews. He would frequently express the following sentiments:

I starved my stomach once and that was the same thing as starving my brain.
Once I suffered from starvation and nearly died.

I did not know that it was not so good for others when I ate all the food in the world and that they would be hungry.

When I filled myself with corn my father nearly starved. I was afraid people would say that I worshiped food.

Once, after talking about his "stories" (that is, fantasies or dreams), he remarked:

All those stories are the same. There is only one story—that somebody was starved. But not really—only inside, in my stomach. And then I ate the corn and all was well. Then I took a good long drink of water.

On another occasion he said the following and again revealed an early oral trauma:

My mother once said to me, "Does that soup belong to you?" I was fooling and said that it did not. She misunderstood me and replied, "I don't see why you want to eat at all." She said she would send the soup to a restaurant—where anybody might eat it.

He went home for a visit during Christmas of 1938 and saw a film about the First World War. Upon his return to the hospital he said:

The movie had submarines in it. People thought the world war was beginning again and that somehow I was responsible for it. The world war broke out when I was eating a beef stew.

The theme of food eaten (or not eaten) recurred in endless variations. Early in 1939 he had had trouble with another patient who had taken a piece of bread from him and upset his food tray. N.N. started a fight with the other patient and later complained to me:

The nurse thought only of the other boy, not of me, whose food had been taken away. It all began a long time ago when somebody in my family—my father or mother—took my food away.

On another occasion he said:

I was eating a kind of chocolate pudding, and there was a slowly acting poison, called "pon-ton," in the pudding. My mother then gave me some soup in a can and asked me, in a sort of triumphant way, what had happened. But I got the better of her that time because I had been eating in the *right way*.

The next statement illustrates that the "food trouble" was not simply a question of nourishment but also a question of love and hate. An attendant had told N.N. that he could not have a second tray of food at breakfast. This rebuff touched off the following emotions in him:

I felt as if the food was a hard lump, as if somebody had put a stoppage into me. The trouble first started when people envied me the food—it suddenly caved in and slipped out. I have had difficulty with the beef stew or the corn soup. I could not eat it and I could not make myself understood. It was like being dumb—like an animal. I felt hungry but it was not like hunger, only a feeling like hunger. As if there was a whole restaurant full of beef stew or corn soup and I could not eat it.

A week later he said:

For three hundred years they let me eat that beef stew or corn soup undisturbed. And then, suddenly, when I wanted to eat a whole restaurant full of food, I was told I couldn't because other people might get hungry or might be hungry. I didn't know that I thought I could eat it all. When I filled myself my father nearly starved.

Some girls did not want me to go out; they are like my mother in this way. One of them *translated* my eating the beef stew as if that meant that I wanted to marry her.

The patient frequently referred to a "big catastrophe," which, as we have already seen, was sometimes described in terms of the First World War:

One Sunday I was trying to eat a beef stew and could not eat it, and I could not make anybody understand what I was trying to say, and consequently the world war broke out.

When I was coming up to the hospital, I ate an ice-cream soda, and it acted different than at other times. It was as if somebody had not wanted me to eat the food, or as if I ought to have gone to court after I had eaten the food.

I was eating a bowl of soup, but at the same time I wanted to eat another food that was on the table. But this other food was behind a sort of curtain or haze.

These statements referred either to real events in his life (as is possible in the matter of the soup or the beef stew), or to a schizophrenic episode which was a repetition of his original trauma, or to pure fantasies based on the trauma. I believe the patient's remarks to mean that there was a sudden cessation of the milk supply, with the result that great aggression was called forth by this frustration and by the fear of rivals (in this case, the father and a younger brother).

It is obvious that the patient equated *cow* and *mother*:

I had eaten a beef stew or some milk, and people thought I meant a whole cow.

[He laughed outright as he continued with the story:] There was a cow that used to put its head through the window, and its face was like my face. The cow walked into the house and people thought it was a person and put it to bed. I suppose the cow was just playing. In olden times there were no houses and no city, only cow paths and trails. I came from those trails—where I had been living with the cows for a long time. In those days I was always drinking milk and churning butter. If I am crazy, then why don't they bring the cow in here from which the beef stew I ate originated? Once I ate cheese and that made me dream that all the food, the whole party, was mine. With milk it was different, that used to disappear or I would disappear. I came into the city with the cows from the pasture, but the milk stayed outside the city—it didn't come in through the gates.

The following statement about the "food trouble" referred ostensibly to a holiday at Cape Cod or rather to a visit home after the holiday:

> When I came home, others had got the better of me. The others had been eating more during my absence, and now I had to catch up with them. This trouble was made all right by somebody telling me to eat alone for a while, so that I could catch up with the others.

This was obviously a fantasy of going back to a period of his life when he was alone and had no younger siblings as rivals.

He frequently referred to an archaic period of starvation:

> After eating the beef stew at noon, I drank a quart of milk the next morning and then I was almost married. The trouble with my stomach is due to the fact that I was once nearly starved. That was fifty years ago—not really fifty, it may be only twenty-five, but it feels like fifty, or perhaps only one. The whole trouble started with a party. People were dreaming that they were hungry, but hungry inside; they were not understood and the police broke it up.
>
> My father and mother did not want me at home, and when I came home they told me that there was no supper for me.

In connection with the oral trauma he introduced the concept of oral omnipotence or, as he expressed it, of being *overweighted*:

> I drank nine cups of coffee or soup instead of one, and then I was *overweighted*.

Only a person of great authority could be *overweighted*: for example, a President of the United States.

There were two other important statements in this connection. One was that the words would not come out when he was *overweighted* and that he could not *translate* them. The other was his explanation of the phenomenon: "*Overweighted* comes from starvation."

The patient was so far removed from reality that I did not think any interpretations could be given or that they would mean anything to him. Once, however, his fantasies came so close to a straightforward statement of the oral trauma that I attempted to convey an interpretation to him. His reaction was quite emphatic:

> I have never had milk of any kind. I was raised on solid food from the beginning.

If we interpret many of his fantasies as an attempted *denial* of the original trauma, this reply is very characteristic.

Having clarified the patient's oral trauma, we turn now to his loss of the object world, with this loss being derived from his oral trauma and his early relations with his mother.

On March 17, 1939 the patient received a letter from his mother, telling him that she was coming to see him. He was surprised and worried:

> So quickly—after only two or three months. I thought it would be a year. It used to be that I upset everything whenever I went home, or perhaps everything looked as if it were upset. I used to practice thinking that my mother would take me home—because then it would come true. I thought my mother did not take me because of the food trouble; and if I ate the food the *right way* and did not make any mistakes in eating it, then it would not thin down and she would take me home.

I asked him if he ever wrote to his family. There was somewhat more contact with reality in his opening remarks:

> It is no good writing home. I would only be asking for things—and then they would become angry. My father might give me a punch on the jaw if I went home. It is just like when I could not eat the food. My father was up here—and the nurse ought to have given me the pills, but they disappeared. I had fifty cents from home. For twenty-five cents I bought candy, and twenty-five cents disappeared. This is like when the food disappeared. Two hundred and fifty dollars once disappeared like that.

He paused and then referred to the extraction of a tooth upon his return to the hospital after his visit home at Christmas, 1938:

> While I am trying to say these things the words disappear from my mouth. My face was swollen; they ought to have made the swelling disappear. There was no reason to pull my tooth. I once had my own automobile and my own trail in life and my own bread and butter. They had no reason to take these from me.

In other words, the original oral deprivation was the forerunner (or prototype) of his loss of normality.

He also expressed the fact that it was difficult for him to endure the separation from his *parents* (that is, from the primary objects of infancy):

> The awful thing is that my father and mother did not know when I left home or when I was away. Sometimes I try to trace the food I have eaten. I try to trace it home. I send it back again on the road to see if I can follow it in imagination as far as Boston. It was easy to leave home but hard to find the way back. My father got angry with me. He took the things away from me.

In explaining this, he made a slip and said "she" instead of "he"; then he continued to make detailed complaints about a basic theme—that his *mother* took everything from him.

The patient's oedipal and preoedipal fantasies will be discussed presently. We must note here that the material on object loss was considerably more abundant than on any other subject. He was always trying to go back to the origins of his trouble and trying to find the way back to normality. Hence there is a strong trend in his fantasies toward *denial* and *restitution*.

There was another way in which he expressed the same thing:

> I had been writing stories like an author, and somebody told me to correct the story because there was *no happy*

ending. Losing my job was like the loss of time or the trouble with the food. Food can make you lose time and lose yourself. I am also trying to think things—then they will become real.

Since the nipple is the infant's first goal, and since many schizophrenics try to regain the object by means of its symbol or image (that is, via magic), our patient's goal is clearly understandable. He is trying to think his way back to the maternal breast. We shall return again to the relationship between thought and magic. For the present, however, it may be noted that the mental image (or magic) mediates between the ego and the libido.

For our patient, *words* constitute the path back to reality—to the world of objects. And, since the images and symbols have been cathected with object cathexis, he can proceed no further. At the same time, the anxiety connected with the original is displaced to the substitute.

He liked to write stories about fantasied voyages and expeditions, but he was fearful that *other people would take these stories away from him and use them as their own.* As indicated, these stories did not have a "happy ending"; rather each one ended with the representation of object loss in the form of a void:

> When I arrived at the mountain it was flat land, but hollow as if it had all been washed out by the sea. It was the end of the world. After that, comes nothing—just miles of desert. The mountain seemed unreal, as in a fairy world.

His relation to reality and to the world of objects was based on his infantile relation to his mother. Every new meeting with her in adult life meant a repetition of the original or fantasied trauma.

On July 7, 1939, after approximately three and a half months of fretful anticipation, the patient told me:

My mother visited me on Sunday. But I have given up all hope of going home. People would notice that I have been here so long. Whenever my mother brings me things, something is always torn or lost.

Approximately two weeks later he returned to this subject and said:

I stopped thinking about things after my mother's visit, but I began thinking again a few days ago. I have been thinking about a place—it is like a big mountain at first. But if it is only a picnic place, you don't want to go back to it. It is like a little hill. This is what happened to my home.

A statement made before his mother's visit clarified the oral basis of his orientation to reality:

I used to try to find out whether the places I used to stay at were right by wandering through these streets (in memory) and by trying to eat at each of these places. It was like a Christmas dinner. I left a little of the food—so that I could be able to identify myself and find the way back.

He sometimes described his anxiety in terms of getting lost, sometimes in terms of losing the object. Both amount to the same thing. Without object there is no ego; without ego, no object.

On one occasion he said:

I have been thinking about the whole trouble, about people not recognizing me, and how I got lost in the woods when I lived with my grandmother. The way the food disappeared in me was like the way I myself disappeared when I got lost. Once I went so fast that people could not see me. That was the same thing as when the food disappeared from my inside. My feeling is like the way you feel when you go into the woods and go deeper and deeper, hundreds of miles, and you feel heavier—and when you come out again you are dazed. Once, when I was at home, I disappeared— I could see the people, but they could not see me. Just as the food disappeared, a mountain that figured in one of my stories disappeared. And the Garden of Eden disappeared too. At home, the furniture disappeared—the piano, everything disappeared.

Sometimes he expressed the problem of object loss in different terms: that the intervening empty space was an *obstacle* that kept him from going home.

When I go home, I find the door shut and I have to jump over space.

[On another occasion he said:] Once I had a shirt on and the nurse—or perhaps it was my father or mother—came and said that it did not belong to me, that it was my father's or brother's or sister's. But then it turned out that I was right after all. The whole trouble started when I came back from a movie and had the wrong shirt on accidentally. It was my mother's shirt or the shirt of a nurse who knew my mother. I was eating very quickly and I changed to that second shirt, and then the doctors noticed that there was something wrong with my insides, with my stomach.

[At a later interview he said:] If I got my job back, that would be like having the whole world—or like being invited to a party. Then I *thought* a brand new job: a big truck going right through the continent. Once I had *all my rights and my name,* but my mother took them from me because I did something wrong! I had a chair and a table and I lost them. I had to leave when the meal was only half finished because my mother did not want me to go on. That chair was part of me. It stopped when I left—like the grandfather's clock that stops when he dies.

We have already seen the degree to which our patient suffered from object loss, and we have also noted that this object loss was expressed in oral language or took place on the oral level. Before we attempt to trace the successive phases in the development of our patient's fantasy systems, we shall first attain some additional insight from his dreams and fantasies. Some of these narratives can best be described as myths. The patient himself referred to them variantly as "experiences," "stories" or "fairy stories," and sometimes as "dreams." Quite apart from these differences, he never doubted the reality of the narrative. These dreams and fantasies are:

(1) I am trying to come back home, but there is a mountain in the way. It is very high and semicircular, like the place where I live. The sun sets on the top of the mountain, and I have an uneasy feeling because I do not know where it will disappear. A man stands on the ground in a lion's skin which is like a coat, and he is leading a pet lion like a dog. Above the hill, in the air, there is an angel—a young girl. Her face was like mine used to look. Still higher up, a skeleton that looked like my father or brother hovered in the air. Then I had a feeling that something came out of me. It was just like another self. It came out of my nostrils, and I felt as if I had fainted. It was just like me, and it stood beside me like an angel.

I call this his *initiation dream* because he himself regarded it as the starting point or origin of his disease. This narrative, with some slight variations, had been entered in his hospital record by the examining physicians. When I asked him to clarify this narrative he said:

It is as if I had been away for many years and could not find my way home. People pass me on the street and they do not recognize me. Something has changed. Once I flew to heaven and once I went to Europe on a ship; and when I came back, people acted as if many years had passed.

He continued to talk about the changed aspect of things and then connected this both with his dream and with his problem about eating things that disappear.

It is instructive to compare this dream with some of the dreams of Pukuti-wara (Róheim, 1934):

Then I flew up to the Milky Way, where there was a black mountain to which the souls always fly [p. 69].
     The soul of a man came in the form of an eagle-hawk having wings but also the penis of a man. It caught my soul with this penis and dragged it out by the hair. My soul

hung down from the penis, and the eagle-hawk flew about
with me, first to the west and then to the east [p. 75].

The eagle-hawk man threw Pukuti-wara into a fire and then
took him to a place where there were many sorcerers. These
sorcerers were skeletons. When Pukuti-wara was hurled
against them, their sharp and spike-like bones went into his
body (*ibid.*, pp. 73-77).

The fainting in our patient's dream agrees with the observations of Boss (1938) on the *autosymbolic* representation of
the death process in schizophrenic dreams. The angel who resembles and steps out of the patient is none other than the
ngantja ("mystic double") of the Aranda or the *puli nyun-
guru* ("stone bad-magic") of the Pitjentara (Róheim, 1934, pp.
32, 63, 128, 153). Finally, the fission that takes place in the
dream suggests the very name of the disease *(schizophrenia)*.

The patient later added:

This dream is like Alaska. I used to live there once, or my
grandfather did. It is like a buried country that belonged
to another people—like Alaska, which once belonged to the
Russians or the Indians. Nothing remains to show the way
—only *hands*. It is like the time I could not get the food
and could not make people understand what I wanted. It is
like somebody starving and people don't know it. It is like
reaching hands right across from one continent to the other,
from here to Russia. But there are so many countries in between, and they all eat different kinds of food. But if somebody is hungry it does not matter.

Hermann (1936) has characterized the primal type of libido
organization as the "hand-mouth system"—that is, the infant
holds on to the mother with his hands and mouth, both by
clinging and by sucking. The hands reaching over continents
in our patient's dream symbolize a painfully perceived distance. The same thing is expressed also in terms of hunger
and the different kinds of food. The *mountain* to which he is
trying to return is his mother's breast. The same symbol is

duplicated in the angelic face of his sister, who is hovering over him. The father or brother, in the guise of death, refers to the obstacles or dangers that complicate the return to his mother or sister.

The next narrative may be based on a dream but is more reminiscent of a fantasy. The patient sometimes dreamed that he was crashing through glass or bricks and that the air was weighing him down. He described the sensation as comparable to "being pulled out of a room by a truck." This theme, it will be noted, enters into many of his fantasies.

(2) Once a priest took me up into the air. I just flew through the sky and disappeared from home, and was away for eight or nine years. Up in the sky I found an angel, a woman called Angel Love. She had yellow hair, a body of gold, and wings made of feathers that covered her completely. She wanted me to go to her house and marry her, but I was detained by other women. One of them was the woman known as Little Depth Koda. These other women were similar to the first one. Sometimes their faces were round, like mine; sometimes, long and different; and sometimes they would disappear altogether. It was an island floating in the air, and I came up there, like the time when I crashed through the stained glass. There were men on the island, and they took me for a walk. Nobody did any work there. Everyone was just free and easy, and they gave me something to eat—orange juice, or berries, or soup.

Then there was a battle up there, like the end of the world. Mussolini or the Romans or the devils were attacking the angels. From that island I could see another land— like a continent—by the sea. I tried to go there but could not. In the other land, people had everything without working for it.

This dream or fantasy has certain typical elements. One of these is the narcissistic love choice: the women who want to marry him are very much like the patient. There is also a tendency to transform the one into the many. There is Angel Love or Little Depth Koda and then many women of the same type. This paradise is the place where he gets the soup (sometimes beef stew or the like) that figures so prominently in the traumatic explanation of his disease. He receives nourishment and happiness at the breast, and all the women (or breasts) want to marry him. This fantasy is an attempted denial of the trauma. But it is not quite successful. Soon there is a battle in heaven (a representation of the oedipus situation), and then there is once again the attempt to reach for another continent —a repetition of the same separation trauma.

> (3) A man was lying in a room in a house, but a private house, not like this one. There were two other boys taking care of him, giving him food. The man might almost have been me, but at the same time I was lying on my bed in the ward. Then I woke and felt as if a bug had jumped at my throat and bit it. Or it might have been a snake—or as if I had bitten my throat with my own teeth.

The associations show that a transformation of affect had taken place in the conscious content of the dream: an original rival or foe has been transformed into an ally:

> The two boys were like my younger brother and my cousin. My cousin is also like my younger brother.
> [He continued to discuss the dream:] At one time I used to live alone in our house with my mother and sister. My brother used to live in another house, not there with us. But then he was there, and I could not figure it out somehow.
> The bug was like an ape, a gorilla, a hairy person—almost like a man—but with a face like my father's. Once I had a fight with my father because I wanted to go to Canada and my father said I owed him a dollar. Another time, when I came home, my father did not want me to stay there; and when I asked for supper, they said there was no supper for me. Before that I had had a fight with my mother. She had not wanted me home either.

> (4) It was not a dream—it was a puzzle. I was in a room. It was all of red bricks, like a fireplace, and no door. How

could I get out? In my mouth there was a bowl of beef stew, but I could not eat it. The stew was covered with wax, and I could not get my teeth into it. In the room there was a tall, hairy thing—or two. Or perhaps more of them. It was a bug with a face like my father. These bugs ran about the room like little dogs. They would pick you up and then put you down playfully. This is like the dream I told you about before, about the bug flying at my throat.

Here we observe again the tendency to transform an enemy into an ally. The bug or ape, symbolic of the father, flew at his throat in the other dream; it is now a doglike playmate. It is also highly significant, I think, that the food difficulties are now placed in a closed room from which there is no exit, no door. I feel that we are justified in interpreting this room as the womb.

Several days later he said:

The brick place I was in was like a room in which I had been before. It was like the fireplace they make at Christmas. I felt as if I were being pulled out.

His vague familiarity with the brick room and his feeling of being pulled out of it are both suggestive. And the supporting association which points to Christmas, the birthday of Christ, is quite conclusive, especially since N.N. referred to himself in some of his fantasies as "Christian, King of the Jews."

(5) I was playing football with two or three colored boys. They were small, like dwarfs. They expected me to pass the ball, but I hung on to it and I would not let it go. It was like the other dream [Dream 4] in which I ate beef stew or corn soup, but somehow I could not eat it and could not make myself understood. It was like being dumb, like an animal. I felt hungry, but it was not really hunger, only a feeling like hunger. As if there was a whole restaurant full of beef stew or corn soup and I was not allowed to eat it.

[When asked about the dwarfs in the dream, he remarked:] At first I was only looking at the game. The

dwarfs played so nicely. It looked as if they were only looking, not playing. I ought to have passed the ball to the
black dwarf, but it seemed that the dwarf was not ready to
take it. So I hung on to the ball and ran down the field all
alone. Then I had a funny feeling—of being all alone on
the field.

The dwarfs on my side were like myself, only much
shorter and black. The dwarfs on the other side were real
dwarfs, however, who were really six feet tall like myself, or
even eight feet tall, but they looked as if they were no
bigger than a child.

We see here once more the autosymbolic nature of schizophrenic dreams, as emphasized by Boss (1938): (a) *He is all
alone* (b) and then the strong narcissistic trend: *Everybody
looks like he does.* We note again the tendency to oscillate between the one and the many.

His retention of the ball clarifies his food difficulties, that is,
the oral trauma. In this connection he added:

The dwarf who ought to have caught the ball was like some
of the others in my dreams, like Angel Love or Little Depth
Koda. These dwarfs were supposed to help me with my
food trouble because they were supposed to be able to
translate what I said and *to know who I am,* like the people
up in the place to which I was transported by Angel Love.

Once I was introduced to a real, heathen dwarf. That
dwarf could help me because he knew lions and dumb animals. Then I was hungry. There were other people present,
and they wanted the same food I did and objected to my
eating. The heathen was able to help me in these troubles.

(6) I dreamed that I had to go to the bathroom to urinate.
I laughed and thought that there was something funny
about this.

The next night I dreamed that I wanted to have intercourse, but I could not see the girl. Somebody must be doing this to me. Then I was awake and my bedcover was
thrown off. A crown prince stood at my bed with a sword,
as if we were equal and going to fight. You know, as if your
father had come in in the morning to wake you up. There

were many girls. They had yellow hair like angels, and their faces were like mine.

It makes no difference whether the crown prince and the duel are a waking fantasy or the continuation of a dream. The dream is a very simple oedipal dream: the patient's sexual desires bring him close to a duel with his father. We find again the narcissistic object choice and the need to change the one into the many. It is also noteworthy that this oedipal dream occurred at the time he was expecting a visit from his mother.

(7) A soldier dressed all in red woke me. He wore a black hat. His red uniform was more like plush—like mixing up all the colors of the rainbow. I was very anxious that he should not make a mistake, because he might mistake me for a United States trooper, whom they fought three hundred years ago. My grandfather was British—and my father. Once I marched with the British soldiers.

(8) A crown prince dressed all in black with a high hat came and woke me. The crown prince handed me a sword to see if I would fight. There was another crown prince there also, dressed in grey, and then several others. I wondered whether the crown prince would stay with me.

He seemed to stay with me after the dream and to take care of me. I was once allowed to dress like that and was almost a crown prince myself.

The first crown prince gave me the sword to see if I would fight, and the other crown princes were ready to fight him if he did.

In connection with this fantasy or dream he explained his theory of dreams, according to which dreams are caused by dreams:

Somebody else might have dreamed of me as the crown prince, and then I would appear in the dream of that other person and wake him. That is how I go home sometimes. Somebody at home—my mother—dreams of me and then I am at home with a broom in my hand, helping her.

(9) Somebody—a former attendant—he looked like you —lifted the boards or the furniture in the room. But at the same time this was also a rock on the outside. You know, rocks sometimes look like furniture. It was as if somebody was lifting your bed and lifting you right up with it. I used to have a snake like that once and I used to play with it, but then it left me. It did not like me so much and tried to poison me. Under the board they found a Teethy—or rather two Teethies. They looked like my father and also like me. They kept jumping up and down and nodding. A voice told me that there was another bigger snake—the size of a man—underneath. I used to know that snake once. It was the snake in the Bible: Satan, the snake in the Garden of Eden. I used to wind it around my body.

[He continued, referring to an event of the previous day:] I had been looking at the rocks in the garden. Some of them were purple, some had other colors. They were pretty. I was turning them over and looking at the crabs underneath. Then I saw something funny. A bird called a "purple crackler" was flying toward me. And behind the bird, sitting on it, was a human figure, an angel with wings. This was my mother's Teethy.

(10) Last night I had a wet dream. But it was no dream because I did not see any pictures. At first I thought it was my bowels moving—because I had eaten green apples. Then it felt the way it was when my father scolded me for masturbating. A girl once accused me of having married her because she wanted to be a mother. My sister accused me of the same thing. Once a girl wanted to marry me, but a crown prince discovered it and we had a duel. Once I was shot and killed for marrying a girl. I came through all right in the duel with the crown prince because I was so very small.

(11) I expect to go home for a visit in a short time. I dreamed that I was at home. All my teeth were replaced and I was ready to eat my Christmas dinner. When I was at home the last time it was Christmas. When I came back here I had to have one of my teeth pulled. It was quite easy this time to dream of going home. At other times it is difficult even to dream of going home. When I had the tooth

pulled, my senses and brain all disappeared. I was numb, like under ether. Then it felt as if somebody had let fresh air in.

He was correct about the visit home at Christmas and about the subsequent extraction of his tooth. In view of the replacement of the teeth, this was a typical restoration dream.

(12) A horse came to fetch me and carried me to an empty carriage. Then a crown prince came and it turned out that the carriage belonged to him. Then another crown prince came, took me by the scruff of the neck, and rushed me to a doctor's office. It might have been you, or Dr. B., or Dr. L. The crown prince looked like you or my father. In the office there was also a nurse. And a young girl—she was funny, like thin air. There were several young girls, and many horses and carriages. Then I was rushed back—by one of the girls, or by the crown prince—to pull a carriage out of a ditch. The horses had run away, and the people wanted to see if I could do it. Then the crown prince came up to the carriage. He was almost French—he was Napoleon Bonaparte. He made me sit beside him as if I were almost a crown prince myself.

I do not like to talk about these things because you or I might be mistaken for a crown prince. I had a horse like that once. It went like lightning. It was quite black. It was a white horse. It was really dark brown, a kind of black. Then I had an awful experience. There was a carriage with a man and a girl in it. The horse broke away like lightning, and I had to rush to the rescue on another horse to catch it. I jumped into the carriage, took the reins, and brought the horse back to normal again.

The carriage in the dream was like a stagecoach or a carriage for royalty. The carriage was stuck in a ditch—and the ditch was like a cow pasture. The stagecoach was like a mountain. But when I awoke it was only a little hill. I used to ride on a cow like that, driving all the other cows to pasture. Or I would ride on a bull and drive the herd. This was when I lived in Alaska.

This was a very funny dream. I have to laugh. All the crown princes disappeared; and all the young girls, like my cousin or sister, were there, and I was married to them. Usually, in a dream—one has either the crown princes *or* the girls. It can't be both.

Before this dream I had another dream. I was being chopped up with an axe. It was just like chopping up your food or bread with a knife. You know how it is when you fill your mouth with saliva and then draw it back. It is cut off with a knife. Your tongue is the knife.

Once—when I had eaten cheese and some other rich dish —this acted like a dream and lifted me right off the bed. In the dream I was trying to pull one of the carriages right off the wall where it had got stuck. The carriage was tilted on the side of the wall as if it had been trying to run over the roof but had stopped half way; and the house was like this house.

This dream shows a faint trace of transference. The crown prince is not the father and himself, but me (or Drs. B. and L.) and himself. The carriage, having made an attempt to pass over the roof of the house, gets stuck half way. Since he is always trying to return to normality, we may reasonably suspect that the carriage that gets stuck on the Worcester State Hospital is his ego, which is stuck in his psychosis.

In another version of the same narrative the carriage is stuck in a cow pasture. Since we know that the cow symbolizes his mother, this would mean that the key to his psychosis lies in mother fixation. A carriage that is easily carried away by wild horses: this indicates a lack of resistance in the ego, and the anxiety of being carried away by his impulses. This is confirmed by his statement that he brought the wild (mad) horse back to normal again.

We defer the interpretation of much of the dream material until we have related more of his fantasies.

In returning to certain aspects of the patient's oral trauma, it is important to note that he felt that his *food trouble* was closely connected with a process that took place within him and with certain internalized mythological beings. After mentioning the difficulty he had experienced with the patient who had taken a piece of bread from his tray, he said:

> It all started a long, long while ago when some member of my family—my mother or my father—took my food away. It happened intestinally, when my food was half digested. There was a time when I could not go to the bathroom to pass stool: it was either very hard or very soft. And that is why I was sent up here.

His psychosis had some relation, he felt, to various introjected objects. As he himself put it:

> There are *bugs* inside me. One of them is as big as me. It tries to eat all the food when it gets into my stomach. There are also several little bugs who also look like me and like the Little Depth Koda. These bugs are the same as the Teethies that I found in myself.

At a later interview he added more information about the excremental aspect of these internalized objects:

> Another story—like that of the *speed*—has to do with the time when I could not use the toilet. I was *obstipated,* and the stool stuck in my spinal column. I took a laxative, but not to make the stool go out. It was to clear the passage so that the food I was eating could go down. It is like cleaning one's teeth. The stool in me was like the speed or gravity. Once I ate chocolate and there was pon-ton poison in it.

This disappearance of food was intimately connected with the core of his mythological beliefs: the bugs. He said that he had always had the bugs. Whenever he tried to eat, a bug would eat the food:

> An apple would lose its weight. They could weigh it and prove that a bug had eaten it. This bug made me get lost—that was three thousand years ago—and it also made the words get lost when they came out of my teeth. I was full of bugs, and the bugs ate all the food. A big one was cut out of my stomach, and another one was taken out of my spinal column. The bug put its teeth into my teeth and ate my food. Another bug that looked like a wasp flew up against

my jaw and knocked my teeth out. There was a second tiny bug in human shape—it was riding on the wasp bug. This bug looked like me. There was another bug that looked like a ship. As I stood on the dock, looking around, the keel of a ship knocked against my jaw.

The words were lost. I was also lost. That was three hundred years ago. And then the bug made me lose myself. But the bug was also lost. I used to have a bug like a lion and one like a monkey, but they took the bug away from me because there was no room for it.

Once there was a bug like a gorilla. It stood in my way, and I almost had a fight with it.

There were occasions when he began to reveal the identity of the bug:

I am afraid to offend the bug. If I did that, I might not be reborn. Some people are not reborn, you know. The bug that governs rebirth is the one that has a head like mine and eats the food when it gets into my insides. The bug looks like my father.

The connection between the parental images and the introjects was quite clear:

Once my father put his head inside me and ate all the food. Once before, when I was walking backwards, I bumped right into my mother. Then I felt as though she had put her head inside mine and had eaten all the food within me. This happened when I went home after the death of the old lady.

I want to know about this business with the teeth—whether other people have the right to put their teeth into mine. The two sets of teeth are apt to knock against each other. I even went to the dentist once, because I felt so uncomfortable.

On another occasion he returned to a discussion of the supernatural beings, called Teethies, who figured in some of his dreams and fantasies:

My own Teethy regularly eats with me. This does not disturb me. But other people send their Teethies into my mouth—these are the ones that make my food disappear. I used to carry a Teethy inside my body—it looked exactly like me and fitted exactly into my body. My father would sometimes let me have his Teethy for a while—this one was called Man-Man. My father used to have lots of Teethies. Then I lost my Teethy, as I lost the snake and the surgeon (sturgeon) fish. Somebody took it away from me.

It is necessary to digress briefly for a preliminary consideration of the theoretical principles which emerge from the data. As the result of an oral trauma, the patient's father and mother have become internalized objects. The patient has reacted to the withdrawal of the nipple by creating a fantasy nipple in himself. We may here refer to the theory of Schmideberg (1930), who has interpreted schizophrenia as a flight to the internalized objects.

I think, however, that the richness of the patient's fantasies permits another theoretical step, namely, that there is some relationship between internalized objects and body-destruction fantasies. Our patient, in the course of his fantasies about the disappearing food or some other trouble with the food, often represented the situation as if these problems were of his own making. That the fault, for example, was the amount of aggression he has shown in eating his food. He also believed that his mother was trying to poison him, but he felt that he could ward off this danger by eating his food in the *right way*.

In connection with one of his mythological creations, the Heathen, who could help him with his food difficulties, I suggested on one occasion that perhaps he thought the Heathen could help him by telling him to go ahead and not to mind the others. He grew angry and said that I had things quite wrong. He added:

I do not like to talk about these things because I might use the wrong words and hurt somebody—you, for instance. My mother does not take me home because of the food trouble. If I eat my food in the right way and do not make any mistakes in eating, it will not thin down when it gets into my insides, and my mother will take me home.

When I had the wet dream I thought I must have eaten green apples and that made the trouble inside me.

The green apples are here identified with the love object, and the love object with the introject.

As indicated, the patient had several theories about his ailment. One was that he had suffered an oral frustration: that his mother was bad and had taken his food away. Another was a functional representation of the aggression aroused in him by this deprivation: his mother withheld the food because he did not eat it in the right way, that is, because of his oral-sadistic trends. He stated quite clearly that he might not be able to control his emotions if he returned to his home. He might, he said, get *mad* (angry) and would have to be brought back. He described the anxiety he had experienced during a visit to his home:

Once, when I went home, I could not pronounce the name of the street where I lived, or my father's name. I said that I had eaten beef stew or milk, and people thought I meant a whole cow. I said that I was through, meaning that I had gone through a street or door; and people thought that I was saying I was through with them, that I was angry. The trouble was that when they were calling me to dinner, I thought they were telling me to go and play. "Dinner time" sounded exactly like "darn time." I had not said that and had not refused to eat.

It is obvious that these are elaborate attempts at denying the aggression caused by oral frustration. First there is an oral frustration, then there are destructive trends called forth by this frustration, and finally there is an attempt to deny this aggression.

Another group of fantasies revealed, as distinctly as some of his dreams, that he was reacting to the appearance of siblings on the scene, that is, that he was confronted with rivals:

The trouble started first when people envied me the food. I was sitting with my father, and when I had eaten the food it suddenly caved in and slipped out. It was like when I was a little child with my grandmother and I went in the opposite direction and hurt myself. Once I came home late and my mother would not give me any supper.

The following statement, frequently repeated, clearly referred to the arrival of siblings:

They let me eat the beef stew or corn undisturbed for three hundred years or even five hundred years. And then, suddenly, when I wanted to eat a whole restaurant full of food, I was told that I could not, that other people might be hungry and might get angry. I did not know that I thought I could eat it all.

We assume that he responded to the oral trauma with aggression. It seems obvious that the hostility and envy that he detected in his father or brother or other members of the family in connection with food was a projection of the hostility and envy which he had felt toward his younger brother. This hostility resulted in the formation of hostile introjects— for example, the Teethy, who envied him his food and who devoured it or made it disappear whenever he ate.

Before taking the next step in our theoretical progression, it is necessary to describe a group of fantasies connected with his sister and with the "old lady" (that is, the mother of his former employer).

He had a number of interesting fantasies about the death of his younger sister, whom he sometimes described as his wife:

My father and mother scolded me because I did not want to marry my sister and went about with other girls. My father and some of the doctors seemed to think it was natural for a brother to marry his sister. This gave me a lot of trouble. I tried to think about what I had done. I must have made a mistake. I mean that it must be something like my trouble with the food. Once—accidentally—I found myself with my head where it should not be: my mouth was touching my sister's genitals. I had other sisters—too many of them—with whom I was actually married.

We observe here the transformation of the one into the many, as in his dreams. He continued:

My mother also asked me to marry her, but she was only fooling. When my sister asked me to marry her, she already had that thing in her stomach—and I was afraid of injuring her or killing her. That's why I did not marry her. The minister and God and the judge would not like it if I married my sister. Dr. B. said that I was guilty of killing my sister, but the judge found that I wasn't guilty.

In response to questions about "that thing" in his sister's stomach, he said:

It was a crown. The crown in my sister's body was due to the fact that I had hit her, or that I was a crown prince, or that she was a crown princess herself and had a crown inside. In fact, I did not put the crown into her—I just pulled it out of her.

The remarks we have quoted illustrate the use of negation as a defense against his fantasied wishes. His remarks that he was not guilty of having married and killed his sister mean that in a fantasy he had had intercourse with his sister (who represented his mother) and thereby killed her. Since he was a crown prince, she thus became a crown princess and had a crown within her. Since the crown was in her because of something he had done, it would seem that the crown is their child. Further—and according to the defense mechanism of negation—the crown was something that he had pulled out of her, not put into her.

His fundamental feelings of guilt would thus be connected with body-destruction fantasies: that is, he had pulled the valuable body contents out of his sister's (or mother's) body and had thus killed her.

The "old lady" of his fantasies plays a similar role. Before the onset of his psychosis, N.N. had been employed by a family as a chauffeur. During this period, his employer's mother, the "old lady," had died. The patient frequently declared that he had been accused of killing her and that he saw a big bug flying from her stomach toward his body. This would make the bug the bearer or symbol of his own body-destruction fantasies.

In connection with his sister's death, he said:

I did not kill my sister. It was Dr. B. who accused me of doing that. It was she who killed me by throwing a truck at me. And then I was brought up here. After my sister's death people did not like me. They did not like my looks. They thought that I was responsible for her death. Boys and girls would hit my solar plexus—or they would only swing at it—and that filled me with hot air.

It is obvious that he connected his psychosis with his sister's death. It is also noteworthy that the attacks against him were directed against his stomach—because his own attacks, that is, his own body-destruction fantasies, were directed against his mother's stomach.

He went on to explain what he meant by "filled with hot air":

A friend of mine first told me, "You are full of hot air." It is a slang expression for "You are telling lies" or "You are crazy." My friend said this when I told him about the swordfish. The whole thing banged my stomach and made me sick.

According to my interpretation, the stomach in this connection is the retributive form or agent of his body-destruction fantasies—that is, of the infantile fantasy system in which the child wants to tear something (milk, siblings, feces, father's penis) out of the mother's body. The following association, containing the idea of eating the swordfish (mother), confirms my interpretation:

I thought how funny it would be if my mother sent me to the shop to buy fish and somebody had caught that sword-fish and I happened to buy it.

To recapitulate the conclusions we have reached at this point: His psychosis had something to do with an early oral trauma. He reacted to this frustration with aggression and body-destruction fantasies. Some of these fantasies were connected with internalized objects that ate his food. These introjects constituted the retributive form of his body-destruction fantasies. Or, to put it in somewhat different terms: He fantasied himself going into his mother's body and eating her (as a response to the oral frustration); and he was now afraid that his mother, father, brother, sister, and so on, being in him, were eating his food as quickly as it got inside him.

I do not assert that the patient never progressed beyond the pure preoedipal phase, as represented by the body-destruction fantasies. We have seen the recurring element in his dreams and fantasies about a duel with his father. In addition, his oedipal fantasies found adequate expression in his own interpretation of the myth of the Garden of Eden. Of course, the choice of this myth was partly determined by the fact that his guilt could here be expressed in oral symbolism.

This business about somebody—my father or brother—putting his head inside mine and making the food disappear was very much like Adam and the apple in the Garden of Eden. It was not just an ordinary apple—it had to be *translated*. You can eat an ordinary apple. But suppose the apple belonged to someone else—was in the other person's orchard—then you couldn't eat it. If you did, the bug would know all about it. Someone wanted to take the food or the apple or Adam's birthright away from him; but the bug would know this and would not permit it.

I myself was Adam years ago, or perhaps a crown prince. We were sitting at home at the table—me, my father, my mother, my brother, my sister. Then maybe somebody—maybe me—would think that the food on my father's plate or my brother's plate looked better and would try to exchange it. Maybe he wanted to get into somebody's head and eat other people's food in their insides. But the bug would not allow this to happen. Maybe I was a bug once or maybe I was in the bugs that destroy people.

Here we have the confirmation of our interpretation, namely, that internalized objects are derived from the mother's body contents. Some time later he described the Garden of Eden in these terms:

Once upon a time I ate an apple that was growing near a farm house. It was not like the other apples that one gets in the market, and the doctors thought it might make my chest broad. I ate the apple. That is why the food would slip right through me.

I saw the Garden of Eden once. It was like an island with trees, but the water around it was not really water. It was like looking at the other shore of an ocean, or like a cemetery with a gate. Nobody could go in and take things away —not even God or Satan. I had been in there once. It was the same thing as Alaska, a place I discovered, where I lived with my grandfather at the beginning of the world.

I connected my eating the apple in the Garden of Eden with my dream about the sunset and the mountain, and with the fact that my mother did not want me to stay at home. They did not like me at home. My father and mother wanted me to go away to this place here—or to another country, or to a place beyond the world.

[He began to laugh and then added:] But the house where I was born is mine, and nobody can take it away from me. My father and brother tried to do that, but they couldn't.

The Garden of Eden—where he ate the apple (or breast) and incurred the wrath of God (his father)—was obviously his own mother. At a later interview he came back to this theme:

The Garden of Eden has something to do with the fact that my mother cannot see me when I am at home. I have the power to be here and at home at the same time.

Once upon a time I got into some trouble—because of eating apples. I ate a lot of them green, and that naturally caused diarrhea. But it would have been all right if the owner of the apples had consented to my eating them. My mother or aunt or father was the owner of the apples. The green apples caused the wet dream and all the trouble with my insides.

At one time the nurses complained that he was behaving aggressively toward the other patients. When questioned about this, he ascribed his behavior to his troubles with *speed* (a problem to which we shall presently return). He also ascribed his aggressiveness to the following causes:

Once upon a time I had six apples. I ate one. Then I was afraid—by the time I came back—that the other apples would not do me any good, because I had eaten other food in the meantime. I was afraid that the apples would disappear.

The significance of the apples becomes clear: it was the original food (breast) to which he always wanted to return after having been weaned, that is, after having eaten other kinds of food. The following sentence indicates his aggression against the breast:

One of the apples was bruised, so they might all be bruised.

He returned to this problem again, further revealing the apples as internalized love objects:

Once I got three bananas—I mean three apples—when my mother was here with her two sisters. I was wondering if the three apples I ate could understand or know what I was saying to other people.

We see again that the apples meant milk to our patient, as opposed to chocolate (feces) or bananas (penis):

Once at night I thought people were talking of chocolate milk, so I went down for the milk, which I used to drink at night, but it was breakfast time and they were talking about coffee and hot chocolate. When I got back to the milk, everything was normal again. When I came up here I had eaten three apples. But my mother and her sisters thought it was three bananas. When they understood that it was three apples, things were all right again.

At a later date he returned to this theme, connecting the Garden of Eden with the end of the world:

There was some trouble because I ought not to have taken the journey to the end of the world. A part of the road—about the size of this room—was private property, owned by a farmer. The farmer was a huge, tall man. He came flying through the air. He might have been God. I was not supposed to pick any of the apples. I used to ask my grandfather and grandmother. They owned the orchard. The path to the orchard was divided like the fangs of a snake and it *came* like lightning.

He frequently returned to the basic aspect of the oral trauma. Shortly after his mother visited him he said:

The whole trouble started at a party. People were dreaming that they were hungry—not really hungry, but hungry inside—and they were not understood and the police broke it up. It all started with the apple, with the Garden of Eden. I was Adam and I thought somebody was trying to take the apple away from me. Then—finally—I gave it up. I did not want the whole world to starve. I spoke to my mother about this, but it is not possible to go back now.

Sometimes he expressed the conflict with his father by playing the role, not of Adam, but of Satan or the primeval serpent:

I once saw God, but I can't say what his face was like—because it kept changing. Sometimes it was like mine, and sometimes long. God had a big beard. Then I saw Satan. He was young, and he looked like me. God gave me some soup to eat. Satan also would give people things to eat, but he would fill them up so as to make them sick. That part of it was very amusing. Sometimes the Devil would let me play that I was the Devil and I would fill people up. I flew up into the air with God—and there was a battle between us. When I was at home, my father used to be like that—like God. I used to ask him if he had had his soup. Satan has a serpent around his body. I used to have a serpent around my body in the Garden of Eden and I walked around like that.

At other times he would describe his oedipal difficulties without the Biblical terminology:

When my mother took away my rights, it had something to do with my father, who played that he was himself and me at the same time.

This was, of course, another manifestation of the technique of displacement, since it was he, not his father, who "played" at being father and son at the same time. At any rate, there were occasions when he blamed his father for his illness, as in the following instance:

I can't get back to normal because of certain pills my father gave me. I *almost* blame my father for all this.

We assume that the patient progressed in his development as far as the oedipal stage, probably beyond that to the super-ego stage; but his mental structure was very weak because of the underlying preoedipal anxieties. Whenever some difficulty would occur in reality—for example, the death of his sister or of his employer's mother—it was necessary for him to make a new adjustment; and he would regress to the oral situation where his fixation was actually conditioned by an oral frustration. As we have seen, he had reacted to this frustration by exaggerated body-destruction fantasies.

In trying to find the cause of his trouble, he consistently emphasized object loss, but he oscillated between two possible attitudes: he ascribed his problems to a basic frustration, that is, starvation, or he blamed himself for the aggressions and body-destructive fantasies caused by this frustration.

One of his anxieties or fantasies was connected with the idea of *speed* (sometimes expressed in terms of *gravity* or *gravitation*). He used these words synonomously, as his remarks will indicate:

> I was playing that this was my home and that the cafeteria was a restaurant where I go to eat. Then I felt a lot of *speed* or *gravitation,* as if the walls were pushing me out.
>
> [At a later interview he said:] Do you know the feeling of stumbling over the furniture before going to sleep? One's feet get all entangled. Sometimes I jump out of my chair and feel as if I were an eagle with wings growing on all sides. It is like the time I came home after having been away for eight or nine months. The eagle-feeling is like the food trouble and like being a bug.
>
> [On another occasion he described the same sensation in these terms:] I was riding in a car with my father. The air began to get thin around me and I felt lost. When I put my coat on—sometimes I do this so quickly that by the time it is on, it is off again.

This *speed,* it will be recalled, also presented itself in the form of aggression. Thus, after the nurses complained that N.N. was behaving as if he were going to jump on people, he said to me:

> There is too much *speed* or *gravity* in me. I feel as if the chair were falling over and throwing me out. It is like one of my dreams or fairy stories. It is like the time when I was crossing the field near my house, when I had the lion, and the *speed* took me away. I disappeared between the sun and the night, and I was not seen again for seven or eight years.

The following remarks, already cited in a different context, are also related to the problem of *speed:*

> Another story like the *speed* was when I could not use the toilet. I was *obstipated,* and the stool stuck in my spinal column. I took a laxative, but that was not to make the stool go out. It was to clear the passage so that the food I was eating could go down. It was like cleaning one's teeth.

What did he mean when he said that the purpose of the laxative was "not to make the stool go out"? It will be recalled that he made similar remarks when he discussed his *food troubles*. He has frequently said, for example, "It was not real food, only like food," or "People were dreaming of eating food." This would seem to mean that he was really talking, not about food, but about introjection—that is, about internalized objects in general, with both "food" and "stool" meaning body contents. The comparison of the laxative with a dentifrice ("like cleaning one's teeth") indicates that he has equated the oral and the anal orifices.

The correlation between *speed* and aggression also became progressively more obvious:

> The stool in me is like the *speed or gravity*. Once I ate chocolate [feces] and there was pon-ton poison in it, and it turned sour. But if I eat chocolate the *right way*, there is no pon-ton poison in it.

The *right way*, of course, means without aggression.

From the point of view of our patient, the *speed* was a force within him. It seems clear, I feel, that he was thus referring to the marked weakness of his ego, with *speed* or *gravitation* describing the dangers inherent in any id activity or impulse, aggression, anal urge, or genital desire. He once compared a nocturnal emission to the feeling of *speed*, but he also ascribed the emission to the eating of green apples. *Speed* generally referred to those *aggressions* that were connected with the *internalized objects*. This interpretation is verified by his correlation of *speed* and dizziness:

> Sometimes I get dizzy from gathering too much *speed*. It has to do with a change in work or attitude. The first time I had this sort of trembling feeling was when my father asked me to help him with some work while I was playing baseball. This is a bad habit of mine—I always go on doing things.

His dizziness was, of course, always connected with guilt and aggression. He always felt dizzy when he had done something wrong or when he was discouraged.

Our conjecture that his *speed* was connected with ego weakness is confirmed by some remarks of Schilder. Schilder (1939), in connection with Hermann's researches, interprets the grasping reflex as a protection or reassurance against the anxiety of falling—of losing the warmth and protection afforded by the mother's body. He cites the work of Bender and Blau to show that infants with a lesion of the cerebellum cling to the mother to protect themselves from falling, and he believes in general that the vestibulary apparatus is an important factor in ego development. The evolution of the ego and independence are interrelated (pp. 59-60).

In this connection our patient once said:

> When I was in the car going home, I felt sick. Not in the stomach, but with this feeling of *speed* or *gravity*. It is a kind of homesickness—I feel as if I were falling forward.

I believe we are justified in assuming that he was trying to cling to (or hold on to) his mother.

Many of his dreams and fantasies were concerned with this feeling of levitation or *speed*. *Speed*—that is, any urge—was connected with his dread of *complete object loss*. This is the same as the *loss of the ego,* as we shall observe presently.

> Once I was putting on my shoes at home. My feet and shoes began to lift themselves up in the air and I thought I would be lifted off the ground. My hat would rise high above me.
>
> Then there was the time I was walking or riding in a car or on horseback. My awful habit of going so fast made me go almost beyond myself or rush off the edge of the earth, like the sun when it sinks.

The technique of projection or fission—by which he invented a fictional person to represent him or to serve as a duplicate of his ego—was frequently called into action:

There was an engineer once. He ran a train, and he almost ran the train off the earth. I almost thought I was that engineer.

[At a later meeting he said:] I was born in Europe and came to America three hundred years ago. This country is different from Europe. Sometimes it feels like a natural country, almost the same as in Europe. Then you are suddenly lifted off and thrown out. This could not happen in New York State, where it was just natural country. I was running too fast. Not me, but a race horse. Then a trainer fired a shot at the race horse, and that made him stop.

As we have observed above, the patient frequently associated his difficulties in eating and the disappearance of his food with an inability to communicate these problems to other people.

I was thinking of how that trouble began. On a Sunday when I could not eat and could not make myself understood it felt as if I were being lifted right out of the house. As I have told you—when I went home I would upset everything, or everything looked upset, or *I* was upset. My shoes were always knocked off, and then there was trouble in my brain—and it would be difficult to say things. So one of the doctors gave me the advice to take off the shoe and put it in my brain. Then the shoe would help me talk. When I say the word "shoe," a shoe would form itself in my mouth. Or I would feel the chair, or the street I was living on. This would happen when somebody who knew me—maybe my aunt or mother—would touch me through the air. When I said "street," the whole street would be in my mouth, and it would be difficult for me to pronounce it. Or when I ate soup, the whole can of soup would be in my mouth. Or a house.

Then I was knocked on the head by a blow. But it was not a natural blow, only hot air. [We have noted above that *hot air*, to our patient, meant to be psychotic. He continued:]

I had the trouble with the sundial. It was like a well— and I was dazed, lost in the shadow. It was like a bug. The words were *angered* in my head—they would not come out.

He said *angered* but he meant *anchored*—made immovable by an anchor. Thus, his words were *anchored,* that is, he could not get them loose. Similarly, he would sometimes say that the food on his plate had been *angered* by a food expert.

To continue with his confusion about symbol and object:

> Pronouncing the word "street" and at the same time feeling the street in your head—that is insanity. I ate a pie and I was too anxious. That is insanity.
>
> When I tell you these stories I am afraid that you might not understand or the words might be wrong. Even my own father might not understand me. Insanity is when I speak through my head. I think I hear the words, but I am not saying anything and people don't understand me. I am talking and eating through some other part of my body than I ought to. Perhaps the bottom of my tongue.

These remarks are of great importance. Our patient has said:

(a) Insanity means the loss of object relations; people cannot understand him.

(b) Insanity means a confusion of symbol and object.

It is unquestionable that this confusion is related to various internalized objects and to the failure of the cathexis to move back from the internalized object to the environment.

To return to his difficulty with words:

> Three hundred years ago a bug made me get lost, and this bug also made the words get lost as they came out of my mouth. Once I said "ten o'clock"—and as the word came out of my mouth, it was lost. So I went to see where ten o'clock was. This was when I had the trouble with the sundial. The word was really lost in my insides—at the root of my tongue. The bug put its teeth into my insides and ate my food. As the words were lost, so I was lost three hundred years ago. And then a bug made me lose myself, but the bug was also lost.

This is not meaningless talk. The word itself is an internalized object. And his internalized objects are not safe in his body but are threatened by his own anxiety. The introjected objects, however, are frequently himself, though they may also be the father or mother imago. In fact, the key to his state of mind appears to be his tendency to identify himself with the introjected objects.

> The way the food disappeared from my mouth is the same as when the words disappeared from my mouth. In school I had to do exercises and draw a table. Instead of writing, "This is a table"—I wrote, "This is no table." This would be corrected afterward. We also had to write stories. Between the stories we used to make music. *Mu* [music] and *me* is the same thing. The word *told* is the same thing as *toll*, the fare you have to pay on a bridge for passing.

The bridge connects one shore with the other, and the word connects one person with another. The money or toll is the effort we have to make, the tension we have to endure, if we wish to be in touch with reality.

He continued:

> This is like a trolley car. I had a trolley car but they took it away from me. Some stories are difficult to tell. They are so broad, one cannot grasp them. Once I suddenly felt a thud on my stomach and head—as if somebody had shaken me up. Then I lost my brains—and, what was worse, the next morning I started eating my food backwards, first the bacon and then the cereal. Finally, after I did get my appetite back, there was still trouble, because I could not find the words. When I tried to get home once, I took the words too lightly. Supposing you read a story, and when you read it again you have to read every word. Once I suffered from starvation and nearly died. After that, I got *overweighted,* eating nine cups of coffee or soup instead of one.

We observe again that the oral trauma is followed by denial in fantasy and by symbolic pregnancy (nine).

The following sentences justify the equation of the word with the internalized object:

I was *overweighted,* and the words would not come out. It could not *translate*—it was like a foreign language.

[This was followed by other remarks, which indicate that sibling rivalry and the resulting anxiety were connected with his problems:] Somebody who was only an ordinary boy said that I had much more than I ought—that I was *overweighted.* If I could correct each word I have ever said, I would come back to normal.

[Discussing his verbal problems, he once said:] The feeling of not being able to go back to a place is like the feeling of not being able to pronounce a word. I think that if I could get the word back, I could also go back to the place.

[I asked him if he had any particular word in mind, and he replied:] "Forgetfulness." Now I can remember it, but I can't pronounce it. I used to try to say the sentence, "I forgot how to say the word 'forget' "; but when I came to the last word of the sentence, I couldn't pronounce it. I used to try to say the word "encyclopedia," where all knowledge is contained, but then I had to go to the encyclopedia to find the word "encyclopedia"—and I could not find it. If I could find the words or remember my old stories, I would be able to go home.

One of the fictional beings of his mythological world is a person who is deaf, or deaf and dumb—obviously a personification of himself in those situations in which people do not respond to him or in which he is unable to make himself understood:

I used to know a person—have you ever met him?—who was deaf and dumb. I began to teach him to read with writing in relief, and he began to be able to speak. This person used to play that he was my brother, and I used to help him to make himself understood. Then I met a missionary who went to foreign lands to make people understand things. I was once a missionary myself.

We have already observed that the words which failed to bring a response from the environment (or were lost within him) were closely connected with his internalized objects or body contents. As the patient himself said:

There are various beings and persons in me. The voices inside me are connected in some way with my difficulty in making myself understood. Once, when I was at home, I asked my mother for supper and she said that I had had my supper already! The trouble was not the actual food—it was the *work in the food*.

If our interpretation is correct, the *work in the food* refers to the psychic energy involved in introjection and in the turning of aggression against himself.

Up to this point we have heard primarily about the various hostile and internalized objects (parents, siblings, Teethies, and so on) who were eating his food or making it disappear—that is, who were leaving him empty. We turn now to another group of internalized objects: these are reparative or restitutive in type. The putative phases in the development of his fantasy system may tentatively be summarized in the following way:

(a) Introjection, the eating of food.

(b) The aggression which is implicit in introjection comes to be represented by hostile internalized objects who eat his food after it is in him, leaving him scooped out and empty, totally deprived of body contents.

(c) Internalized objects of the restitutive type attempt to cope with the anxiety that is connected with the hostile introjects.

One of the benevolent voices or persons within him was Little Depth Koda. He identified her with Angel Love, the woman in the dream in which he flew up to heaven.

She is called Depth because "depth" is like "deaf," and I sometimes feel deaf with all the noise around me. Depth Koda is a tiny person who speaks in my insides and is connected with the food trouble, as if she were trying to fix it and make me well again. She is like a doctor.

[On another occasion he explained her name in the following way:] Depth means something deep, like the ocean. Koda is an island in the ocean, or a photo—like Kodak.

There is something like a diluted reel of film in my brain, and the reel and the photo are like the doctors—trying to tell me what to do.

He could hardly have expressed himself more clearly, because mental images *were* working against his anxiety.

In connection with these benevolent images he said:

I have a photographic machine that takes pictures of people eating. This machine is like the one in the movies. The doctors built it—to see who was putting his head inside me and eating my food. When I ate a cereal it would thin down to coffee, and when I drank coffee it would evaporate into smoke.

It may be noted that on one occasion when the food he was eating disappeared and he could not make himself understood, he tried to convey his problem by drawing pictures.

The identification of introject and imago (or mental image) means that in an infantile fantasy these images appear to be emanating from within. The image may represent the memory of gratified desires for food, of people eating. They not only serve as a protection against anxiety but are also identical with the patient. As he himself described it, these inner voices or images tried to explain things to him in exactly the same way in which he tried to explain things to the members of the hospital staff and to his father.

The mechanisms of introjection and projection are complementary. An effort is made to fantasy "good body contents." The possibility of separation is thus avoided. However, since these "good body contents" are also cathected with aggression (derived both from their capacity to thwart satisfaction and from the aggression in the subject caused by this frustration), they become dangerous (that is, "bad body contents") and an effort is made to get rid of them by projection.

The patient remembered that on one occasion, when he was at the movies, he heard the voices on the screen and became quite alarmed:

I did not know if the voices came from my insides or from the outside. Then I saw Little Depth Koda walking into my mouth. She was trying to fix the trouble with the food.

Another person or voice inside me is a little man called Jew or Jewel. He acts like a Jew.

[I asked him how a Jew acts, and he replied:] Well, trying to help me. I was nearly a Jew myself once—when I lived in Jerusalem. A rabbi or a doctor circumcised me because he thought there was something the matter with my foreskin.

The hospital records indicated that he had previously accused a rabbi of *castrating* him. This leads me to assume, therefore, that these benevolent introjects of the restitutive type were originally hostile introjects.

In view of our patient's identification with words (that is, the word gets lost in him, as he gets lost in the world), these benevolent and internalized beings also represent inherent libidinal (magic) power. We may thus consider the schizophrenic as a magician who fails.

Before analyzing our patient's magical manipulation of words, we digress briefly to consider the ontogeny of speech. At an early phase of the infant's mental development, all objects are "internalized," as it were, because there is no clear-cut division between "inside" and "outside." According to Wundt (1911), the first sounds produced by the infant are those of crying or screaming—that is, these sounds represent an attempt to ameliorate a situation of pain or tension. Sound production that is definitely connected with external objects, with the attempt to name things, comes considerably later (pp. 284-285). In psychoanalytic terminology this indicates a gradual increase in the reality content of fantasy objects.

Spielrein (1922), in an interesting paper on the origin of the infantile words for father and mother, shows that the infantile syllables "mo-mo" (or "ma-ma") and "po-po" (or "pa-pa") are both derived from movements made by the lips in connection with sucking. With this difference, however: when the infant is happy it says "pa-pa"; when it is in a state of tension, "ma-ma." The word "ma-ma" or "mo-mo" closely approximates sucking, while "pa-pa" or "po-po" corresponds to the playful moving of the lips when the child is satisfied and is merely playing at the nipple, catching it with its mouth and then dropping it again (p. 365). The mother, therefore, is the object in the environment that can satisfy the fundamental tension, while the father is an object of secondary importance. However, the difficulty is that these results can be demonstrated only in some linguistic groups and are by no means valid for *all* the languages of the world.

At any rate, there is one time or another when the infant is hungry and feels empty—that is, anxious and aggressive. He cries or shouts, but the environment (mother) fails to respond and he has had his first and greatest disappointment.

It is very significant that our patient was always talking about the words that could take him back to reality, about stories without a happy ending, and about the difference between himself and a minister: "People listen to the minister, but they do not listen to me." This is an infantile grievance, but it is one which clearly reflects an archaic (infantile) logic. His early environment failed to respond to him and he has been expressing a great and real disappointment.

Under ordinary conditions the maturing infant gradually differentiates himself from the environment, with all the personal and cultural consequences that follow, including the development of the ego, the capacity for sublimation, and so on. The schizophrenic, however, remains at (or reverts to) the level of infantile word magic, where the ego is weak (or absent) and the self is not differentiated from the environment.

In several previous publications I have discussed the problems of sublimation (Róheim, 1943a), culture (Róheim, 1943b), and magic (see Part I). To recapitulate briefly, sublimation is creative, something tangible is produced: for example, a house or garden. Other sublimations—a language or a myth—are more like symptoms, but they differ from symptoms by their distinct *social nature*.

Freud explained how the superego originates: libido is withdrawn from the object, and the love objects are introjected into the ego. As Freud (1923) wrote:

> The transformation of object-libido into narcissistic libido which thus takes place obviously implies an abandonment of sexual aims, a process of desexualization; it is consequently a kind of sublimation. Indeed, the question arises, and deserves careful consideration, whether this is not always the path taken in sublimation, whether all sublimation does not take place through the agency of the ego, which begins by changing sexual object-libido into narcissistic libido and then, perhaps, goes on to give it another aim [pp. 37-38].

Ferenczi (1924) has expressed similar views: libido is genitopetal or genitofugal, which is the same as calling it objectpetal or object-fugal—that is, there is an oscillation of libido between object and ego (p. 51). Hermann (1936) has emphasized clinging and withdrawal from the clinging position as a fundamental aspect of the libido.

In addition to this tendency of the libido to oscillate between object and ego, we have come to understand another fundamental aspect of our make-up, namely, that we find substitute objects for the mother. As Waelder (1933) has indicated, a little girl playing with her doll is re-enacting the mother-child situation, but she puts herself in the mother role as a protection against the danger of losing the mother or of being left alone in the dark (p. 209).

In analyzing pregnant women or young mothers, we soon find the similarity between the cultural object and the child. We notice that the child, being closer to the original, replaces the sublimation or the hobby in the mother's life. In being or becoming mothers, women relive their own infantile situation in a biologically determined manner. Men, on the other hand, require substitutes. For example, they "give birth" to culture. Thus, a poet of the Somali tribe told me that he felt pregnant, like a woman, before he sang one of his songs; and in ancient Egypt *to make or to fashion a statue* was apparently the same as *to give birth* (Róheim, 1943, p. 76).

In describing the cultural object as analogous to a child, or in considering the relation between the bearer of a culture and the culture itself as analogous to the child-mother situation, we have in mind Ferenczi's description of parental eroticism as a happy combination of object-seeking and narcissistic trends. (Unfortunately, I have been enrolled from time to time among those who believe that every man is envious of women's ability to bear children. I do not hold this view. As I see it, paternal love is a reaction formation or, as it has been described, a "cultural artifact.")

We conclude that the cultural object partakes of narcissistic and object-erotic qualities. The oscillation between ego and object is thus stabilized, with an intermediate position being taken between the two. However, reality is faced, and it becomes possible for a larger group of people to share in the same sublimation and to have an outlet for their own fear of object loss.

We now apply this interpretation to the problem of the internalization of *the word*. It would seem that the function of the word as a cultural object is to link the internal to the external world—in other words, to summon the mother when the child is hungry. Some libidinal cathexis is thus withdrawn from the mother and invested in the word—in the reprojected internalized object (sensation). This serves to bridge the period of tension (from desire to satisfaction) and also helps to lay the basis for deferred wish fulfillment, that is, for the reality principle. But if the infant cries in vain, if he is not understood, reality fails at the outset to fulfill its function of reassurance and a secondary reinvestment of cathexis in the word concept takes place.

Instead of the purely oral trauma that our patient was talking about, we assume a negativistic environment. His dreams and fantasies completely confirm this view, since he was confessedly and avowedly trying at all times to find his way back to normality by repeating the right words or the right stories. When he declared that the *right way* to pronounce the word "shoe" was to take the shoe off his foot and put it into his brain so that the object could help the word come out of his mouth, it was obvious that he was trying to re-establish the connection between word and object. He was also groping back to the object through the word when he thought that everything would be all right if he could remember the word "encyclopedia"—because that contained everything in the world. Unfortunately, however, the word "encyclopedia" was in an encyclopedia which he could never find.

Our data permit further conclusions, especially since the patient identified the words that disappeared in him with the food that similarly disappeared. And, as we have already observed, he was lost in the world, as the words were lost in him. That is, he identified *himself* with the lost words. A psychosis, therefore, represents not only the withdrawal of libido from the environmental to the incorporated object but also the failure to maintain the *link* that connects these incorporated objects with the environment. This withdrawal to a kind of fictional autarchy corresponds in some ways to the essence and core of magic. But in magic the seeming "autarchy" is merely a device for *returning* to the environment. In a psychosis, however, the return is virtually blocked.

It is interesting in this connection to see how N.N. constructed things out of phrases after the ties between word and object were lost. Thus, when someone described him as being "full of hot air," he took this literally and developed a theory that being "full of hot air" meant "to be insane." Similarly, because he had heard the mental hospital described as "a bug house," he came to believe that a psychotic was a person filled with bugs. And from this he inferred that he was himself a bug or that there were bugs in him—or that the mythical bug of his dreams and fantasies was a kind of protective genius, or that he himself was Christian of Jerusalem, the destroyer of bugs, who takes them all to a bug house.

It would be a mistake, however, to assume that our patient's whole mythological complex about "guardian spirits" and other internalized beings was simply derived from the phrase "bug house." Rather, his use of this expression indicated his tendency to treat words as if they were objects, and it was for this reason that he frequently described his internalized beings as "bugs." Actually they appeared to him in all sorts of shapes (as wasps, fish, eagles, lions, apes, human beings, angels, devils, and so on), and he frequently explained his psychosis by reference to these internalized beings. In any case, if language had not offered him this metaphor, he would not have described these beings or forces as "bugs."

We shall presently return to the bugs and the other supernatural beings. For the present it is important to discuss a group of beliefs connected with his name and also to clarify the anxiety associated with the dreaded loss of his name. During one interview he gave me the following information about his name:

> My real name is N.S.N. But I have different variations of my last name. Sometimes my last name is N-x, or N-y, or N-z. I have finally decided to change my last name to "Athol." That is the name of a carpenter's drill. It is also the name of the cough drops you are eating.

It is obvious that his name represented his personality. In this instance the name was both a drill (a penis) and some food that I was eating (that is, introjecting).

> My mother and grandmother always scared me about my middle name. I was always afraid that I might spell it wrong—and I always do. Once I called myself "Reedville" instead of S. That's a town but it also sounds like my middle name. Once I changed my middle name to "Sherborn." That is also a town, but the feel of it is just as if you had been through a swamp and did not feel so good afterwards.

The point is that his middle name, which represented his mother's family, was equivalent to a place or town (that is, a mother symbol). His tendency toward object-ego identification was also expressed in the various fantasies about his name. It will be clear that the object was introjected in each case:

> I called myself "Race Track," because I would have liked to be on a race track going fast in a car or on horseback. Then I called myself "Hubert," and that really sounds like ice cream. In my language, N. really means blood or the food one eats. There was also an N. the Great of Orange or of Russia. My middle name S., like "Sherborn," in my language means the woods in which you are or the air around you.

As indicated, his middle name, which referred to his mother, has encompassed him in this fantasy.

Our interpretation is also confirmed by a narrative in which he was in the woods and the woods were in his body, and by numerous anxieties associated with a change of air or environment. The "name" myth was also connected with a fantasy about another man who bore the name N.N. or even N.S.N. (His name, incidentally, though obviously and properly "Anglo-Saxon," was in no way common enough to convince me that he had ever encountered someone in reality with the same complete name.)

> The other N.N. looked like me and told me his name. I frequently met people like that, and I would go up to them and ask them about it. But then they would change their name. Then I would ask them again, and they would change it again. I don't like that.

I got my name at the beginning of the world, when I began to live. Sometimes I thought it was dangerous to have
my name, and I have tried to get rid of it. Once, in a shop,
I saw the other N.N. There was a girl with him—she was
Mrs. N.N. She was like my mother. Then people let me
play that I had money and that the other N.N. had taken
it away, and that made me mad. My father or grandfather
gave me my name. Sometimes my father did not like me to
be at home—as if I had no name! I had no name for a
time, and my father fought me and would not let me stay
at home.

At another time the question of his name became involved
with a loss of balance and with the situation in which he
could not make himself understood. He concluded:

The word I could not take off my lips was my uncle's name,
or my father's name, or the name of a street where I lived
with my father, or the name of a street that sounded like
my uncle's name. The sound came from the back of my
head—or as if I had food in my mouth.

His name meant contact with society, with the world of
objects and reality. He returned to this problem at a subsequent meeting:

There are several people who have my name. I met one of
them a long time ago. This other man who had my name
could get automobiles and property and whatever he
wanted, and I was angry because I could get none. This
other fellow had no right to my name—but it is no use, it
can't be helped. You can't go back further than the beginning of the world.
[Showing me his chin, he added:] People used to fight
with me, and I was injured—because they all wanted to
take my name. Then there was a nurse whom I used to
know in olden times. She was almost like my mother—she
would have died for me, to save me. And she told me that
the best thing for me would be to give up my name. Then
people would not want to fight me. They were always trying to take my name away. They tried to take my name
from deep down, from inside me.

I met many N.N.'s. When I went home, my family did not recognize me. Or I could not find my way home because my name was lost. Once I fell off a slope or a hill and banged myself. I lost my name when I was banged, and the same thing happened to another fellow, so that our names got exchanged. I met some girls who also had the same name, but it turned out that they were Mrs. N.N.—and they were all men. They all looked like me, both the girls and the men.

When I found out that others had got my name, I decided to change it. I turned my first name around and it became "Dilahad."

[When I pointed out that his first name spelled backward was *not* "Dilahad," he agreed but promptly disregarded it:] I saw a picture of this "Dilahad" once in a museum. It was a boy who had run away from home. He also called himself "Chauncey" or "Pierpont Morgan," and he was once arrested for it. He also took his father's name. He had no right to do that. Nobody has the right to take another person's name.

The problem of his name was similar to that of the word. His name was a place or town where he would like to be: the symbol of his mother. When he fantasied himself as a horse let loose on a race track, the horse meant his unbridled impulses, while the race track was his mother (or his own body, since he identified with her). His name sometimes symbolized food and blood—that is, the introjected mother in him. His name also meant the link between the internalized object and society; and to have a name was to have a house and other property. The basis of all reality, as he saw it, was the mother concept; he therefore fought for his name against his father.

Another of N.N.'s myths could also be traced directly to the oral frustration:

All this trouble about the food and the bugs and about losing the wall and about things closing in on me—it is all the same as the trouble with the sun-dial. People thought that kind of funny, too. I was trying to make it stand straight at twelve o'clock and to stop the sun while it was hurrying in the sky. There was a girl—she thought it was about her and that I was trying to catch her.

It was the same thing as the Fourth of July. People had lost the Fourth of July. It did not come when it ought to have come, and many people died of hunger as a result. I was examined, but it was found that I had got the *right date*. This was proved when I showed what I had eaten on the first, the second, the third, and the fourth.

These remarks indicate clearly that his confusion about time ("There is something wrong with time") was connected with hunger, and that he was denying something. *"Others* had some trouble, and *others* suffered from hunger": this was his formula. He continued:

When they found out that I was not wrong about the date and that I had eaten something or everything, I became President of the United States. Although I was *nearly* in the same condition as those people—the ones who died from hunger because they could not find the Fourth of July. Once I was out of date by six or seven years, and I was told that it was caused by a bug.

[Then he went on to discuss the bug, whose main function seemed to be protective:] I am always in touch with the bug. I know the bug, and the bug knows me.

The bug, as we shall presently observe, provided a protection against the danger of the patient's disappearing or of not being seen or understood. After expounding on the bug, he added:

When the trouble started I went to the sun-dial—which is opposite the sun and like the sun. I wanted to set something right. The sun-dial directs all the automobiles and ships. I was told that "time and tide wait for no man." So I wanted to see whether this was true, and I tried mentally to reach out for a ship at sea. This was at noon and I was taking my food too seriously. This was in the year 1894, but people had lost part of the time—they thought it was 1849. I couldn't trust the clock that was in the house, but I could trust the sun-dial because it looked like a drinking fountain.

As the reader will recall, the patient had once said the words "ten o'clock," but they were lost as soon as they were spoken, and he had gone to find ten o'clock. This, too, recurred in connection with the sun-dial.

In trying to explain the basic cause of his confusion about time, he said:

I thought it was breakfast time and it was really dinner time. So I lost track of time completely. First it was only eight or nine years, but then it amounted to one hundred years. This loss of time happened because somebody was hungry. Some people thought that I was hungry.

I was allowed to keep track of time by keeping track of ships coming and going from Europe. I did the same with the sun. But then I would look at the line made by the sun, or at the railroads, because the clocks were not reliable. Once I was so happy that I flew into space like the sun. Food can make you lose time and lose yourself. Losing your job and losing time is the same thing, and both are the same as the food trouble.

Once I was away for seven or eight years—in a place like this. Somebody asked me what time it was. It was noon and I was eating my noon meal. But I was fooling and said that it was breakfast time the next day. Then the whole trouble started by somebody's eating the soup that I was eating, but eating it in the opposite direction. I am always trying to find out the mistake I made—perhaps it was with the food. I used to travel about, and a man whose name was Teethy used to go with me. He was eating a beef stew and it was full of bugs—but not real bugs, you know.

[After trying to indicate that he meant "metaphorical bugs," he continued:] At the same time I moved the sun-dial. I wanted to take the sun off its course. They did not like that. It was as if I had eaten the stew and accidentally splashed it on someone else. I thought that there was something wrong with time. I was not born at the time people said I was born. That is why I tried to take the sun out of the sky.

How could his *food trouble* be related to his attempts to regulate the course of the sun? Like Joshua and Maui, he was trying to prevent time from passing too quickly (Bergler and Róheim, 1946, pp. 193-198). The answer to this problem may be found in some of N.N.'s straightforward remarks. He has told us that the loss of time occurred because someone was hungry. Therefore, when he said that he was trying to find out if time and tide would wait for him, this really meant that he had had to wait too long for his food—or that time had passed very slowly. But in his magical or fantasied omnipotence this painful experience of his infancy was transformed into a great victory: time began to pass very quickly, and it was *he* who prevented the sun from setting too rapidly.

It should also be noted that he was always eating his lunch or dinner at breakfast time. That is, it might be dinner time in reality, but he fantasied that it was already breakfast of the following day. In fantasy he was always ahead of time. He was thus able to make a complete denial of the original trauma—of the pain and anxiety of having to wait for his food. However, he was still aware of the fact that he took his food "too seriously." (An unusual resemblance exists between some of our patient's fantasies and the events in Lewis Carroll's *Alice in Wonderland*. To avoid a lengthy digression at the present time, we shall keep this problem in abeyance and return to it later.)

At any rate, it would appear that we are justified in equating his food difficulties with his sun-dial problems. As indicated, we assume that his tensions had accumulated unbearably while he was waiting for nourishment in his infancy. His fantasies of denial came to serve an important function: they negated the original deprivation and made him *the master of time.*

To continue with his solar mythology: In some of these fantasies he identified himself with the sun. It will be recalled, for example, in connection with his remarks about *speed* and *gravity,* that he had experienced sickness and dizziness during an automobile ride. The *speed* theme was also reworked in solar terms, as the following remarks will indicate:

> This was the trouble with the sun-dial or saint dial. Once I looked at the sky. I saw the sun rising suddenly and then going down in flames. This was as if I had been driving a car on the curve of a race track. I am the sun. The sun is speeding too fast. It will disappear from the sky, and I will disappear from the earth.
>
> Once I went out into the street and it felt as if I had stepped into hot glass—it scorched my body. Once I was looking up into the sky with one eye closed, and I saw an eagle near the sun. It was huge—like an airplane. From that distance it looked about as big as my tooth. It was as if I was looking at myself. This is not Alaska, and the sun-dial is not sun-dying, but I am afraid that the sun will die. This means that I will die or disappear.
>
> [On another occasion he said:] When I look for food or look for time, the food that comes into my mouth makes a trail. Sometimes one loses the trail of the words that come out of one's mouth. They stick in a tube. And then I look for a trail, but the trail is broken off. There is a trail on the earth—like the path of the sun in heaven. It is as if somebody had been throwing flowers on the earth. And then I lost my mother, but she did not know it. She thought I was at home, but I was with my grandmother. I lost my brain when I put a fork into my hat. If you dust a couch with a duster, then the sun and the rainbow and everything go out—like a pool that stands still. Later my mind was brought back.
>
> Once I was so happy that I flew into space. Like the sun. But the food dies in me, like the sun sets in the evening.

In this connection it is noteworthy that Bak (1939) has discussed schizophrenic patients who identify themselves with the sun. One of Bak's patients suffered from megalomanic delusions: he was identical with the sun, and he had the power to resurrect the dead, to create new solar systems, and to thaw out the old solar systems when they were frozen. Light, sun, and warmth were in his hands, and it was his duty to "give sun." He gave the history of his divine role in these words:

When after birth I became conscious, I found myself in a locality, in which I gave light and warmth to myself and to others. The bigger the Universe, the more predominant the sun-giving becomes. I started sunshine. At my birth I produced it, along with atoms, light and warmth. At the beginning the Universe was a canoe, in which I alone had a place. This was the first building. The caul was the canoe and this was also the first Universe [p. 67].

Bak explains this by assuming a primary or *thermic* ego and libido organization:

The moment of being separated from the mother involves amongst other things an immense decrease of temperature. We know that the foetus has a much higher temperature than the mother. After delivery, its situation is catastrophic; to use an exaggerated expression, it is in danger of freezing. The temperature of its body falls rapidly, and in the six hours after birth it has dropped one and a half or two and a half degrees. We see therefore that among the various environmental traumas there is an immense change of temperature against which the infant is defenseless. At the same time there is the phenomenon of thermo-lability, which means that the infant's own temperature depends on the temperature of its environment. In its thermo-regulation it is not yet separated from the external world and has a tendency to merge into the temperature of its environment [*ibid.*, p. 69].

Other students have shown that a similar condition exists in schizophrenia. For example, Gottlieb and Linder (1935) write:

Schizophrenic subjects are unable to comply normally with the homeostatic principles concerned with the regulation of heat. Their homothermic stability seems to have been replaced by a lower phylogenetic type of adjustment mechanism, resembling poikilothermism [p. 785].

On the basis of this evidence we can make two assumptions: that the schizophrenic's regression toward infancy is not only psychological but also physiological, or that there is an original organic difference, an inherent weakness. With our patient, his solar identification appears to be a denial of the trauma of birth (or of loss of temperature), just as his fantasies of enormous eating are a denial of the trauma of starvation. We may assume that his oral fantasies were conditioned by the experience of starvation; but on the other hand we may also assume that these fantasies were the result of an inherent inability to cope with even those small quanta of tension that are an inevitable aspect of the oral situation in infancy. At any rate, the connection between the solar identification (or thermic orientation) and the birth trauma is quite evident.

To recapitulate briefly, our patient has told us that he manipulated the sun because there was something wrong with time. He also contended that he was not born at the time people said he was born. Sometimes he dreamed that he was crashing through glass or brick, and that the glass or brick or air was weighing him down. Sometimes this experience felt as if he were being pulled out of a room by a truck. Once, he said, a priest took him up into the sky. He just flew through the air, and he was absent from home for eight or nine years. I assume, in this connection, that these various pressures indicate and refer to the trauma of birth, while the flight into the sky and the pulling by the truck are similar to his solar identification.

It is probable that this solar identification is related to the dreamlike quality of his fantasies. In our study of mythology we have seen that the sun frequently refers to the moment of awakening (Róheim, 1952, p. 370). If our patient is the sun, then he is awake—not asleep (in utero), not dreaming.

He said on one occasion:

My father and mother wanted me to go to a place beyond the earth. But the house where I was born is mine, and nobody can take it away from me. I once found an entrance to the Garden of Eden. It was a hole or a ditch in the earth and I nearly fell through. This is the place where I came out, the place where I was born—in the Garden of Eden. It is as if you are driving a car through a dark forest and suddenly you go through a tunnel and fall forward, head first, with great speed.

Once upon a time I came out of a place where there was no door. That was before I had a name. Some people thought that I was born like that—in the desert or in the woods, like a wild animal. Or maybe I was born in the Garden of Eden and had no mother. I came right up through a tunnel, right through the earth, somewhere near the Mississippi, and there was a great mountain there to stop me. I had no name for some time, and then my father fought with me and would not let me stay at home.

We have seen that his omnipotence in regulating time rested on the same denial (or compensation) that characterized all his fantasies. His assumed mastery over time was a denial of the great tension he experienced in the past when he had to wait for the gratification of his desires. In a similar way, the shock of a sudden cooling at birth was denied by his identification with the sun.

We turn once more to the problem of the "bugs" and the other internalized animals. These are variations of the "bugs" (about which we shall have more to say). In addition to the small bugs and other creatures within him (wasps, Teethies, and so on), there were also large bugs in the environment— and a number of other animals which were somehow connected with the bugs.

In a frequently repeated story, which I have already cited in one of its many variations, we are able to observe a link between the small Teethies within him and the huge eagle in the sky:

I was looking up into the air one day, with one eye closed, and I saw an eagle about where the sun was. It was huge, like an airplane; but from that distance it looked about the size of my tooth. When I looked at the eagle it was as if I was looking at myself, and the eagle knew when I did something wrong.

We can clearly see that the eagle functions as the superego. In addition, the following remarks reveal the oral origin of his guilt feelings:

When someone was accidentally trying to eat a bowl of soup or an apple, the eagle would see it. The eagle would send a dark fairy, a flying thing, or a bug like a moth—so big, about two feet. It came and hit me. It flew right through my body and came out at the other end. The eagle was also like a fish—and he looked at the sea. The fish was big, like a boat. The eagle, the bug, the fish—they were all mine, they knew me, they saw when I did wrong and wanted me to do right.

[After a pause he said:] This eagle was not a natural eagle, and I ought not to tell anybody about it.

[I may note that this last remark is exactly what a Yuma medicine man once told me about his guardian spirit!] But I had another eagle, a smaller one. I kept this one floating in the air. My father shot it. Now I haven't got it any more.

His father kills the small eagle, but the big eagle represents the father. The remarks which follow reveal an attempt to deal with the father in a negative oedipus fantasy:

The big eagle wanted to prey on me like a fish. It also likes to prey on women.

Then he turned at once to the deepest root of all these fantasies:

Perhaps all these stories are the same story. That somebody was starved, but not really—only in his insides. And then, when he ate the corn, all was well again; or, after nearly dying with thirst, he had a good long drink of water.

It was also the bug that caused his difficulties with time (he was out of date; rather, other people were out of date).

He had had a bug ever since he was born, and he was still in touch with his bug. The point that he kept emphasizing was that he knew the bug and the bug knew him, or that he was constantly in touch with the bug.

We may assume that this clinging to the bug was a compensation for the patient's withdrawal from reality. This was indicated by a characteristic remark:

> I passed by my uncle without seeing him [but] I am always in touch with the bug. [He did not say *but*. This was my interpretation.]

The connection between the eagle and the sun became quite evident. On one occasion he gave me a different version of the eagle myth:

> I am trying to regulate myself. Before, I often *lost the dawn* and would oversleep myself. The eagle was in the east and looked like a human eye. It was preparing to swoop down on somebody—maybe on me. It belonged to some country, like the land belongs to some country, maybe to the United States. No, it did not belong to the United States—it was black, it belonged to space.
>
> [He followed this with a very interesting attempt to test the relationship between his fantasies and reality:] I was trying to find out how big eagles really are, so I asked for the smallest eagle. It's about the size of a medium-sized book. They showed me the bigger ones, until finally I was told that the biggest eagle was the size of a man or an airplane. I had one myself that used to prey on sheep. Then there was the lion, the king of the beasts, who had escaped from a tropical country. And there was the big fish. *If I could put these three together (including the bug) and make one story out of them, I would go back to normal again.* When I was at home the last time, I hoped I could suddenly go back to work again without having to think of these things. The lion, the eagle, the big fish.

It becomes progressively more obvious that the lion, eagle, and fish were all repetitions of the bug (rather, of the *big bug*), who, as we have seen before, was like his father but also an exact copy of himself. At a later date he identified the big bug with an ape:

> The trouble started when I met a big bug—a gorilla. But it was very beautiful, and it had nice smooth fur. I was at home, trying to find my way with the sun-dial or compass. The bug knows me and sends other animals who walk about with me and know me. One of these was a lion—but not a natural lion. It was a wolf-dog nine feet long. It was a wolverine—almost a wolf. Then there was an eagle, but not a natural eagle; it was as big as a room. Then there was also a little bug, but in my insides. It looked like the big one but did no harm.
>
> The gorilla bug came from the south in a boat, and it started a fight with the crew because it caught my scent and wanted to go with me. I have to be careful and watch out for these animals, or they might take me away altogether into their country. All these animals were about me, and I was the little child that leads them.
>
> One of these animals was a snake, the snake in the Garden of Eden: Satan. I was once found asleep with this snake coiled around me, to fight off all the others. One of the animals sent by the bug—or by a zoologist—was a good fairy or angel. This was a fairy godmother who used to feed me everywhere I went, and I stayed with her once for a hundred years. Then they took her away from me.
>
> There was a crown prince who was interested in me because I had this story, and the first crown prince wanted to find out if I had not met another crown prince who was the wrong one.
>
> [Then he added very mysteriously and with a great deal of hesitation:] This second crown prince was called Christianoff! They almost let me play that I was a bug once. I had a swordfish with a human face that followed me everywhere I went. But the gorilla-bug did not like him and wanted to fight with him.

The quotation from the Bible about *the little child that leads them* throws some light on our patient's animal fantasies. The child leading the wild animals undoubtedly means that the wild impulses have been tamed! This Little-Lord-

Fauntleroy fantasy is the key to his entire animal mythology: the nice big bug (or gorilla) wants to play with him but fights with the tame swordfish that follows "the little child" about.

In some versions told by N.N. at other times, the swordfish was not a tame animal who followed him constantly but a dangerous monster:

> I had a collision with the swordfish when I was swimming in the sea. This had something to do with a fluid like blood, but it was black—because it came from a black swordfish and it was called *blackmor*. The blackness of the swordfish reminds me of the black eagle.

It is noteworthy that many dramatic events were softened in the retelling by the generous use of "almost." Thus, in one version of the collision with the swordfish, he said:

> Once I was at the beach and a big fish—black like the air or the sky—rose out of the sea. I bent forward to see what it was like and nearly lost my balance. Later on, when I *almost* collided with the swordfish, I thought it was the same animal.
>
> Then there was a lion once—he was in a cage and had been brought over here from Europe or Africa and wanted to go back. The lion was the king of beasts and wanted to make himself understood by the other beasts, but he could not. This was when the lion was eating.
>
> [He bent over and said:] The lion bent over and looked into the sea. He thought he was something else—a leopard or a tiger or a human being. Or a bug. And then he was almost like me. When I heard this story, people told me to be cautious.

He has clearly revealed that one of the animals is identical with himself. However, since the animals represent aggression, he felt that he would become normal only if he could integrate his aggression into his ego.

There were also times when he related a terrestrial parallel to the collision-in-the-sea myth:

Once I was driving and there was something in the way. It was like a big bug or an ape or Christian of Jerusalem, a crown prince. People thought he was Christian. He was also regarded as being a German crown prince, as having led the German boats in the big war, or as having piloted them and thereby having sunk the Lusitania and the Titanic.

[The same theme was developed in the following version:] There was a black crown prince from Ethiopia—like the colored dwarfs in the game I told you about. He *almost* had the same experience. I mean the trouble with the beef stew. He came to Boston. His boat was the Hesperus. It was shipwrecked, and people didn't know who he was. Christian, Prince of the Jews, was in the same situation. I used to know him, but I don't know him so well now.

It is interesting to observe that, even in these primitive fantasies, we are able to trace the transformation of themes and motives. The boat theme is derived from the collision with the swordfish; and the black prince as well as the black dwarfs develop from the black swordfish and the black eagle. But what was the origin of the black swordfish and the black eagle?

In consulting some of the patient's past interviews with other members of the hospital staff, I came across the following:

April 2, 1934:
N.N. says that he saw a man who was dark but resembled his father. When he was out walking he would meet this man, and the man would offer him a drink of some reddish-orange liquid. When he attempted to take some of the drink he could get none of it, but this man would sometimes put his head inside his and drink it, and in this way he might be able to drink it too. He said that at times the man would appear to sit on the window sill or on his bed at night.

A comparison of this data with his dreams and fantasies will clarify the identity of the patient's father. We may also note in passing that the sunset in one of his dreams was described as "reddish orange" and that he received a "reddish colored" drink in the otherworldly narrative about Angel Love. The black Angel of Death is probably his father; and it is noteworthy that N.N. once declared:

> I have been offered the job of Angel of Death, but I cannot accept it now because of lack of practice.

We are able to observe how the black man (father) becomes a black fish, a black eagle, and then a ship. On the other hand the patient himself is the black prince or Christianoff or Christian. In the animal version of the collision, the obstacle on the road or the opponent is the bug or ape. Here, too, the path leads from the father to the bug, as we shall presently note more clearly.

The patient earnestly aspired to return to reality, but inevitably the *bugs* kept driving him away from the world of objects. He expressed this dilemma in the following way:

> I was not thinking of anything—I was trying to think of normal, natural things like the snow, or working in the woods. Then the mistakes with the food would be over, and I would be like I used to be again. While I was trying to do this, I saw the big ones, like a man flying toward me. It was as if they were going to attack me. I was afraid that if I told people about the bug they might take it away from me. The bug knows who I am and would lead me home when I got lost. When I was trying to think of natural things and the bug flew toward me, it was like the time I had the fight with my father because he did not want me to stay at home. I also had a fish once. It used to go about with me, and the fish knew who I was, like the bug. I also had an eagle, but not like these eagles. I had one that used to fly high. *My father used to shoot eagles!*

These are the steps taken in the transformation: The dark man (father) becomes a dangerous animal, whether bug, wasp, ape, lion, eagle, fish, or the like. Aggression is then replaced by protection (and submission), and the hostile animal becomes a guardian spirit or a foreign prince. But the patient himself remains in a state of identification both with the aggressor (and protector) and with the victim.

In another version of this problem he developed the theme along more realistic lines:

> My whole trouble is due to an accident. I had something on my back—a tin can or a suitcase or an ash can that belonged to my father. It banged up against my back when I was driving very quickly in my car. I made a mistake: instead of sitting on a chair, I sat on a tin can and I felt it pressing against my back. The main trouble I have is too much *speed* or *gravitation*.
>
> This is how the accident happened. It was not I who was driving, but somebody else who was sent by some people. There were three ladies, and I just wanted to pass them. There was a train—it crossed the road before my car. But when I was on the other side it seemed as if I had passed first. I was *not* scared of my father. An invisible person passed on the road before me—perhaps it was an angel, but it felt like thin air. I must have bumped up against somebody when running—probably my brother or perhaps my father.

At one session I asked him to tell me about the swordfish again. This experiment was of interest because he always produced new combinations of old themes, thus confirming our interpretation of the links that connected all his myths. This is what he said in response to my question:

> I was swimming to the Barbados Islands about twenty years ago from Australia or South America. Only a peak was visible. I met a shark, and the shark looked like a school of fish. A swordfish came up from the other side, and I collided with it. But I had a knife, too. You can't swim in the deep sea without a knife. The shark was a man-eater. I was afraid of him because he might eat me all up and then I would not look so good afterwards. The one shark was like a whole school of fish, and it acted like a girl who wanted to marry me. The swordfish merely wanted to bite my leg off. The real trouble was that there was a bug—it looked like a gorilla or a bamboo [baboon]—swinging on

the trees from the island to the mainland. Now this bug or swordfish thought I had no right to go on that island. The school of fish was almost a ship, and the bug acted like a train that crosses the road [cf. these themes above]. The bug was a yellow adder—a big spider who thought it owned the place and would make for you like a train. The trouble was that on the road somebody made me eat yellow apples, thinking that that would help me to get back to normal. But they were not natural apples—they were full of castor oil. But the whole thing made me feel yellow [afraid]. I used to live on that island once. I was born there, and I thought nothing of swimming in the deep sea.

The fundamental theme was always his desire to reach a place (his trend toward the object). On the way he always encountered an enemy who prevented him from reaching this goal. The enemy was a bug, an ape, a negro, a lion, an angel, a train, and so on—but fundamentally the father. As we have already noted, a further process of transformation took place when this enemy became a kind of guardian spirit, a protector in danger—indeed the very bond that connected him to the outside world.

"The bug knows me, I am in touch with the bug," and so on: this was a formula of denial, an inversion of the original setting in which the father or the symbolic animal was driving him away from home and blocking him from contact with reality. Frequently, too, he was identical with his mythical protagonist: he himself was a bug or wild animal, or a crown prince or angel.

In all these dreams and fantasies we see one thing very clearly: the lack of differentiation between object and ego. If a person in a dream looks like his father or a doctor, this person also looks just like the patient. The same is true of the girls and women: they all resemble him very strongly. This is not surprising in a narcissistic state; and in a psychosis we should expect a narcissistic object, both in the heterosexual and in the homosexual object formations—that is, if there *is* any object choice to speak of. Interestingly enough, the girls whom he saw in his dreams not only resembled him but also his mother and sister; and he generally described these girls as having "yellow hair, like angels."

He frequently described a sensation which was common in both his dreams and fantasies, that of being irresistibly drawn toward something:

> I was rolling toward the wall, and it felt as if I could go into it. But there was no woman.
> [Another common sensation was described in this way:] I felt as if I had stepped into glass that was broken and melting hot, and scorching my body. This was like an experience I had before I was little. There was a mirror, and I walked into it—drawn by the suction. It was a convex mirror. It was my mother's mirror, and it was very hard for me to get out again.

The mirror to which he was drawn may be understood as the mother's imago (or his own) and represents both narcissism and dual unity.

The same theme was retold at another interview in the following form:

> The whole trouble started when I came back from the moving picture and had the wrong shirt on accidentally. It was my mother's shirt, or the shirt of a nurse who knew my mother.

We are already familiar with the "accidental" wearing of his mother's shirt. It is another indication that his basic troubles stemmed from mother identification (or introjection).

At this point we can proceed in two ways. We can go "out of context" and use the materials of anthropology and folklore as an analogy, or we can remain "in context" and try to explain our patient's statements in their own terms.

In a previous publication (Róheim, 1919) I have discussed various forms of divination and love magic that require the use of the mirror, and I have indicated that the mirror is taboo in connection with many rites of marriage (pp. 91-162). Thus, according to the Polabs (or Elbslavs), the bride and groom should not look back when they go to church, or both might die (Tetzner, 1902, p. 372). In Worcestershire, the bride should not look into the mirror after being fully dressed for the ceremony (Addy, 1909, p. 345). According to Hungarian belief, a girl who sits under the mirror will never get a husband (Nagy, 1896, p. 181). The main point in all of these taboos is the *regressive* aspect of the mirror. Similarly, our patient feels himself being drawn by an irresistible force toward a fantasy object which is both a narcissistic copy of his ego and a representative of his mother. Rosenzweig and Shakow (1937), it may be noted in passing, have made an interesting and suggestive study of the behavior of schizophrenics before a mirror (pp. 171-174).

At any rate, denial and negation are important defense mechanisms, and we are justified in interpreting our patient's fantasies about the mirror and his mother's shirt in terms of these processes. This may be put in another way, namely, that the strong identification in fantasy covers a lack of identification in reality.

We return to context—to what he said immediately after his troubles with his mother's shirt:

> I was eating very quickly and I changed to my mother's shirt. The doctors noticed that there was something wrong with me inside, in my stomach. I had forgotten to finish the food! I was eating corn or carrots. But then I corrected that and went back, and everything was all right again.

In his language this meant that he was normal. But since everything was obviously *not* "all right again," we may go on and say that he had *never* "corrected his mistake." It was not he who had forgotten to finish his food; rather the food had been withdrawn from him. As we know, the strong tendency toward a fantasied identification with his mother was a compensation for the lack of real acceptance of the mother. And this lack of real acceptance may well have been based on the oral frustration.

We reach the same conclusions if we examine his mirror problem in context. Immediately after his statement about going back into his mother's mirror, he spoke about being lost in the woods, about the woods pressing in on him, and then about being lost in the open and about the general difficulties of *transition*.

The problems of *transition*, it should be noted, were equal in importance to the *food trouble* and were often combined with it in his narratives. As he put it:

The whole trouble started when I walked away from home and got lost in the woods. At the same time my senses got lost in my brain. I was out there to do calisthenics and to find myself; but when I was out there, I came to a place that was all apart—it was beyond the world, like an Indian reservation, like a place that was *caged in,* like a wall of solid wood. Somebody thought I did something wrong there, and that is why I could not find my way back. They thought I had taken an apple from somebody's orchard, and a policeman took me to court for it [guilt]. I had had the right to take that apple before; but when I came the second time, I had not. I would have to build a house and stay there always—to convince people that I had the right.

They gave me four or five apples and carrots. It was like playing with the cow—they thought I had no right to do it.

My father did not want me to stay at home. It was like the time I went on the trail and when I saw the mountain that could show me the way out of the woods. In the middle of Massachusetts, I dropped into a deep canyon, and it was hard to get out.

[He continued, clenching his fists:] It was like when you cling to a town and are fixed to it right in the middle. I was trying to get busy with the stories so that my mistake would be all right. When I was in the woods I lost my speech.

[Ten days later he gave me the following version:] The trouble was that I once stopped between two jobs and could not gain my balance. I went to school, but I did not finish school and was given credit for the rest of it. I had been

going to school for some time, but then my father and
mother began to handicap me. They took me home because
somebody—my sister—was sick. But then I got all my
school and all my credit back because I went to court about
it. I lost my first job, but then I *thought* a much better one
of the same kind and I had that one.

The awful thing was that I once stole four or five apples
that belonged to my father or mother, or I stole seven or
eight years.

[The identification of time and food is noteworthy.] The
awful thing was that I left home and did not tell my
mother, and then she did not like me to stay at home. I
thought—on one of those trips I had taken, like when I
collided with the fish—that the swordfish was really doubt
and fear, and that that was the trouble on the way. The
trouble was that I was always doing two or three things at
once. When I was working, I was daydreaming and playing
that I was somebody else.

This problem of *transition* occurred, in one variation or
another, in nearly all of his narratives. In one version of it he
said:

I used to live in Alaska. That was a buried country and
belonged to other people—the Russians or the Indians.
Nothing remained of it, only hands—to show the way. It
is like the time when I could not get food and when I could
not make people understand what I wanted. It was like
somebody starving and people did not know; like reaching
with my hand from one continent to the other, from here
to Russia. But there were so many countries in between,
where they eat different kinds of food. But if one is hungry
it does not matter.

I once skipped two classes in school, but they said I
could not do that. It is like hands reaching over—or like
passing—the frontier. Once, when I was passing through
Russia, I bumped up against a girl who was like my sister.
I want to collect all my dreams because all the countries
would unite against me. Something similar happened three
hundred years ago—the time I came over on the Titanic.
I came over from Europe on a sailing boat, but the boat
had been taken away from me. They let me go very quickly

from one country to another because I was just like a refugee. I had lost my parents and was looking for them. Then I was introduced to the President who had been shot, or perhaps I had been shot, or perhaps I was the President of the United States.

Before resuming our analysis of these fantasies, it is necessary to clarify our theoretical assumptions. Hermann (1923, 1936a, 1936b), in a series of papers dealing with the early organization of the ego and libido, has shown that the primary organization should be correctly described, not merely as oral, but as oral and manual, and that the infant at this phase of organization obtains nourishment, warmth, support, and security in all its aspects from the mother. A human being, as compared to the higher apes, is separated prematurely from the mother and retains, therefore, a strong tendency to go back to the mother. If the mother does not hold his hand, the child complains that he cannot give up the need to hold on to something (or to suck his thumb) before going to sleep. The typical sleeping posture of the infant, with fists clenched and hands lifted up to the shoulders, is not the intrauterine position but the position of an infant clinging to its mother.

Hermann regards the grasping reflex as a part of the grasping impulse, with the latter again being an aspect of the general tendency to cling to the mother. The reaction of an infant to alarm is the Moro reflex, which is a *clinging* to something. The frustration of this grasping or clinging to the mother leads to a *seeking* tendency, to pleasure in migration, or to a desire to go away. This subsequently culminates in the finding of a new object—to a new grasping or clinging. It is the *seeking* phase that I have described as *transition*. In this phase of its existence the infant is in a stage of object loss or depression.

Hermann interprets neurotic symptoms—such as nail biting, tearing one's hair out, or picking on the skin, that is, the human equivalents of anthropoid grooming—as the functional representatives of *separation,* the mother having been identified with a part of the body's surface. At first there is an original and biological unity of mother and child. The disruption of this unity begins at birth and grows worse each time the infant is separated from the nipple or the mother. And then there are the various mechanisms or fantasies that function to bridge over or to deny this phase of separation. The original ego of the infant is a dual unity: it consists of infant and mother. This phenomenon is based on a biological reality, the uterine situation, that is maintained psychologically after it has ceased to be wholly true, as in the early infantile situation. The lack of integration in the schizophrenic personality would then, from this point of view, be a failure to tolerate (or to compensate for) the amount of tension involved in the separation from the mother. The schizophrenic cannot regard himself as complete, as a whole, without the mother; he has not succeeded in overcoming the trauma of separation.

If we attempt to interpret this situation from the Kleinian point of view, we could proceed somewhat differently, beginning our argument with the infant's aggression in the phase of frustration or separation. Thus, the object of aggression is the mother's body; and the infant's aim is to take all the "good contents" out of the mother's body and to possess them for itself, to keep them stored up safely in its own body. This flight to the internalized object must fail because the quality of the object is conditioned by the quality of the emotions. The result is that the internalized "good object" must automatically be transformed into an internalized "bad object." Projection would constitute the means of ridding one's self of the internalized "bad object." And the identification of this internalized object with the surface of the body might be an "arrested projection," a compromise between the desire to rid one's self of something and the desire to retain it.

However, since we do not wish to oversimplify the problem by reducing everything to one formula, we must consider both the real situation of the infant and the data supplied by the fantasies of the patient. We find that the infant is actually in contact with the mother in two ways: through the milk it imbibes (we regard this as the reality basis of all fantasies of introjection); and through the warmth, contact, and support furnished by the mother's body. (It is the latter which provides the reality basis for the other type of identification, that is, the nonintrojective, surface, or clinging type.)

We can now return to our patient's fantasies. He said that he went into his mother's mirror and could not get out again. This going back into the mother was a defense against the tensions generated by the absence of the mother.

Another characteristic feature was the quick succession of fantasies or defense mechanisms. He was eating very quickly (introjection); he put on his mother's shirt (contact identification); there was something wrong in his stomach (introjection); he had forgotten to finish the food (denial of an environmental frustration); and the mistake was corrected (fantasy as a camouflage or denial of the trauma).

We can demonstrate the same processes in the fantasies of transition. The trouble started when he walked away from home (not when his mother left him). When he was lost, his senses were lost in him (the separation from the object is compensated by the internalized object and then followed by the loss of the internalized object, with the sequence being similar to the one which takes place in "the return of the repressed"). He made an attempt to regain his strength by calisthenics (narcissistic investment); he found himself in a place beyond the world (complete object loss); he had a fantasy of being in a cage (reaction to object loss; an intrauterine fantasy). He took the apple illegally (oral guilt, and the clarifying sequel: people thought he had no right to play with the cows). Then there were the trail and the *journey* (the period of transition), the mountain that showed him the way out of the forest (the breast), the deep canyon (uterine fantasy), and the very revealing statement about the *trail*: "It was like when you cling to a town and are fixed to it right in the middle" (clinging to the mother). His acting out of the Moro reflex indicates that this was a technique of *denial*, because the trail was really an interruption of the clinging to the mother. Then he got busy with his "stories" in order to correct his mistakes (this indicates the *function of fantasy*: to regain the object world; that is, the "autarchic fiction" or magic).

He stopped between two jobs (between one object-related situation and the other) and lost his balance (the failure of narcissistic independence). He failed to finish school but got credit for the rest of it; after the loss of his job he *"thought a much better one of the same kind and had that one"* (fantasy compensation). This was followed once more by a reference to the apples (oral guilt) and by his departure from home (the denial of frustration). On the trip he collided with the swordfish (father). The swordfish, as he so insightfully pointed out, was really representative of doubt and fear (that is, the conflict with the father developed during the oedipus phase, thus repeating and explaining the original situation of tension and frustration).

Alaska was lost (loss of the original object) and only *hands* showed the way (the desire to cling, as indicated by Hermann). The trauma of starvation followed, and he collected his dreams in order to cope with his enemies (fantasies are used to fight reality; or, as I have attempted to demonstrate elsewhere, the dream provides a new reality or new libidinal environment: cf. Róheim, 1952). He journeyed from Europe, with the subsequent loss of the ship in which he came (object loss); he went very quickly from one place to another in search of his parents (the long interval from one breast feeding to the other); he was shot (starvation, death); he was the President of the United States (overcompensation, or denial of helplessness) or he was introduced to the President (fission, lack of integration in his fantasies).

I think that we can accept Schmideberg's (1930) interpretation of schizophrenia as a flight to the internalized object, but I should like to add that this mechanism of defense shows a particular lack of stability and constitutes a quick shift which accompanies a lack of integration in the personality. The oral introjection or internalization is a denial of a *minus*—of an oral frustration. The aggression called forth by the oral frustration transforms the "good object" into a "bad object," as we have already noted, and introjection is followed by projection. This projection again lacks stability (in contrast to the more paranoid types of projection), and there is a constant tendency to reintroject these projected aggressions or to identify one's self with them. The so-called introject is really the same thing as the "intermediate object" and the "autarchic fiction." Insufficient object love on the part of the mother is compensated by a fantasied identification with her. In other words, the inroads made by reality on the pleasure situation (that is, the painful *dependence* of the infant) is compensated by a fantasied omnipotence, with the tensions involved in change being made up for by the fantasied resistance to change. As our patient once explained it:

> In my mind I always linger on—I am still doing the things I have finished. Once I had to change this system, and it was like changing from one state to the other.

This was followed by remarks which indicate that object loss was at the back of this resistance to change; or that he still lingered in the object-possessing phase of his existence when he was already in the phase of tension or frustration:

> I had an awful experience once. It was like phantom lyrics, like a ship approaching—coming nearer and nearer, but you never catch it.

Then he immediately describes an injury to himself, which clarifies how frustration is followed by aggression, with the consequent inversion of aggression against the ego:

Then I had a cut on my hand, but it was invisible—like when you cut a boil on your hand and the pus comes out. Sometimes I had a feeling of being thrown out of a closed car into the open.

[He then explained this dizziness or *speed* in terms of *conserved attitudes*:] I used to be driving a car, and now when I am not doing that any more, my head still has the old *speed* or *gravity* and keeps falling backwards or forwards. Suppose you had a fight with somebody and they banged you on the head and held you down—you would still feel as if you went on fighting after the whole thing was over.

He has here clarified the function of these *conserved attitudes*: it is a delusion, a wish to cling to a more favorable situation, thereby denying the existence of a worse situation.

Like all schizophrenics, he was practicing magic: that is, he reacted to infantile helplessness by a fantasied omnipotence, and to object loss by a fantasy of object identification.

On one occasion he described his problem in this way:

I had an iron ball, and I used it to find a hole or other place. I played that the room was a city, and then I used to roll another ball, a tennis ball, to track the first one if that one had not found its way into the net or basket. The ball was like me, and this was like being away from home and trying to find the way back.

We emphasize again that all these fantasies are *an attempt to find the way back*. They are "autarchic" only in the sense of being efforts to work a change in the environment *via* a change in the ego. Thus, he spoke a bitter truth when he said:

People thought I was acting funny. I am like a compass without marks.

In view of his attempts to return to the breast, I shall close this chapter by quoting some of his most frequent complaints:

The awful thing is that my father and mother did not know when I left home or when I was away. I used to sit on a chair at home and play that I went to Canada and came back again, but they did not know.

Sometimes I try to trace home the food I have eaten. I send it back on the road to see if I can follow it in imagination to Boston, where my family lives.

Finally, we cite some remarks which indicate quite clearly that magic (or schizophrenia) is based on the flight to the internalized object:

Once I got three apples when my mother was here with her two sisters. I keep wondering if the three apples I ate could understand or know what I was saying to other people.

I am expecting my mother to come and fetch me home. I am trying very hard *to make things come true*. In my dreams and stories, I mean. Because then I would be able to go home.

The three apples are again the "three mothers," that is, the three internalized objects.

CHAPTER THREE

Further Insights

Before turning to the final summation, I wish to deal briefly with several problems which have been kept in abeyance. These are: the relationship between thought and magic; the comparison of our patient's fantasies with the events in *Alice in Wonderland*; and the psychocultural meaning of our patient's "bugs." All these linguistic or literary data will provide us with valuable supplementary insights into the problems we have been considering.

In regard to the first of these problems, the relationship between thought and magic, I have dealt with this matter at greater length in Part I. Here I wish merely to note that Freud (1911) has defined thinking as "an experimental way of acting " (p. 16). Hermann (1940) has described thinking as the process in which the mental image is separated from the object and independently manipulated. The first image must certainly be the breast or nipple, and the infant thinks of it because he desires it. If a separation from the object exists in thinking, there is also an attempt to return to the object *via* the image or in other words, via magic, which is an important component of thought (see Part I).

Some interesting linguistic data appear to confirm these assumptions. Thus, in the Duau language of the Normanby Islands, *nuanuago* means "I desire" or "my desire," and *nua* is the "mind." In the Maori tongue, *aro* means "to face," "to turn toward," "to favor," "to be inclined" or "to be disposed." *Whaka-aro* means "to think upon," "to consider." The related word in Samoa—that is, *aroa*—means "the underside" (as of cloth or the belly of a fish), "a chief's belly," "the child of a chief," "the seat of the affections and feelings" (that is, the belly), and "to be pregnant" (of a chief's wife). In Hawaii, *alo* means "breast" or "belly." Other words derived from the same root are: *whaka-aro-rangi* ("to think about continually," "to love," "brooding affection"); *aroha* ("to love," "to pity"); *aropiri* ("to cling," "to be attached") (Tregear, 1891, pp. 24-25).

Classical philology is even more convincing. The *genius,* the serpent that is coeval with man himself, is obviously the libido. Rose notes that "the genius is the life, or reproductive power, almost the luck, of the family" (1923, p. 59) or perhaps of the clan (1930, p. 135). Lovers invoke the genius (Tibullus, *Elegiae,* II 2.5), and the genius of the husband is invoked on the wedding night (*ibid.,* III 11.8). In the sense of the phallic serpent, the genius is the *fons et origo* of the genius or great thinker.

In Latin, the head is frequently a symbol of the genitals (as in dreams and so on). *Caput limare cum aliqua* (or *aliquo*) means "to file away (diminish) one's head with someone," that is, to make love (Onians, 1951, p. 123). Similarly, *cerebrum,* the word for brain, is a cognate of the old Latin word *cereo* (or *creo*), "I beget," "I engender" (*ibid.,* p. 125).

The cerebrospinal marrow was, for the Romans, the stuff that connects the head and the genitals, and the seat of passion, whether of love or warlike fury. Onians describes "frenzy" as "a becoming active, a burning and, as it were, eruption" of the procreative power (p. 150). In the following lines of Horace, *ira* is libido, not anger:

Diceret haec animus: "Quid vis tibi? numquid ego a te magno prognatum deposco consule cunnum velatum stola, mea cum conferbuit ira?" [*Satires,* I, 2, 69-71.]

And Virgil's famous lines about Dido's love are recalled:

> ...*incendat reginam, atque ossibus implicet ignem* [*Aeneid*, I, 660.]

and:

> *Est mollis flamma medullas interea, et tacitum vivit sub pectore volnus uritur infelix Dido totaque vagatur urbe furens* [*ibid.*, IV, 66-69.]

Bruni, in early English, meant "burning," "heat," "burning passion," "lust," and the like; while *brundr* meant "seed" (animal) (Onians, 1951, pp. 155-156). German *brunst* is similar to the English expression "to be in heat." From here we can see the transition to the concepts of the halo or nimbus or the related flame (or sparks) of genius. Onians points out in this connection:

> It is in harmony with the belief that radiance about the head was an expression of the divine power, the *genius* there, and with the argument about *numen* and *capita deorum* above, that we find, e.g. on the wall paintings at Pompeii and Herculaneum, the immortal gods, including those who had no obvious connection with the heavenly fires or with other fire, represented with a *nimbus* or with rays about their heads, and in literary records the faces of divine images are gilded [p. 166].

It is apparent that there has been a transition from desire to thought by means of a displacement upwards. We suggest, therefore, that *thinking*, which at its apex is very much an ego activity, is deeply rooted in the libido, and that between the two we must place the mental image as magic. It means both "away from the object" and (by means of the image) "back to the object."

Since the image (or magic) mediates between the ego and the libido, it is significant that, for our patient, words constitute the path back to reality, to the world of objects. But, as we have pointed out above, the images and symbols were cathected with object cathexes, with the result that he could proceed no further than his "stories"—and the anxiety connected with the original is displaced to the substitute. It will be recalled that his stories either lacked a happy ending or were taken from him by other people who used them as their own, and that object loss was represented in the form of a void.

We turn now to the writings of Lewis Carroll, where a literary parallel may be found to our patient's schizophrenic manipulation of time, food, words, and reality. Interestingly enough, the patient himself once told me that his experiences in life were similar to those of *Alice in Wonderland*. The comparison is not a forced one, and I am not the first one to explain Lewis Carroll's work along psychoanalytic lines. Schilder (1938) has already discussed the oral and destructive nature of *Alice in Wonderland*.

In Lewis Carroll's writings the oral trauma (or the oral situation, to express the same thing more cautiously) is always breaking through the polite superficialities. For example, we attend a "Mad Tea-Party" with Alice, the March Hare, the Mad Hatter, and the Dormouse. It is a *mad* tea party. The March Hare *is* as mad as a March Hare, and so is the Mad Hatter; while Dormouse (dormeuse), with his continual tendency to fall asleep, represents withdrawal. In view of all this we expect to find a duplication of schizophrenic mechanisms in this part of the narrative, and we are not disappointed.

The March Hare reproves Alice for not saying what she means.

"I do," Alice hastily replied; "at least—at least I mean what I say—that's the same thing, you know."

The Mad Hatter objects that this is not the same thing. What, we may ask, are they quarreling about? The real meaning of the dispute seems to point to the ancient problem of words and meanings.

"Not the same thing a bit!" said the Hatter. "You might just as well say that 'I see what I eat' is the same as 'I eat what I see' " [Dodgson, 1931, p. 60].

The main thing about this tea party is that time has stopped. It is always six o'clock, and they are always having tea. Alice is told that if she were on good terms with time, rather than beating or killing "him," she could (instead of doing her lessons in the morning) set the clock for half past one and it would be dinner time. The Hatter, it may be noted, originally went mad when the Queen said: "He's murdering time! Off with his head!" (*ibid.*, pp. 63-64). If "time" here means the ends of tension, or oral satisfaction, we can see that the Hatter's aggression touches off anxiety and counteraggression in the Queen.

The Mad Hatter appears again at the trial scene. The trial is about some stolen tarts:

> The Queen of Hearts, she made some tarts,
>   All on a summer day:
> The Knave of Hearts, he stole those tarts
>   And took them quite away (*ibid.*, p. 98).

The Mad Hatter is asked to testify:

> "I'm a poor man, your Majesty," the Hatter began in a trembling voice, "and I hadn't begun my tea—not above a week or so—and what with the bread-and-butter getting so thin—and the twinkling of the tea."

This is followed by the schizophrenic play on words that runs right through the entire book.

Aggression plays an important role in our theory of the oral trauma. The infant's aggressive tendencies are mobilized by frustration; but, in view of the expected retaliation and the identification with the mother's body, this aggression results in anxiety. In Chapter VI of *Alice in Wonderland* we encounter the Duchess who is a counterpart of the Queen, both with her motto "Chop off her head" and with the baby who is really a pig. The Duchess sings a lullaby, shaking the baby violently at the end of every line:

> Speak roughly to your little boy,
>   And beat him when he sneezes:
> He only does it to annoy,
>   Because he knows it teases [*ibid.,* p. 53].

Since they are busy putting pepper into the soup to make the child sneeze, the cycle of aggression and counteraggression is complete.

Lewis Carroll, though strongly attracted to little girls, disliked little boys. On one occasion he declined to see a friend's boy and said:

> He thought I doted on all children but I am not omnivorous like a pig. I pick and choose [Schilder, 1938, p. 160].

(It may be noted parenthetically that the infant at the breast is a pig—or he is an omnivorous pig in relation to the other children in the family. This is very similar to our patient's complaint that people thought he ate like a hog.)

The whole story of *Alice in Wonderland* begins with the problems of time and orality. The Rabbit takes his watch from his pocket and finds that it is late. When Alice falls down the hole, the first thing she notices is a jar labeled "Orange Marmalade." To her very great disappointment, the jar is empty (the oral trauma). She is afraid that she will drop the empty jar and kill somebody underneath her (aggression). Then she hopes that the people at home will not forget to feed Dinah, her cat (that is, give it some milk at tea time), and she continues in a dreamy sort of way:

> Do cats eat bats? Do bats eat cats? [*ibid.,* pp. 6-7].

The same theme of oral tension may be found in a famous poem by Lewis Carroll, "The Hunting of the Snark." It begins with a play on the words "fuming" and "furious," which are condensed into a new word, "frumious," very much in the way our patient played with words and coined neologisms. The poem then introduces a person who enters a ship and has completely forgotten his name. He answers to any loud cry such as "Fry me!" or "Fritter my wig!" (*ibid.*, p. 396). His intimate friends call him "Candle Ends," while his enemies refer to him as "Toasted Cheese." The journey is full of oral difficulties. The Baker can only bake a bridal cake; the Butcher can only kill beavers. What is the mysterious Snark they are pursuing? It seems to symbolize food because the first mark of a Snark is its taste, which is meager but hollow and crisp (*ibid.*, p. 404).

The Snark is also connected with the anxiety about disappearing. Some Snarks are Boojums; and if you happen to see a Snark who is a Boojum, you simply disappear. When the Baker finally finds the Snark and it turns out to be a Boojum, he vanishes in the middle of a word. (This is exactly similar to our patient's anxiety that the words will disappear in him, or that he will disappear in the world. It is our interpretation that the patient deals with the oral trauma by identifying himself with the *vanishing breast* or nipple, which is the source of life. When the breast vanishes, he himself vanishes. The awful thing, he says, is that his parents did not know it when he left home.) During the Barrister's Dream in "The Hunting of the Snark," the Snark defends a pig in court— the pig is charged with *deserting his sty* (*ibid.*, p. 418). This is also of great interest because the pig is a symbol of the baby in *Alice in Wonderland*.

But the significant person in "The Hunting of the Snark" is the captain of the expedition, the Bellman. In addition to his remarkable lamp, in which the Snark-disappearing motive is indicated—because there is no shore, no goal, only the sea— his ideas about reaching his destination are somewhat peculiar: his navigational charts are blank.

This was charming, no doubt, but they shortly found out
    That the Captain they trusted so well

Had only one notion for crossing the ocean,
    And that was to tingle his bell (*ibid.*, p. 402).

The interpretation I suggest is that the Bellman is hungry, he is a child crying for food.

This is clarified by a passage in one of Lewis Carroll's letters:

You know I have *three* dinner-bells—the first (which is the largest) is rung when dinner is *nearly* ready; the second (which is rather larger) is rung when it is quite ready; and the third (which is as large as the other two put together is rung all the time I am at dinner [*ibid.*, p. 429; Carroll's italics].

The importance of the oral trauma and the similarity of Lewis Carroll's literary fantasy to schizophrenic fantasy are further illuminated by a reading of *Through the Looking-Glass*, a sequel to *Alice in Wonderland*. At the beginning and end of this book, Alice is playing with her cat, Dinah, and with Dinah's kittens. Alice is half asleep. In the dream that follows, the black kitten turns into the Red Queen; the white kitten, into the White Queen. At the end of the dream Alice herself becomes a queen; with the result that there are three queens, the Red Queen, the White Queen, and Queen Alice. The obvious conclusion is that the two kittens are Alice's siblings—the situation is one of sibling rivalry.

Early in *Through the Looking-Glass* Alice is scolding Kitty, alias the Red Queen, for her faults:

Number two: you pulled Snowdrop away by the tail just as I had put down the saucer of milk before her! What, you were thirsty, were you? How do you know she wasn't thirsty too! [*ibid.*, pp. 171-172].

The kitten's punishment is that she will have to go without her dinner; and then Alice meditates on what would happen if she herself had to go without her dinner. We conclude, therefore, that the Red Queen is Alice and that she is trying in the fantasy to keep all the milk for herself, so that her sister should have none. We recall also that Alice had once frightened her old nurse by suddenly shouting in her ear that they play a game in which Alice would pretend to be a hungry hyena and the nurse would be a bone!

It is significant that Lewis Carroll (Charles Lutwidge Dodgson) had ten siblings. He was the oldest child in the family, and he therefore had plenty of opportunity to feel jealous of his younger siblings and (we conjecture) to develop cannibalistic fantasies about the rivals who took his place with the mother. In *Through the Looking-Glass* there is the well-known story of the Walrus and the Carpenter. They take all the little oysters for a walk and then, although they "deeply sympathize," they eat the whole lot. There is also the very significant passage at the end of *Through the Looking-Glass,* where Alice is Queen and a feast is given in her honor. The first course is a leg of mutton. The Red Queen introduces them to each other: "Alice—Mutton, Mutton—Alice." Having been introduced to the mutton, Alice cannot eat it. In this way she is in danger of missing her entire dinner; so when, notwithstanding the introduction, she cuts a slice of pudding, the Pudding says:

> What impertinence! I wonder how you'd like it if I were to cut a slice out of *you,* you creature! [*ibid.,* p. 285].

If the successive courses at the dinner represent the siblings whom Alice wanted to eat, we can understand why she cannot eat them after being personally acquainted with them, or after being introduced to them. This would mean that the siblings, instead of being mere fantasy objects, have become personal and real; they are friends and cannot be eaten.

It is worth recalling in this connection that, among the Pitjentara of Australia, every second child is eaten by the siblings and parents in order to give them a kind of double strength; but if the baby survives until it acquires a name, the period of danger is over and it will not be eaten (Róheim, 1932, p. 80).

But what happens at Alice's banquet? The Red Queen and the White Queen, her rivals in this situation, are transformed into soup and a leg of mutton, thus confirming our interpretation of the nature of the courses at the dinner.

In Chapter V of *Through the Looking-Glass* the White Queen goes rushing through the woods and keeps whispering something to herself that sounds like "Bread and butter, Bread and butter." This is followed by the theme of disappearing food (or breast). The White Queen offers to engage Alice as her maid. The salary is two pence a week and "jam every other day." The Queen explains that there is jam tomorrow and jam yesterday, but never jam today. The Queen eventually turns into an old sheep in whose shop Alice experiences some interesting difficulties: everything that Alice tries to take hold of disappears, and the egg she finally buys becomes Humpty Dumpty.

The disappearing food also explains Alice's anxieties at the beginning of *Alice in Wonderland*. She dwindles when she eats one kind of food, and she becomes so tiny that she is afraid of disappearing. Another kind of food makes her so big that there is scarcely any room for her in the house. Diminution in size is the opposite of growth and refers to the oral situation in which one is subject to attack. When Alice is so big that she fills the whole house the Rabbit throws a cartload of pebbles at her. These are transformed into cakes; but as soon as she eats a cake, she begins to shrink (*ibid.*, p. 401). The food that makes Alice small is the disappearing nipple (subject-object identification), while her colossal size represents oral aggression and body-destruction fantasies.

In Chapter V of *Alice in Wonderland* Alice is so tall that she reaches above the trees. The Pigeon says that she is a serpent and must be after her eggs (that is, the young ones). The whole narrative deals with creatures whom one ordinarily eats, or who are eaten by the cat and dog, and with whom Alice is required to meet on terms of friendship and equality. This touches off guilt feelings of the oral type. In Chapter X of the same book the Mock Turtle tells Alice that "perhaps you have never been introduced to the Lobster." Alice is just going to say, "I once tasted—" and then checks herself in time (*ibid.*, p. 87). The same thing occurs with the Whiting. Similarly, Alice's idea of starting a pleasant conversation with the Mouse (who may be French) is to ask, "Où est ma chatte?" (*ibid.*, p. 18).

We see that oral destructiveness and sibling rivalry must have played a part in the formation of these fantasies. Their similarity to schizophrenia is equally striking. First of all there is the continual play on words. What does the Whiting do under the sea? It does the boots and shoes. Boots on land being done with blacking, they are done under the sea with whiting. Likewise, the shoes are made of soles and eels, and it is impossible to do anything without a porpoise (purpose), and so on *ad infinitum.*

After the episode with the "Looking-Glass Insects," Alice comes to the country where things lose their names and she loses her name. We have adequately described our patient's fears of losing his name. As indicated above, the loss of one's name reflects the separation of words and objects. In schizophrenia, the connection between the preconscious cathexis and the world of objects is lost at first and then there is an attempt to restore this connection; but this attempt is only half successful and the words are dealt with as if they were objects.

The restoration of these destroyed connections, *the way back,* is represented by Humpty Dumpty. He overemphasizes the connection between word and object.

"*Must* a name mean something?" Alice asked rather doubt-fully. "Of course it must," Humpty Dumpty said with a short laugh: *"my* name means the shape I am—and a good handsome shape it is too" [*ibid.*, p. 234].

Humpty Dumpty represents an attempt to return to the world of object relations, but it is an unsuccessful attempt. The reinvested cathexis is now in the words, and these become persons and depend on their master, the subject.

When I use a word it means just what I choose it to mean— neither more nor less . . . When I make a word do a lot of work like that I always pay it extra [*ibid.,* pp. 238-239].

It is appropriate that Humpty Dumpty should be made the representative of an unsuccessful attempt at restoration. This is undoubtedly determined by the rhyme from which he originates. We all know that Humpty Dumpty sat on a wall, had a great fall, and that all the King's horses and men could not put poor Humpty Dumpty together again.

In the parallel we are drawing between Alice and our patient there is an additional and very striking feature. In *Through the Looking-Glass* Alice too has her "bugs." A hoarse voice speaks and Alice thinks, "It sounds like a horse." And an extremely small voice close to her ear says, "You might make a joke on that—something about horse and hoarse, you know." The owner of the small voice must be inside Alice because he repeats her thoughts. When it does this once again, Alice says, "Don't tease so; if you are anxious to have a joke made, make it yourself." The little voice sighed deeply; it sounded very unhappy. It was such a wonderfully small sigh that Alice would not have heard it at all had it not come quite close to her ear. "I know you are a friend," the little voice went on. "A dear friend and an old friend. And you won't hurt me, though I am an insect." Then Alice sees the insect: it is a gnat, the size of a chicken (*ibid.*, pp. 196-197).

A discussion follows about insects and their names. In this country, we learn, there is a Rocking-horse-fly instead of a horse-fly; a Snap-dragon-fly (its body is made of plum pudding) instead of a dragon-fly; and a Bread-and-butter-fly instead of a butterfly.

> Its wings are thin slices of bread-and-butter, its body is a crust, and its head is a lump of sugar [*ibid.*, p. 201].

The Bread-and-butter-fly, it may be noted, lives on weak tea with cream in it.

The bugs, as in the case of our patient, are internalized objects. The similarity goes even further. Our patient's bugs have to do with the disappearance of food. Alice's bugs are made of food. The patient's bugs are closely connected with his dread about the loss of his name. The Gnat, while humming around Alice's head, says to her: "I suppose you don't want to lose your name?" (*ibid.*, p. 202).

Additional examples could easily be adduced. They would only be supernumerary at this point. There is no doubt that there are numerous and striking similarities between the fantasy world of *Alice in Wonderland* and the fantasies of our patient.

The relationship of the internalized to the external objects is a problem that also deserves further clarification. In other words, we are interested in learning whether the little bugs within our patient are the antecedents of the big bug; whether the animal mythology deals with projected internalized objects; and whether symbol formation in the external object may be independent of symbol formation in the internalized object.

In American slang a "bug" is an insane or simple-minded person, and a "bug house" is not only a lunatic asylum but also refers to the condition of a crazy, idiotic, or simple-minded person. Since words are objects for our patient, he came to believe that he was actually full of bugs. In other words, he borrowed a word or phrase from the language and made it a basic element of his myth formation. The origin of the expression, "crazy as a bed bug," is attributed to a certain "Boston Mary," a famous tramp character of seventy or eighty years ago. She is said to have coined the word when she imagined that insects were crawling about in her skull (Irwin, 1931, pp. 38-39). The interesting thing is that an element of a psychotic fantasy became a slang expression, and then the slang term became an element of a psychotic fantasy.

As Apperson (1929) indicates in connection with the expression "to have a bee in one's bonnet":

> In 1553: "Ye must perdonne my wyttes for I tell you plaine, I have a hive of humble bees swarmynge in my braine" (*Respublica*, I.1.). In Herrick's *Mad Maid's Song*, (1648): "Ah! woe is me, woe, woe is me, Alack and well-a-day! For pitty, Sir, find out that bee, Which bore my love away. I'le seek him in your bonnet brave, I'le seek him in your eyes." A. Behn, *False Count*, II.iii. (1681): "What means he, sure he has a gad-bee in his brain." Reade, *Cloister and Hearth*, Ch. XCVII: "He may have a bee in his bonnet, but he is not a hypocrite." Weyman, *Ovington's Bank*, Ch. XXXII, (1922): "What mare's nest, what bee in the bonnet was this?" Another form of the phrase with the same meaning is "His head is full of bees" ("cares, fancies, or, he is restless"). Also 1546, Heywood, *Proverbes*, Part I, Ch. XII: "Their hartes full heavy, their heades be full of bees" [p. 33].

Borchardt (1894) notes that in Germany the cricket is the universal explanation of eccentricity. *Grillen fangen* means "to be moody" or "to be wrapped in one's own thoughts." The cricket, of course, is only one representative of a group of small creatures which buzz about in one's head like thoughts. If one is crazy, these small beings are in one's head (*dagegen den Narren, den Affen im Leibe*) (p. 184). According to Borchardt, one of the oldest records of the concept of insects in the skull is found in the *Zimmerische Chronik* (I, 130) of the year 1220:

Marchiam quoque Anconae et principatum Ravennae Conrado de Lützelhardt contulit, quem Italici Muscam-incerebro nominant eo, quod plerumque quasi demens videretur [ibid., p. 184].

Borchardt also indicates that the same meaning is intended when a person is said to have pigeons, birds, mosquitoes, or worms in his head. Other versions of the same expression ascribe the blame to gnats *(Mücken)*, caterpillars *(Raupen)*, or bumble-bees *(Hummeln)*, while the Parisians attribute the problem to spiders *(avoir une araignée dans le plafond)* *(ibid.,* p. 185).

Richter believes that these phrases may develop a new meaning as a result of a linguistic misunderstanding (much in the manner of our patient's attitude toward "bugs"): a phrase is taken in the literal sense, or a misunderstood word will give rise to a personification. According to Richter, *Mücke* (gnat) and *Mucke* (mood, whim) are probably related to each other, as are *Lunen* (sparrows) and *Launen* (moods) in the Luneburg dialect.[1]

However, the etymological explanation may merely be *a posteriori* in nature, a folk etymology. In the case of *Mücke* and *Mucke* there appears to be some confirmation in view of the fact that *musca* (fly, insect) figures in Italian beliefs as early as 1220. And there is some evidence that these sayings are based on actual beliefs. Thus, the Hungarian word *bogaras* means "having an insect" and is used in the sense of the "peculiar." In Kapuvar (Hungary) the peasants actually say that lunatics and imbeciles "keep insects." They carry these insects about wherever they go, and they must obey the whim of their insects or the devil will take them (Varga, 1914). This takes us into the midst of medieval witchcraft and into its modern survivals. In Guernsey, for example, some families

1 *Editor's note:* Róheim cites A. Richter, *Deutsche Redensarten*, 1921, pp. 71-72. The book being unavailable, it has been impossible to verify this reference.

had the reputation of being hereditary sorcerers, and they were furnished by Satan "with a familiar, generally in the shape of a fly, so that the phrase *avoir une mouque* is well understood as meaning that the person of whom it is said is one of the infernal fraternity" (MacCulloch, 1903, p. 331).

It seems very probable that witchcraft had something to do with the belief that abnormal people were being influenced by a small creature within them. According to testimony given in 1584 at Kolocsvar (Hungary), the witch-soul enters the body of the sleeping witch in the shape of a big fly, after which she awakens and talks (Komáromy, 1910, p. 49). In another case which occurred in 1744, in the County of Bihar, a girl accused of witchcraft was said to have been a good "maker of mice" (*ibid.*, p. 513). In Oldenburg, "making mice" was a proof that someone was proficient in the art of witchcraft (Strackerjan, 1909, p. 367; Soldan-Heppe, 1911a, p. 324). In French folklore, anyone who suddenly became rich was said "to have a cricket," that is, he has made a pact with the devil (Sébillot, 1906, p. 314).

Further information about the witch and her familiar creatures is found in the Essex trials of 1645:

> . . . the said Elizabeth desired this informant, and the rest that were in the roome with her, to sit downe, and said she would shew this informant and the rest some of her impes . . . and being asked, if she would not be afraid of her impes, the said Elizabeth answered, "What, do yee think, I am afraid of my children?" . . . And the said Elizabeth also told this informant, that she had three impes from her mother, which were of a browne color, and two from old beldam Weste . . . and that her impes did commonly suck on old beldam Weste, and that the said beldam's impes did suck on her [Murray, 1921, p. 214].

Teats were found about the privy parts of her body, and this was where the imps sucked her. The imps, little dogs or kittens, were fed with milk and behaved like children (*ibid.*, pp. 214-215).

Anne, the wife of John Cooper of Clacton, was also accused of being a witch:

> Confessed unto this informant, that she the said Anne hath had three black impes suckled on the lower part of her body [*ibid.*, p. 216].

The three imps of another witch were called "Littleman," "Pretty-man," and "Dainty." Two of them were said to be smaller than mice. However, some imps were believed to be bigger and longer than mice, while others were like moles, except that they lacked tails and required a diet of milk (*ibid.*, pp. 216-217).

One witness at a witchcraft trial swore:

> That she had been a witch about twenty yeers and hath three familiars, two like mouses, and the third like a frog [*ibid.*, p. 218].

And one witch, in addition to her mouse-like familiars, had one that resembled a sparrow (*ibid.*, pp. 218-220).

Silvain Nevillon, tried at Orleans in 1614, confessed:

> . . . qu'il y a des Sorciers qui nourissent des Marionettes, qui sont de petits Diableteaux en forme de Crapaux, et leur font manger de la bouillie composée laict et de farine [*ibid.*, p. 221].

When these marionettes looked happy, their owner would go to the market and carry on his affairs; otherwise, he would stay at home (*ibid.*, pp. 221-222).

Finally, it may be noted that some witches actually gave birth to snakes, lizards, and frogs, while wizards sometimes had to content themselves with familiars who resembled ordinary flies (Soldan-Heppe, 1911b, p. 174).

We have tried to indicate that, in European folklore, people who are somewhat peculiar or abnormal are believed, as in the case of witches, to possess a small creature who is responsible for their deviant tendencies. There is, however, a difference between witches and psychotics. Thus, while the small creature owned by the witch may reside in her body or in a glass, or may merely be in her service, the small creature that causes a psychosis is regularly within the head or body of the afflicted person.

It is also notable that two insects, the bee and the cricket, are especially prominent in these beliefs and play a role both in magic (that is, in personal, familial, and group rituals, as well as in witchcraft or wizardry, which is generally described as *black* magic) and in all sorts of mental aberrations. For example, it was once a custom in Wales for the head of the household to inform the bees whenever a death took place in the family. Similarly, at the death of the head of the household, the widow knocked several times on the beehive, saying, "He's gone! He's gone!" The bees hummed in reply, and in this way she understood that they had decided to remain where they were. It is still believed in Wales that bees and crickets bring blessings to the house, and it is unlucky to kill them (or to kill spiders) (Trevelyan, 1909, p. 86).

In France the cricket is associated with the luck of the house. They are called *petit cheval du bon Dieu;* and in Béarn they say, "God lives where there are crickets" *(Où il y a des grillons, Dieu habite).* Wizards have no power over a house in which there is a cricket. If the cricket sings in a house, all is well; but if someone is ill, it lowers its voice and becomes scarcely audible. After a death, the crickets in the house are believed to mourn and to stop singing for six weeks (Sébillot, 1906, pp. 314-315).

There is also a connection between the prosperity of the beehive and the health and strength of the master of the house. When he gets old, the number of bees decreases. If the master dies, the bees die also; and conversely, an empty beehive is an augury of death in the house. It is also important for the bees to know about everything that happens in the house, with the result that births, marriages, and deaths are announced to them. In Normandie the bees are addressed in the following way:

Mes petites belles, votre père ou votre oncle, ou votre soeur, etc., est mort [*ibid.*, p. 319].

At Ille-et-Vilaine they say:

En ménage, mes petites,
Montez, mes petites, en ménage,
En ménage, en ménage [*ibid.*, p. 319].

German customs and usages are very similar in this respect (Sartori, 1910, pp. 129, 144; 1911, pp. 118, 127, 132-133). Thus, the cricket called *Heimchen* (or *Hausgrillen*) should not be killed because it brings luck to the house; and if one of them is killed, the others will eat up all the clothes in the house (Wuttke, 1900, pp. 113, 206; Sartori, 1911, p. 22). These crickets are identical with the souls of the unbaptized children who follow Holda (or Holle) in her nightly revels (Wuttke, 1900, p. 26).

If we recall that the small familiar creature of the witch is called her child and is suckled by her, it would appear that the bees and crickets of white magic also represent children. We agree, therefore, with the original interpretation suggested by Rank (1929), that the small animals in a myth represent small children or siblings (cf. Bernfeld, 1929, pp. 234-235).

In discussing the fantasies of our patient, we conjectured that the bugs in his body really mean (or represent) the mother's body contents—that is, the siblings torn out of his mother's body and safely stored in his own. Dual unity, therefore, seems to be the real explanation of *schizo*phrenia, a unity that is not complete but is also a duality.

Having a bug (or toad, imp, and the like) would mean, from the functional point of view, that one is partly a little child; and from the viewpoint of content that one is both mother and child at the same time (that is, dual unity).

We can now clarify the meaning of such expressions as "a bee in the bonnet." The explanation appears to be that for normal people the bee or the cricket (as the incarnation of the soul) was the object of a certain cult. But for the psychotic this connection with society or ritual was broken off, and he turned exclusively to the internalized object. Thus, a psychotic is a person who has failed to reproject his internalized objects into the environment in concert with other people; rather he keeps these objects within himself.

Our patient's bug, which resembles his father or a gorilla, is an internalized object that *has* been reprojected into the environment. But it has been reprojected in a manner that is neither socially acceptable nor ritually coherent, and without any ego-syntonic advantages.

But other processes of secondary elaboration are also at work. When our patient describes the lion as a dumb animal and then adds that he himself is dumb, we are observing the operation of another process, that of fission or lack of integration—the failure to admit that certain part components of his personality, notably his aggressions, form part of his ego. We do not know what the historical relation of these two mechanisms may be. They are related to each other, but it is impossible to say as yet whether they are independent or are different phases of a single process. At any rate, they interact with each other. And when the patient equates the eagle with his tooth or Teethies, he is combining both mechanisms.

Finally, it should also be noted that the three typical animals of his fantasy—the lion, eagle, and swordfish—are the respective rulers of the land, air, and sea. Each is the strongest and most dangerous animal in its own sphere. They are, therefore, mutually interchangeable.

CHAPTER FOUR

Conclusion

We have assumed that an oral trauma is at the base of the schizophrenic process. We have also assumed that object relations in general are based on relations to the mother—that the mother is the prototype of Mother Nature (cf. Róheim, 1921). Since the original object relationship to the mother is obviously oral, it would seem evident that man's relations with his environment must be conditioned ontogenetically by the attitude of the mother toward her child.

As I have pointed out elsewhere (Róheim, 1934), the Central Australian tribes reside in a desert area where death by starvation is well within the range of possibility, yet they have no anxiety about starvation. On the other hand, the natives of the Normanby Islands live in a fertile region, practice agriculture, and have plenty of fish, game, and jungle food— but they are continually and anxiously practicing magic both to increase the food supply and to spoil their appetites. The explanation of this apparent paradox lies in the infantile situation. In Central Australia the mothers are permissive and yielding, and there is no weaning trauma; children can obtain milk, not only from their own mother, but from all the mothers of the tribe. In the Normanby area, however, nursing is systematically interrupted and there is a sudden weaning at the end of the first year.

In the light of our patient's fantasies and dreams, it is unquestionable that his loss of the object world is based on an oral trauma and on his early relations to his mother. His en-

221

tire fantasy system is, in fact, centered around object loss and *food trouble*. Object loss means the loss of the mother, and the *food trouble* refers to the loss of the internalized object. The two anxieties run on parallel lines and are accompanied by a third of the same order, the loss of the self (or the fear of being lost). The internalized object is really the internalized mother—or rather, the internalized body contents of the mother. This is borne out by the patient's repeated statements that his difficulties arose out of his own aggressions. It would seem, therefore, that we must concur in Schmideberg's (1930) theory that schizophrenia is a flight to the internalized object.

However, it remains quite uncertain whether (and to what degree) we are justified in ascribing all this to an exogenous trauma—or in the patient's language, to "starvation." This may well be; and in this case the oral frustration would be responsible for the extraordinary amount of destructiveness directed against the mother's body (and followed by the corresponding amount of talio anxiety and by the loss of the integrity of the ego). On the other hand, it may also be postulated that our patient had an organically weak ego, whatever the organic basis of this ego weakness may be.

In either case he would not be able to tolerate even a normal degree of aggression without reacting to it with the utmost anxiety. The formation of symbols for his aggression may perhaps be explained on this basis: that he is not a wild beast (for example, a lion), but that there is a lion in the environment who is either his ally or his enemy, as the case may be. If ego weakness is inherent in an individual, he is more dependent and he needs more object love or support than other people. Failing to obtain this, he reacts with a strong identification; and he thus resists the acceptance of reality by restoring the original child-mother, or subject-object, unity in fantasy. However, if there is no inherent ego weakness but a real trauma—that is, an event in the life of the infant that approaches starvation—then the result would be quite similar. The incorporation of the mother or the identification with the mother would be the fantasy protection against the recurrence of the trauma.

If we remember that the first form in which reality presents itself to a human being is the breast (mother) or the absence of the breast (or mother), it seems to follow automatically that in a psychosis, where contact with reality is lost or seriously impaired, we must find a revival of these fantasy formations or a regression to those fantasy formations that characterize the infant's primal relation to reality. In every psychosis, therefore, we should expect to find oral fantasies and anxieties, body-destruction fantasies, the talio form of these fantasies, and fantasies of omnipotence and identification. I believe that this expectation is amply supported by the evidence.

On the other hand, it is also true that we all go through this early phase of development and that these fantasies can similarly be found in normal and neurotic individuals, and not merely in psychotics. Gerö (1939), for example, has described a didactic analysis. The analysand was normal in every respect. The only remarkable thing about him was a certain coolness or reserve, and a considerable pride in this peculiarity. We may find parallel tendencies and mechanisms in a schizophrenic, though we must first disregard the quantitative differences and relations in the omnipotence fantasies and withdrawal of the schizophrenic. In due time, Gerö's analysand revealed a milk-phobia, based on an abrupt weaning in the sixth month. He had reacted to the weaning by refusing all nourishment and by spurning the mother's breast when she wanted to suckle him again. His mother had originally refused him the breast because she was pregnant again and because he bit her nipples. Gerö's analysand felt terribly disgusted by newborn cats and dogs, and as a child he had always refused to eat chocolate-babies. (He flew into a terrible rage when a woman wanted to practice fellatio with him, and this aggression obviously covered an underlying anxiety.) When he had been approximately four years old he broke a globular aquarium and killed all the goldfish with the greatest glee. This memory was linked with his hatred of all his younger siblings. Similarly, his coolness or reserve, like the more exaggerated withdrawal of a schizophrenic, was connected with an oral fixation (pp. 241-251). The pathological phenomena are, of course, only a caricature or exaggeration of processes that also occur in a normal individual.

Fenichel (1937) has described the infant as being born in a state of relative immaturity or helplessness. It has no ego— that is, it has not developed the capacity to endure suspense. The aim of its psyche is the speedy elimination of tension, and this is achieved by food and sleep. Therefore, the origin of reality and the origin of the ego mean the same thing, because the ego is that part of reality that is incorporated into the psyche (or is that part of the psyche that represents reality). Schizophrenia is thus a regression to the phase that precedes the evolution of the ego or to the phase that represents the testing of reality. We are a person if we perceive ourselves in contrast to others.

Rado (1926) regards the desire to regain a lost phase of narcissistic omnipotence—the moment of eliminated tension, of gratified hunger—as a fundamental feature of human life (pp. 409-411). This omnipotence, however, is really object-directed: it aims at the restoration of the mother-child unity.

All this points to the same conclusion: that the oral function of obtaining nourishment is one of the earliest and most important nuclei of ego development. And, since this oral function is really the most important ego activity of the infant from the point of view of reality and survival, it is not surprising that we should speak of the *oral basis of the ego*. In the language of our patient, he is lost when the food in him is lost or when he is left alone by his mother. We conclude, therefore, that the ego, which is the extroverted part of the id, originates in the same way as the superego, that is, through introjection. It is the act of thumb sucking rather than the clinging to the nipple; it is the temporary independence achieved by an identification with a part of the body, with the pleasure-giving object. The infant forms an ego by introjecting the part object; and the resultingly more integrated psychic unit (infant plus nipple) forms a superego by introjecting suspense in the form of the father (the animal on the road in our patient's mythology). If we consider the preoedipal superego, we should say that the infant forms a superego by introjecting the "bad" mother (or the "absent" mother) during the phase of oral frustration and tension.

If we regard the ego as evolving on the basis of object-directed trends, on the basis of the introjected "good nipple," this would explain the essential synthetic (integrating) function of the ego, as Nunberg (1948, pp. 120-136) and Anna Freud (1936) have emphasized. And the ego is a synthesis because it owes its origin to the mouth-nipple synthesis. This synthesis, in fact, explains the intimate relationship between the ego and the acceptance of reality. Reality means the tolerance of frustration, of suspense, of pain; and we assume that this becomes possible on the basis of retained sensations of pleasure. Pain becomes bearable because the recurrence of past pleasure is expected; and, as in the therapeutic use of the epic incantation, it is the magic of libido and of memory that makes existence tolerable.

We have good reasons to assume that the infant passes through a fantasy phase in its adaptation to reality and that the psychoses represent a recurrence of (or a regression to) the fantasy level of infancy. It is obvious that there is an analogy here with the magic of nonliterate societies. When the medicine man or sorcerer pours water on himself, he believes that the same results will visit his victim or the world. Object cathexis is withdrawn into a secondary narcissism. It is quite clear that the genesis of these fantasies may be found in the oral stage (see Part I). But it is equally clear that the oral phase of development is *the first step toward reality.*

Our patient did not come to dinner when called but continued to play. He denied that he refused to eat (in his terms such a refusal would appear psychotic). But he went on "playing," that is, leading a life of fantasy, when he ought to have had dinner. However, he wishes to return to the world of objects, and *thinking about things* is the magic he performs to get them back.

It is also notable that our patient's dreams confirm the theories I have postulated in *The Gates of the Dream* (1952). His dreams about his birth and about the sunset and the mountain indicate a uterine regression. But his typical dream experience is a rushing, flying, and rising in the air; this is *the basic dream* as a countermove against uterine regression. The dream in which he says that *eating lifted him up into space* illustrates the two stages (oral and genital) of the trend toward the object. Another feature of his dreams and fantasies is the identification of himself with the space in which he moves. His dreams or "stories" are ultimately his attempts to return to reality and normality. It is for such reasons that we have assumed that the dream is a defense against uterine withdrawal and that the world of reality is rebuilt on a libidinal basis. This same process is valid for schizophrenia and has frequently been emphasized.

Primitive magic follows a more or less similar technique and proceeds in this fashion:

(1) Originally, there is an object-directed cathexis.

(2) Then a withdrawal and a secondary narcissism.

(3) And then a movement back from the "autarchic" position, a return to the object.

But it is also important to point out the difference between schizophrenia and primitive magic. In primitive magic the processes just described are generally ego-syntonic, and they are dramatized and shared by the social group. (In unconscious magic these processes are sometimes dramatized and may be ego-syntonic; or the opposite of these processes may or may not be shared by the social group). But in a psychosis, these processes, though they are generally dramatized, are not ego-syntonic and are not shared by the social group, while the return to the object is usually unsuccessful.

BIBLIOGRAPHY

Addy, S. O. (1909), Scraps of English Folklore, III. *Folk-Lore, 20*:342-349.

Apperson, G. L. (1929), *English Proverbs and Proverbial Phrases.* London: Dent.

Bak, R. (1939), Regression of Ego-Orientation and Libido in Schizophrenia. *International Journal of Psycho-Analysis, 20*:64-71.

Balint, M. (1942), Contributions to Reality Testing. *British Journal of Medical Psychology, 19*:201-214.

Bergler, E. and Róheim, G. (1946), Psychology of Time Perception. *Psychoanalytic Quarterly, 15*:190-206.

Bernfeld, S. (1929), *The Psychology of the Infant.* London: Kegan Paul.

Bleuler, E. (1911), *Dementia Praecox or the Group of Schizophrenias.* New York: International Universities Press, 1950.

—— (1912), *The Theory of Schizophrenic Negativism.* New York: The Journal of Nervous and Mental Disease Pub. Co.

Borchardt, W. (1894), *Die sprichwörtlichen Redensarten im deutschen Volksmunde.* Fourth edition. Leipzig: F. A. Brockhaus.

Boss, M. (1938), Psychopathologie des Traumes bei schizophrenen und organischen Psychosen. *Zeitschrift für die gesamte Neurologie und Psychiatrie, 168*:459-494.

Bychowski, G. (1930), A Case of Oral Delusions of Persecution. *International Journal of Psycho-Analysis, 11*:332-337.

Dodgson, C. L. (1931), *The Lewis Carroll Book,* edited by R. Herrick. New York: Dial Press.

Fenichel, O. (1937), Early Stages of Ego Development. *The Collected Papers of Otto Fenichel.* Second series: 25-48. New York: Norton, 1954.

Ferenczi, S. (1924), *Versuch einer Genitaltheorie.* Leipzig: Internationaler Psychoanalytischer Verlag.

Freud, A. (1936), *The Ego and the Mechanisms of Defense.* New York: International Universities Press, 1946.

Freud, S. (1911), Formulations Regarding the Two Principles in Mental Functioning. *Collected Papers, 4*:13-21. London: Hogarth Press, 1925

—— (1915), The Unconscious. *Collected Papers, 4*:98-136. London: Hogarth Press, 1925.

—— (1923), *The Ego and the Id.* London: Hogarth Press, 1935.

Gerö, G. (1939), Zum Problem der oralen Fixierung. *Internationale Zeitschrift für Psychoanalyse und Imago, 24*:239-257.

Gottlieb, J. S. and Linder, F. E. (1935), Body Temperatures of Persons with Schizophrenia and of Normal Subjects. *Archives of Neurology and Psychiatry, 33*:775-785.

Gruhle, H. W. (1932), Die Psychopathologie. *Die Schizophrenie,* 135-210. (*Handbuch der Geisteskrankheiten,* Vol. 9, Part 5, edited by O. Bumke.) Berlin: Julius Springer.

Hajdu-Gimes, L. (1940), Contributions to the Etiology of Schizophrenia. *Psychoanalytic Review,* 27:421-438.

Hermann, I. (1923), Organlibido und Begabung. *Internationale Zeitschrift für Psychoanalyse, 9*:297-310.

—— (1936a), Sich-Anklammern—Auf-Suche-Gehen. *Internationale Zeitschrift für Psychoanalyse, 22*:349-370.

—— (1936b), Neue Beiträge zur vergleichenden Psychologie der Primaten. *Imago, 22*:442-456.

—— (1940), Studien zur Denkpsychologie. *Acta Psychologica, 5*:22-102.

Irwin, G. (1931), *American Tramp and Underworld Slang.* London: Eric Partridge.

Katan, M. (1939), A Contribution to the Understanding of Schizophrenic Speech. *International Journal of Psycho-Analysis, 20*:353-362.

—— (1940), Die Rolle des Wortes in der Schizophrenie und Manie. *Internationale Zeitschrift für Psychoanalyse und Imago, 25*:138-173.

Kempf, E. J. (1920), *Psychopathology.* St. Louis: C. V. Mosby Co.

Komáromy, A. (1910), *Magyarországi boszkányperek okléveltára.* Budapest: A Magyar tud. akadémia.

Levin, M. (1930), Archaic Regressive Phenomena as a Defense Mechanism in Schizophrenia. *Archives of Neurology and Psychiatry, 24*: 950-965.

MacCulloch, E. (1903), *Guernsey Folk-Lore.* London: Elliot Stock.

Murray, M. A. (1921), *The Witch-Cult in Western Europe.* Oxford: Clarendon Press.

Nagy, J. (1896), Bácsmegyei babonák (Bács superstitions). *Ethnographia,* 7:176-181.

Nunberg, H. (1948), *Practice and Theory of Psychoanalysis.* New York: Nervous and Mental Disease Monographs.

Onians, R. B. (1951), *The Origins of European Thought.* Cambridge: Cambridge University Press.

Rado, S. (1926), The Psychic Effects of Intoxicants. *International Journal of Psycho-Analysis*, 7:396-413.

Rank, O. (1929), *The Trauma of Birth*. New York: Harcourt, Brace.

Róheim, G. (1919), *Spiegelzauber*. Leipzig: Internationaler Psychoanalytischer Verlag.

—— (1921), Primitive Man and Environment. *International Journal of Psycho-Analysis*, 2:157-178.

—— (1932), Psychoanalysis of Primitive Cultural Types. *International Journal of Psycho-Analysis*, 13:1-224.

—— (1934), *The Riddle of the Sphinx*. London: Hogarth Press.

—— (1943a), Sublimation. *Psychoanalytic Quarterly*, 12:338-352.

—— (1943b), *The Origin and Function of Culture*. New York: Nervous and Mental Disease Monographs.

—— (1952), *The Gates of the Dream*. New York: International Universities Press.

Rose, H. J. (1923), On the Original Significance of the Genius. *Classical Quarterly*, 17:57-60.

—— (1930), Ancient Italian Beliefs Concerning the Soul. *Classical Quarterly*, 24:129-135.

Rosenzweig, S. and Shakow, D. (1937), Mirror Behavior in Schizophrenic and Normal Individuals. *Journal of Nervous and Mental Disease*, 86:166-174.

Sartori, P. (1910), *Sitte und Brauch*, Vol. 1. Leipzig: W. Heims.

—— (1911), *ibid.*, Vol. 2. Leipzig: W. Heims.

Schilder, P. (1928), *Introduction to a Psychoanalytic Psychiatry*. New York: International Universities Press, 1951.

——(1938), Psychoanalytic Remarks on *Alice in Wonderland* and Lewis Carroll. *Journal of Nervous and Mental Disease*, 87:159-168.

—— (1939), The Relations between Clinging and Equilibrium. *International Journal of Psycho-Analysis*, 20:58-63.

Schmideberg, M. (1930), The Role of Psychotic Mechanisms in Cultural Development. *International Journal of Psycho-Analysis*, 11:387-418.

Schreber, D. P. (1903), *Denkwürdigkeiten eines Nervenkranken*. Leipzig: O. Mutze.

Sébillot, P. (1906), *Le Folk-lore de France*, Vol. 3. Paris: E. Guilmoto.

Soldan-Heppe, W. G. (1911a), *Geschichte der Hexenprozesse*, Vol. 1. Munich: G. Müller.

—— (1911b), *ibid.*, Vol. 2. Munich: G. Müller.

Spielrein, S. (1922), Die Entstehung der kindlichen Worte Papa und Mama. *Imago*, 8:345-367.

Strackerjan, L. (1909), *Aberglaube und Sagen aus dem Herzogtum Oldenburg*, Vol. 1. Oldenburg: G. Stalling.

Tausk, V. (1919), On the Origin of the "Influencing Machine" in Schizophrenia. *The Psychoanalytic Reader* (edited by R. Fliess), 1:52-85. New York: International Universities Press, 1949.

Tetzner, F. (1902), *Die Slawen in Deutschland*. Braunschweig: F. Vieweg.

Tregear, E. (1891), *The Maori-Polynesian Comparative Dictionary*. Wellington: Lyon and Blair.

Trevelyan, M. (1909), *Folk-Lore and Folk-Stories of Wales*. London: Elliot Stock.

Varga, T. (1914), *Kapuvári népszohások* (Manuscript, Folklore Fellows, Hungarian Collection). Budapest: Hungarian National Museum.

Waelder, R. (1933), The Psychoanalytic Theory of Play. *Psychoanalytic Quarterly*, 2:208-224.

Westerman Holstijn, A. J. (1934), Oral Erotism in Paraphrenia. *International Journal of Psycho-Analysis*, 15:160-186.

Wuttke, A. (1900), *Der deutsche Volksaberglaube der Gegenwart*. Third

Wundt, W. (1911), *Völkerpsychologie*, Vol. 1. Leipzig: W. Engelmann. edition. Berlin: Wiegandt und Grieben.